Praise for Michael Gu

From the beginning of time, parents and sensitive teachers have observed differences in the behavior, learning styles, and focused interests of girls and boys. Defying the political correctness that is today's common wisdom, Gurian and the contributing authors draw on emerging neuroscientific data to justify these perceptions. While never allowing us to lose sight of the reality of individual differences, they suggest creative ways to modify the learning environment to encourage a broader spectrum of achievement in both gender groups.

—Edward Zigler, Ph.D., Sterling Professor of Psychology, Yale University; one of the original planners of the national Head Start program

Nurture the Nature is a beautifully written guide to raising children. It is as scientifically sound as it is humane. Michael Gurian provides invaluable insight into how understanding our children's unique core natures can help us raise happy, successful, and emotionally fulfilled children."

—Harold S. Koplewicz, M.D. Founder of the ChildMind Institute

Leadership and the Sexes is extremely valuable in two ways. Not only can everyone recognize something of themselves in it, but its numerous engaging examples of communication between women and men will help people interpret communication in the workplace more effectively.

—Sandra F. Witelson, Ph.D., Albert Einstein/Irving Zucker Chair in Neuroscience, Michael G. DeGroote School of Medicine, McMaster University

It's a Baby Girl! is thoughtfully research-based, yet perceptively practical for any parent who has just been blessed by the gift of a girl. Parents will close the book truly understanding why boys and girls are different in so many ways, and how to nurture the nature of their daughter."

— Fay E. Brown, Ph.D., Director of Child and Adolescent Development Program, Yale University

I found the *The Wonder of Girls* to be a wonderful addition to the literature already available on raising girls. What I liked best was its constant correlation of developing biology in women to their psychological struggles, giving the authenticity that is sorely needed. I heartily endorse this new balanced way to understand how wonderful the capacities of girls and women are, and so vital to the nurturing of their infants, families and society. Bravo!
　　　—Deborah Sichel, M.D., author of *Women's Moods: What Every Woman Must Know About Hormones, the Brain, and Emotional Health*

Leadership and the Sexes unlocks gender truths for the workplace. Every business-man or woman needs to read this book!
　　　— Louann Brizendine, M.D., Neuro-psychiatrist and Clinical Professor, University of California-San Francisco; author of *The Female Brain and The Male Brain*

THE MINDS OF GIRLS

PREVIOUS BOOKS BY MICHAEL GURIAN

Child Development and Parenting
Saving Our Sons
The Purpose of Boys
Nurture the Nature
The Wonder of Girls
The Wonder of Boys
Raising Boys by Design
The Wonder of Children (previously published as *The Soul of the Child*)
A Fine Young Man
The Good Son
What Stories Does My Son Need? (with Terry Trueman)
It's a Baby Boy!
It's a Baby Girl!
(by the Gurian Institute, with Adrian Goldberg, ACSW, Stacie Bering, MD)

Education
The Minds of Boys (with Kathy Stevens)
Boys and Girls Learn Differently!
(with Kathy Stevens, Patricia Henley, Terry Trueman)
The Boys and Girls Learn Differently Action Guide for Teachers
(with Arlette C. Ballew)
Strategies for Teaching Boys and Girls—Elementary Level
Strategies for Teaching Boys and Girls—Secondary Level
(with Kathy Stevens, Kelley King)
Successful Single-Sex Classrooms (with Kathy Stevens, Peggy Daniels)

Psychology
Lessons of Lifelong Intimacy
The Wonder of Aging
How Do I Help Him?
What Could He Be Thinking?
Love's Journey
The Invisible Presence (previously published as *Mothers, Sons and Lovers*)
The Prince and the King

Business-Corporate
Leadership and the Sexes (with Barbara Annis)
The Leading Partners Workbook (with Katherine Coles, Kathy Stevens)

The Minds of Girls

*A New Path for Raising Healthy,
Resilient, and Successful Women*

By

Michael Gurian

The *New York Times* Bestselling Author of
The Wonder of Girls and *The Minds of Boys*

Copyright © 2018 Michael Gurian. All rights reserved.
Published by Gurian Institute Press
The Gurian Institute, LLC
Send postal mail to: P. O. Box 8714, Spokane, WA 99203
Email directly: michaelgurian@comcast.net or through: www.michaelgurian.com

No part of this publication may be reproduced, stored in a retrieval system, or transmitted in any form or by any means, electronic, mechanical, photocopying, recording, scanning, or otherwise, except as permitted under Section 107 or 108 of the 1976 United States Copyright Act, without either the prior written permission of the publisher, or authorization through payment of the appropriate per-copy fee to the Gurian Institute. Requests to publisher for permission should be addressed to Permissions Department, Gurian Institute, P. O. Box 8714, Spokane, WA 99203, or michaelgurian@comcast.net.

Readers should be aware that Internet Web sites offered as citations and/or sources for further information may have changed or disappeared between the time this was written and when it was read. Readers should be aware that some of the anecdotes in this book, including some gathered from media reports, are composites of two or more comments or stories that needed to be shortened for narrative flow. In no cases have meanings been changed, and no changes involved changes in statistics. In case studies in this book, names have been changed, as well as details that might invade the confidentiality of the person or family.

Limit of Liability/Disclaimer of Warranty: The advice and strategies contained herein may not be suitable for your situation. This publication is sold with the understanding that the author and publisher are not engaged in rendering medical, health, or any other kind of personal professional services in the book. The reader should consult his or her medical, health, or other competent professional before adopting any of the suggestions in this book or drawing inferences from it. The author and publisher specifically disclaim all responsibility for any liability, loss or risk, personal or otherwise, which is incurred as a consequence directly or indirectly, of the use and application of any of the contents of this book.

Books and other materials by Michael Gurian and the Gurian Institute can be accessed through most brick-and-mortar stores, most online outlets, and the websites: www.michaelgurian.com and www.gurianinstitute.com.

Printed in the United States

ISBN: 978-0-9839959-7-5

Dedication

For Gail, Gabrielle, and Davita,

and

Kathy Stevens, in blessed memory

Table of Contents

Preface

"There are things you can't reach,
but you can at least reach out to them."
—Mary Oliver

ONE OF MY CLOSEST FRIENDS, KATHY STEVENS, passed away at 62 after a two-and-a- half year battle with cancer. She was our Gurian Institute Executive Director up to the moment she died—answering emails from school principals just an hour before—and loved her work. She came to us after seven years as Executive Director of the Women's Resource Agency, in Colorado, having developed and taught an empowerment program for teen girls there. When she was out doing training and speaking, Kathy loved to open her presentation with this story.

"A couple from Minnesota went to Florida to thaw out during one particularly icy winter. They decided to stay at the very same hotel where they had spent their honeymoon two decades before. Because of hectic work schedules, it was tough to coordinate flying down to Florida together, so the husband flew first, with his wife ticketed to come the next day. When the husband got to the hotel, he found free Wi-Fi access in the room, so he sent his wife an email from his laptop. However, he accidentally left out one letter in her email address. Without realizing his error, he sent the email.

"Meanwhile, in Houston, a widow had just returned home from her husband's funeral. He was a minister of many years who died after a sudden heart attack. The widow decided to check her email, expecting messages from relatives and friends. After reading the first email, she fainted. Her grown children rushed into the room, found their mother on the floor, and saw the computer screen which read:

To: My Loving Wife
Subject: I've Arrived
Date: February 2
I know you're surprised to hear from me. They give free Wi-Fi access in the rooms here so I am sending you an email. When I checked in, I saw that

everything has been prepared for your arrival tomorrow. Looking forward to seeing you then! Hope your journey is as uneventful as mine was.
P.S. Sure is hot down here!"

After her audiences laughed out loud, Kathy would say, "A little thing can have big consequences. One missing element in an email address can reconstruct a whole reality. It's the same thing in parenting, in education. A little change can make a big difference. Today, we're going to talk about what a difference it makes to really study the female and male brain. It can lead to whole new ways of raising and educating children."

Kathy was right, and along with my wife, Gail, and daughters, Gabrielle and Davita, this book is dedicated to her.

* * *

In the thirty years that I have been working with children and raising daughters, I have become increasingly optimistic about the lives of girls. Compared to what parenting and education were like when I was born in 1958, there are now thousands of resources to help our daughters, from upgraded traditional organizations like Girl Scouts and Girls Clubs, to new paradigms and curricula in schools for STEM and STEAM, to girl-sensitive approaches in non-profits, faith-communities, public and private schools, and homeschool Co-ops. There is still much work to do on behalf of girls, but the last few decades have been amazing in their opening to girls a new and passionate freedom to thrive.

As a child of first-wave feminists, I'm particularly impressed that the idea of girls as second-class citizens in America does not resonate for most Millennial or Gen X/Y/Z girls and women. Empowered young women still see some bastions of sexism in America and they call us out for those, but they do not believe women are victims at every turn anymore. Kathy was often heard saying to girls, "If there's something wrong, fix it. Don't be the victim. That's not the female role we all fought for as young feminists."

Yet, despite gains for our daughters in the last three decades, our girls are faced with multiple issues on multiple fronts because of which they need us utterly and, sometimes, desperately. Katey McPherson, a Gurian Institute director and the mother of four girls, recently put it this way: "In most ways girls' lives are much better than they were, but especially if you have daughters, you see their multiple needs, some of which, especially because of the digital world they like to live in, are very new needs."

Parenting girls, like parenting boys, is a new art form in many ways. Among changing landscapes for our daughters is the pressure of the multiple changes in systems themselves. The human family and workplace are no longer a singular "the family" or "the workplace." Each system is diverse in required outcomes and performance standards and many of the systems we have built to help girls do not fully understand who girls are and what girls need. Depression, obesity, anxiety, and other mental and physiological disorders haunt girls' lives, and social media and technology in general has become for girls both a blessing and a curse.

New science can help us protect and nurture our daughters into healthy adulthood. That science—and its application in the everyday lives of girls and women—constitutes a new path to raising healthy and happy daughters. In the following chapters, I will share with you this path. As a philosopher of science and a practicing family counselor, I have written this book to help you as a parent or professional to use brain and behavioral science immediately and practically as you interact with girls in your life. My interest in the practical grows not only from my profession but from raising two daughters to adulthood. You'll meet Gabrielle and Davita in this book too.

I wrote *The Minds of Girls* at the same time as its mirror book on raising boys, *Saving Our Sons*. If you have read *Saving Our Sons*, you will see some of the same child development themes and material in this book. A few sections of these books echo one another, but they are also tailored for gender in the same way as *It's a Baby Girl!* and *It's a Baby Boy!*—the two Gurian Institute/Jossey Bass publications. Boys and girls are like two interlocking Venn diagrams, and even allowing for a broad gender spectrum in which some space is shared by both, boys and girls still require gender-specific attention. You'll notice in all my work that, rather than seeing boys' and girls' (or women's and men's) lives in opposition, I see them as complementary.

In that vein, we will look together at the newest research, insight, and practical strategies you can use immediately in your family, school, and community to help girls. We will look at the difficulties in a present-day girl's life, including an honest look at neurotoxins, technology, and social media use—areas in which girls and boys share space. If you've read my earlier work, *The Wonder of Girls* (2002), you'll find that I am not trying to repeat that book here, but instead to update the research and advance best practices with the same science-based passion.

In *The Wonder of Girls*, I wrote, "Even while the bulk of this book is written to help parents and other caregivers with the daily raising of girls, for those interested in social theory, I will very clearly be calling for fundamental changes—not only in patriarchy, but in feminism." That same blend of science, strategies, and social theory will appear in this book as well, but with a new emphasis on what I believe is the revelation of a potential new path in parenting in the last decade and a half, since the mapping of the human genome in 2003. In exploring this new path for parenting and educating girls, we will look at research on XX genetics, the female brain, and science-based strategies for nurturing our daughter's deepest needs.

As in *Saving Our Sons* (2017), there are sections of this book that reveal decades of controversy surrounding science-based advocacy for girls. As a philosopher of science, I have briefed U.S. Congress members, provided information to two White Houses, and spoken for the U.N. on gender issues. From top to bottom, Americans and world citizens are searching for answers to questions like, "What do we mean by girl and woman?" "How do we raise healthy resilient daughters?" "What is female identity and what is gender identity?" There is, as you know, a battle in our culture between different ways of seeing sex and gender.

Some of the controversies I've been involved in grow from my nature-based philosophy of child development, the idea that to raise healthy children, 1) we should use all three assets—*nature, nurture, and culture* (the three parts of this book reflect all three of these assets) and 2) we ought to begin our journey by understanding our children's *nature*. In my previous books I have argued that rather than "nurture vs. nature," "nurture *the* nature" is the most useful foundation for social health of children. The sciences grounding our understanding of that "nature" are neurobiology, neuropsychology, ethology, and epigenetics, among others. This book, like my previous ones, hopes to build bridges between different viewpoints on gender issues, through a scientific, practical, and holistic parenting lens.

In every chapter, you'll meet girls and women I've had the honor of working with in my private practice over the last 25 years; in Fortune 500 companies where I worked as a gender consultant for ten years; in hundreds of schools that I and our Gurian Institute team have visited; and among scientists with whom I've collaborated. You'll also meet my wife, Gail, a family therapist in private practice. A few of our family stories will augment the other research and stories in this book with some good humor and fun anecdotes of one family grappling with girls' lives together.

The opening quote from the poet Mary Oliver is a basis point for my own parenting—I reach for perfection but do not expect to ever really reach it. Parenting is not a perfect proposition. It is messy and it can become even more messy when our minds are constantly battered by new theories, concepts, anecdotal experiments, and ideas about how to be the best parent.

You'll find that my approach is somewhat different. I will not ask you to trust myriad experts without confirming what experts say. I'll help you study your own homes, schools, communities—and your girls as a *citizen scientist* who is focused on how girls thrive. The best science available to us shows us that unless we are abusing our children, most of our ideas on parenting, no matter how disparate, ought to be considered potentially worthwhile. Our parenting instincts are generally quite good. Because parents, teachers, extended family members, and professionals are attached and bonded to girls, we can instinctively become scientists of their development. By becoming scientists, we can trust ourselves and, when we see that we are making mistakes, correct them.

As I help you become a "scientist," I will ask you to use your new wisdom to judge for yourself what experts and social media trends claim are "good for girls." If your own science proves *me* wrong, I hope you will toss out the concept you have disproved. Meanwhile, if I bring up something that does not sit well with you at first, I hope you'll read on. I will back up even my controversial ideas with science.

The Dominant Gender Paradigm

In subtle ways throughout the book, and then fully in the last chapter, I will explore with you what I call the "Dominant Gender Paradigm" (DGP). This paradigm controls certain areas of academics, government, and the media (what I call "the Big Three") and from that dominance, it makes a nature-based approach to girls' development difficult today. The DGP, among other things, perpetuates the idea that sex and gender are mainly socialized, not natural. Even some academics who have access to all the science in this book manipulate data to pretend that nature plays a limited role in sex and gender.

A recent example appears in a small group of academics who formed the American Council for Co-Educational Schooling to fight the innovation of single-sex schools and classrooms. The group developed a small meta-analysis for *Science* that cherry-picked data so that it could claim that sex and gender differences had little to do with the education of girls and boys. While nearly every other gender scientist disagrees with the minimalist findings of the group regarding sex differences in the brain, the group's attempt to push ideology on our school systems penetrated the media and government, and various school districts are now spending millions of dollars fighting against the ACCES attacks. Sadly, the people perpetrating the DGP mainly sit behind desks—they don't focus on researching homes, schools, and communities themselves—and from that seat, they create thin and unnatural stereotypes of girls and boys.

The Minds of Girls does not grow from a DGP approach to children's lives. Growing instead from an alliance between hands-on research and human biology, it asks you to be somewhat political in advocating for girls around you. As you use natural science to help create family and school systems that work best for girls and boys, you'll also be protecting vulnerable populations among both. You'll be asserting that both sexes have existed for millions of years and will exist for as long as humanity survives. They are templated to work together, in complementarity, rather than in opposition. Their sexual baseline is binary, you'll be empowered to say, even while certain aspects of gender can become fluid. Seeing both the binary and the fluid at once is the "small thing" that is revolutionary for our children.

In pursuit of that small but tenacious revolution, I hope you will read this book on your own when you can, but also in book groups with other parents, educators, and mentors. Science is a communal profession—we all get to use it! Please feel free to reach out to me and our Gurian Institute team via www.gurianinstitute.com, www.michaelgurian.com, and through our social media. You'll find resources in our "Gurian family" that you can use to further your work—online courses, a subscription service that provides you with video clips or new strategies every month, and many other assets. We at the Gurian Institute are your companions in this journey. Thank you for joining this cause.

—Michael Gurian, the Gurian Institute, 2018

PART I

NATURE

Chapter 1

The Natural Girl:
New Brain Sciences and Your Daughter

"The new sciences of human nature…expose the psychological unity of our species beneath the superficial differences of physical appearance and parochial culture. They make us appreciate the wondrous complexity of the human mind, which we are apt to take for granted…. They identify the moral intuitions that we can put to work in improving our lot. They promise a natural-ness in human relationships, encouraging us to treat people in terms of how they do feel rather than how some theory says they ought to feel."

—Steven Pinker, Author of *The Blank Slate: The Modern Denial of Human Nature*

"COME PLAY WITH ME, DADDY," Gabrielle, 4, invited me one sunny spring day in her childhood. On this day, she wore her a ruffled blue skirt and a white t-shirt that hugged her torso like skin. Her brown hair fell in waves behind her and her hands were too small to clutch more than one doll at a time. She was the kind of little girl who looked her parents directly in their eyes, and they adored her for it.

I heard her playtime from down the hall, so I had tiptoed out of my study and into her doorway. Before she saw me, I stood there watching her interactions with her dolls and stuffed animals. She was healthy, growing, and already resilient, having survived a very difficult birth on a cold, snowy February day, four years earlier. On that day, I stood in blue hospital scrubs watching Dr. Peter Fern's scalpel cut through Gail's abdominal flesh. After a grueling labor of 34 hours, a C-section on Gail had to be ordered. There were worries over Gail and the baby. Now Dr. Fern smiled behind his blue mask as he successfully lifted our bloody Gabrielle out of the darkness.

"Is she okay?" Gail whispered from behind the cloth wall between her face and her stomach. Under an array of local anesthetics, she was groggy but present.

"She's gorgeous," I gushed.

The doctor and nurses echoed, "Very beautiful."

"Yes, yes," Dr. Fern confirmed as he worked.

"Here you are," a nurse said to me, handing me the scissors (more like shears) so that I could, with trembling hands, cut her umbilical cord. When that task was finished, nervous and anxious, I gave the scissors back to the nurse, then held our baby daughter while Dr. Fern cleaned out Gail's cavity so he could drop her uterus back off the ledge of her stomach and down again into the dark. Bringing Gabrielle to Gail, I watched my wife touch our miraculous first child until the nurse took Gabrielle to a metal table, cleaned her with a towel, wrapped her in a thin blanket, and brought her swaddled body back to a medication-numbed but still awake Gail. After Gail touched Gabrielle to her face, the nurse put our baby in a square plastic bucket on a cart and wheeled her away. As I stood, amazed, my latex gloved palms still tingled from the feeling of having held my first child in my hands. I did not know it, but I would become a "citizen scientist" of girls' lives almost immediately.

Which is exactly what I was, four years later, as my daughter noticed me and asked me to come play with her. I grinned gladly and entered a world of ponies and unicorns, books on tables, papers and crayons in neat piles or strewn around, colored Legos in a plastic carton, pictures she had drawn hung by her parents on her walls—a room she alternatively made into a house, hospital, school, or family. Sitting down next to her, I asked, "What are we playing?" She answered by explaining the complex veterinary game she was involved in. The animals to the right were making their way, like animals entering Noah's Ark, toward the dolls to her left, where the hospital was.

Because Daddy is a philosopher of science, I often had a bit of a hidden agenda in playtimes with Gabrielle and Davita, who came to us three years after her sister. From earliest toddler playtimes and coaching the girls at soccer to helping them with *bat mitzvahs* and analyses of boyfriends, a part of me observed our scenes together with scientific eyes. Playtimes got recorded in a gray matter area of my brain called "research" and their rooms became laboratories.

"What should we do with this truck?" I asked. Three inches long, the truck was part of a set of two Mack trucks and two Mustang cars

I had bought my daughters, not only to encourage them to play with trucks and thus avoid gender stereotypes, but also to test the nature-based theory of gender I was developing. "Should I move the truck over here?" I asked.

She pondered this a second, then offered me a trade as she lifted a curly-haired doll (Ainsley) out of the nest of dolls and instructed me to comb Ainsley's hair while she took the truck in her hand and said, "I think I'll name him Larry." She then placed the truck on the floor and put another doll, Sarah, into the truck bed. Once Sarah was well-placed, Gabrielle smoothed Sarah's dress out. For my part, I continued combing Ainsley's hair, curious about what Gabrielle would do next. Gabrielle finished fluffing Sarah's dress, then drove the doll-laden truck toward the pile of Legos to her left.

"Where's Sarah going?" I asked.

"To the school," Gabrielle responded. "Larry's taking her."

"That's great. I bet she'll really like school."

Now came the next part of the experiment. I set Ainsley down to my right and picked up two figures, Winnie the Pooh and Chewbacca. When Sarah arrived at the veterinary hospital, I swatted Winnie and Chewbacca together with my hands so that the two creatures made a kind of muffled slapping sound.

"Daddy, don't!" Gabrielle yelled.

I did it again.

"You'll hurt them!" Gabrielle insisted. She grabbed at them to get them away from the misguided father.

"Okay, sorry," I deferred, and handed them back to her where she hugged both stuffed animals to her chest protectively and with some irritation.

"What was I thinking?" I grinned apologetically.

"I don't know!" she exclaimed like her mother, who has more than a few hundred times sighed, "*Michael, what were you thinking*?!"

"But look," I smiled to my daughter, "They're okay, see?"

Gabrielle brought Pooh and Chewbacca away from her chest with a forehead-crinkling frown. Perhaps because we had executed this experiment a few times in her life already, or perhaps because she was just in a forgiving mood that day, she said, "I guess so."

But she set the two animals safely beside her, as far away from her savage father as possible.

* * *

This kind of playtime with Gabrielle and Davita was different than what my brother and I experienced in our childhoods, though I didn't understand the science of it back then. For me, as a boy growing up in the sixties, GI Joe, Superman, Batman, and Fantastic Four action figures were sacred play things. While my parents, Jack and Julia Gurian, moved us around America and the world many times in our boyhoods (just before her death, my mother joked with my father that they had lived in forty different houses while raising their children), there was not one country or culture in which boys and girls played in exactly the same way. Perhaps my first unconscious "scientific" observation about gender differences was one that most parents understand instinctively—boys don't form communities of constant emotion-talk with our held-objects like my daughters did with theirs.

Phil and I formed deep bonds with our toys, of course, but often by swatting our action figures together, throwing them at one another or up in the air, pulling them apart to peer inside, battling them against (and thus, with) one another, and then leaving them in corners or in piles to be battered and experimented on the next day. For Phil and me, the hair of certain dolls we found lying around did not exist to be quietly combed in the back of a toy truck, then neatly placed in the school, but instead, to be caked with mud.

Phil and I were not macho boys. We were socialized by our parents to be more like girls in our play than many boys were. Because they were feminists, my parents taught us to nurture dolls as much as possible. They wanted us to be gentle boys, to talk about what we felt, search for inner landscapes of emotion and relationship at all costs. Both Phil and I gained from this effort, but already as toddler males we did not feel, at a cellular level, the need to put as many feelings into words with our objects as girls did. We were more physically active in our games, throwing objects through the environmental space around us more than girls did.

While we were being raised in the 1960s, some brain research was already showing the female proclivity to focus more on people and more sedentary games, and the male proclivity to focus more on gross motor movement and "things." But we didn't know this. We were just kids living out our natures. Not until the early 1990s, just after Gabrielle's birth, did I begin to fully comprehend girls and boys from a scientific perspective.

By the time Davita was born in 1993, I had confirmed clinical and laboratory research in comparative gender studies in cities of the U.S. and villages of eastern Turkey. Mirroring the lab research, I found that there were consistent differences cross-culturally in nurturing style, spatial play, emotive verbalization, and general behavior between boys and girls. I realized that if human social systems did not re-form toward understanding these differences, our children would potentially not thrive. Girls who need resilience-building would get enabling and those who need more encouragement might receive harsh and destructive influence. Boys who need to learn kinesthetically would be taught in ways incorrect for their brain anatomy.

Davita was born under less tense and frightening circumstances than her sister's (Her C-section was planned; thus, Gail did not go through the two days of excruciating labor). As I cut Davita's umbilical cord, and held her in my hands, I felt the love of this baby equal to my love of her sister while also realizing I was even better prepared now to raise a girl. I understood that there is a distinct "mind of girls" that needed to be savored, nurtured, and grown consciously.

* * *

If you are parenting or work with girls, I think you may have, even if unconsciously, wondered, "What is a girl?" and "What is a woman?" Everywhere around us is research on the minds of girls and women, but everywhere too is cultural noise that can, at times, try to stop us from answering these questions deeply. This chapter will help you answer the questions for yourself. Our Gurian Institute database, which includes survey instruments and brain-based cadres in parenting, education, mental health, and business development, reveal facts and applications of the answers we and our teams have developed—answers that you too can develop in your own home and neighborhood. But first and foremost, the answers must be *yours*.

Become a Citizen Scientist

Almost fifty years ago, Albert Einstein said, "Science should not be left to scientists." He was not denying the genius of scientists; rather, he posited that science should not remain in the laboratory because even people who are not scientists can model from scientific study to create their own studies and experiments.

You are that person. You can use the sciences of nature, nurture, and culture to answer for yourself, "What is a girl?" and "Who is a woman?" Because you are a parent, educator, or mentor of children, you have access to a laboratory. You can play on the floor with your daughters; volunteer at your children's school and study the children there; observe your children's car pool conversations, chores, and work time; study their media time, bedtime, and homework experiences. You can see how your kids interact on the playground with each other as four-year-olds, then move some of their social life to smart phones as fourteen-year-olds. Wherever you live or travel, and in whatever you do, there are girls and boys, and women and men—all can be your test subjects.

To become a citizen scientist, you need a keen eye, a resource of some kind to guide you (like this book), a yellow pad or new document in your computer, and access to the Internet. There have been citizen scientists of children since there were parents, but the Internet and our open social dialogue today have made it possible for each of us to make conscious what we are studying. You can use this book as a model for reading and integrating meta-studies of laboratory work I have provided in the Notes and Resources at the end of this book. I have also provided more than 1,000 clinical studies for you to look at on: www.michaelgurian.com/research.

Over the last thirty years, I've asked tens of thousands of parents and teachers to replicate the kinds of experiments I did with my daughters in their playtime, as well as many other experiments that provide "data" on their children, their students, and their communities. From the trenches, these people have helped academics, governmental officials, and the media to push beyond encrusted and ideological gender theories by developing wisdom of practice research (citizen science) in their own local environments.

As you continue reading this book, begin your citizen science by observing children around you. If you notice that they are in distress, try to analyze what may be causing it. Continue researching, observing, increasing your pool of laboratory subjects and scientific tools, and discuss what you learn with others who are in the trenches with you. We have come to a time in history when we must become citizen scientists if we are to do best by our children. The Internet has provided us with millions of different viewpoints which we can and must assess through a scientific lens.

What is a Girl? Who is a Woman?

These are questions of female nature (sex) and female identity (gender). As a person who is constantly answering these questions, I have come to believe that those answers are crucial to a safe and stable childhood for both girls and boys. Why would we apply parenting and teaching techniques to girls without understanding who girls are? Even if you have a trans girl, sex and gender play a huge part in that child's upbringing—why not focus on it? There is a great deal of public confusion about who and what our girls are. Because of that confusion, our families are making health-related errors that cost some girls their lives and other girls their success and happiness.

Should We Move Beyond He or She?

To develop and use a constructive parenting philosophy without understanding girls and women is like setting out for another country without a map. *Time* recently published a cover story, "Beyond He or She," that illustrates very well our cultural confusion about female nature. The editors introduced and summarized the articles in the issue this way:

"*Time* interviewed dozens of people around the U.S. about their attitudes toward sexuality and gender, from San Francisco to small-town Missouri. Many said they believe that both sexuality and gender are less like a toggle between this-or-that and more like a spectrum that allows for many—even endless—permutations of identity. Some of those young people identified as straight, others as gay, still others as genderqueer, gender fluid, asexual, gender nonconforming and queer. Several said they use the pronoun *they* rather than *he* or *she* to refer to themselves.

"This variety of identities is something that people are seeing reflected in the culture at large. Facebook, with its 1 billion users, has about 60 options for users' gender. Dating app Tinder has about 40. Influential celebrities, such as Miley Cyrus (who spoke to *Time* for this article), have come out as everything from flexible in their gender to sexually fluid to 'mostly straight.'"

The articles in *Time* reflect the editor's desire to explore the attitudes of a relatively small group of people who responded to the surveys. If you get the issue and read it, you'll notice that the issue has an ideological bent and avoids looking at sex on the brain (female/male brain spectrum). The issue avoids scientific analysis regarding the minds of girls because the editors wanted to offer up to readers the idea that humanity is ready to finish with "He" or "She."

I will take a different tack in this chapter by helping you go deeper into the female and male brain. However, I will also agree with the *Time* editors that "He" or "She" can be relegated to human history—the new natural sciences prove to us that we live in a world of "He" *and* "She." A responsible scientific approach to "What is a Girl, who is a Woman?" will encounter three sets of sciences interwoven in this book:

- the sciences of nature
- the sciences of nurture
- the sciences of culture.

We will apply insights from each and all of them in order to understand girls' assets and to help girls meet the challenges they face. The word "or" is no longer needed for this work. Daniel Amen, M.D., neuropsychiatrist, and author of *Unleash the Power of the Female Brain,* explored this point with me recently.

"The time has come to stop believing there is a single way of defining a girl or a woman," he said. "There are multiple ways, beginning with exploring the female brain."

Research from brain scans—the kind of research on which this book is grounded—reveal that "She" and "He" have been used since the beginning of time because they accurately represent the chromosomal pattern we are born with—XX for female, XY for male. Numerous scientists, including Dr. Amen, study these gene-based female/male patterns by exploring both sex and gender.

The Four Aspects of Sex/Gender

In the natural science approach, there are four aspects (quadrants or *chambers*) of sex/gender. Without overusing the metaphor of the four chambers of the human heart, I do think there is some resonance with the heart since everything about sex and gender does relate in some way to human love. Because scholarly and public literature use the terms "sex" and "gender" relatively interchangeably today, I will do the same in this book. But first, let's define what we mean by each one. All four of these chambers or aspects together provide answers to "What is a girl, who is a woman?"

Sexual Anatomy. The first of the aspects or "chambers" in sex/gender is, obviously, *anatomical.* A girl is a girl and a woman a woman because of her body. While there are always exceptions to a rule (some girls are XXY and some are XYY), 99.9 percent of females are anatomically female because the XX creates that anatomy during its gene expression throughout a lifespan. This anatomy is, for nearly every human being, controlled by reproductive organs that are binary, *in utero,* then in childhood and adulthood. Binary means that they are significantly different between females and males. These sex-different human organs work along a hypothalamic-pituitary-gonadal axis to control the binary female/male.

David C. Page, M.D., professor of biology at the Massachusetts Institute of Technology, recently captured this aspect of She/He. "Our genomes are 99.9% identical from one person to the next as long as the two individuals being compared are two men or two women. But if we compare a woman and a man, the genetic differences are 15 times greater than the genetic differences for two males or two females."

Page's reference to genetics is crucial to raising girls, and so it is crucial to this book as well. Genes really do matter. In her book, *Eve's Rib,* Marianne J. Legato, M.D., warns us to be careful about pretending this is not so because the pretense can negatively affect both women and men.

"Everywhere we look," she writes, "the two sexes are startlingly and unexpectedly different, not only in their internal function but in the ways that they experience illness. To care for them, we must see them as who they are: female and male."

Page and Legato are talking about what used to be called sexual trait differences, now called *gender trait differences*. It should be obvious, of course, that female and male anatomy are not the same, and that females and males experience various different traits. And it is obvious, at least in the science itself, because this first chamber or aspect of a girl's and woman's identity also hides other elements of nature within it, including aspect 2: the female and male brain.

Sexual Anatomy of the Brain. Sex on the brain (recently altered in public discourse to "gender on the brain") is the second aspect and, like human sexual anatomy, it is binary (gender trait differences are clear and robust between females and males). The reason for this is that sex/gender differences begin chromosomally, as we just noted, then become "expressed" (generated) in utero via the XX and XY chromosome markers that direct the fetus to differentiate male/female in Mom's womb before the child is born. Over a period of months in utero, the differences between female and male brains get pre-set. They will mix with personality genetics and environmental influences once the child is born to get further expressed, but their gene expression begins in utero.

Some examples:

- XY children (he) come out processing language mainly on the left side of the brain while XX children (she) come out of the womb processing language and word production on both sides of the brain.
- Female brains process their daily experience through up to 10 times more white matter activity than males.
- Males generally utilize up to 7 times more gray matter activity to process daily life and learning than their sisters do.
- Females are driven more by oxytocin than testosterone and males more by testosterone than oxytocin.

As this book continues, we will go even deeper into these female/male brain differences and I'll help you apply them to better give your daughters what they need. We will also explore the pitfalls of *not* integrating female/male brain difference ("sex on the brain") into child development philosophies and teacher, parent, and corporate training.

Because the XX and XY brain differences are trans-cultural (existing across the globe), females and males are who they are in all cultures. The X and Y chromosomes transcend culture-difference, and a great deal of sex/gender comes in on the human genome. This is why school-wide training about "sex on the brain" has been proven so effective by our Gurian Institute team and others.

While culture controls a great deal of how gender roles play out, culture does not change the fact that the female brain processes words on both sides of the brain, or that the male brain processes them mainly on the left. These brain differences are binary, and school systems that do not take them into account will likely create underachievement in students, both female and male.

Courageous Conversation

LGBT Are Not a "Choice"—They Are Natural

Sexual Orientation. This third aspect of sexuality/gender includes the LGB portions of LGBT (Lesbian, Gay, Bi-Sexual, Transgender). We will look at the T (Transgender) in a moment, as well as gender fluidity.

Approximately 5 - 10 percent of mammals, birds, and primates are LGB. They have a homosexual or same-sex biological attraction. Their sexually dimorphic nucleus (SDN) in the medial preoptic area (POA) of the anterior hypothalamus (the densely-packed cluster of cells in the part of the brain that controls sexual orientation) is shaped like the same nucleus in the other-sex brain. This means, for instance, that a lesbian's SDN is the same size as a man's. Meanwhile, a LGB person will likely still have a male or female brain (e.g. verbal centers gender differentiated) but can have a cross-sex SDN such that aspect 1 of sex/gender generally replicates itself in the SDN of the brain for 90 to 95% of humans, primates, and other animals, but not the other 5 – 10%.

This is an example of the crucial idea in our citizen science, and throughout the field of sex/gender on the brain: exceptions prove the rule. Every exception to a rule that emerges through science does not de-activate or destroy the rule, but rather proves its prevalence. There are some males who do some language and word production on the right side, but most males do most of that on the left side: exceptions prove the rule. Most people are heterosexual, but some are homosexual: the exceptions prove the rule. Simultaneously, the exceptions create mysteries that hopefully will continue the human process of activating new scientific principles and ideas with which to develop policies that include both the rules and the exceptions.

The exact reason for the SDN exception (homosexuality) is yet unknown, but we do know that homosexuality is at least partially genetic. The Harvard Medical Letter publicized the genetic component of homosexuality (and thus, heterosexuality) in the early 1990s. Since gene mapping in 2003, geneticists have been looking at various X chromosome clusters, such as the Xq28 marker, to try to discover the elusive "gay gene." These genes, which run in family lines, appear to develop gay/straight SDNS via in utero hormonal surges that format various parts of the brain, including the SDN, before the child is born.

Homosexuality then, is, like aspects 1 and 2, mainly biological. In the battle for equal marriage rights for gays and lesbians, the brain science has been very helpful. Being gay, lesbian, bi-sexual, and transgender is not a "choice" but a fact, and LGBT and other gender-spectrum individuals are just as human as anyone else.

Gender Fluidity. The fourth aspect of He and She is the one the *Time* article mainly discussed. While reproductive sex hormones exist in each male and female cell, they exist in differing quantities between human beings so that the extent to which each individual brain is sexualized pre-birth for female/male is vast enough to include variety and diversity among the more than 7 billion people on earth. The term "gender fluidity" was initially used to represent this gender spectrum, but lately it is being used as a way of arguing that there is no female and male. But this is just ideological experimentation with no real science behind it.

Because they don't analyze the four aspects of sex and gender, magazine articles like the one in *Time* confuse people. They argue rhetorically that there is little or no "sex" on the brain, only "gender," and that gender is not binary but completely fluid. Some people in power, including well-respected academics in Ontario, Canada and at Oxford University, have bought this conceptualization so fully they have lobbied for "outlawing" he and she as pronouns.

Their mistake grows from the pressure of ideological conformity. They are willing to bypass science, nature, and common sense to say there is no female and male. They don't realize that the existence of gender fluidity and a gender spectrum does not deny the binary nature of sex on the brain or vice versa. Even transgender people, who are exceptions to the rule in their matching of aspect 1 and 2, feel the pull of the female and male brain. They are people with female anatomy carrying self-defining aspects of a male brain or male anatomy carrying self-defining aspects of a female brain. They know it and want to match body with brain.

A girl's identity is both a matter of being female-not-male *and* of constantly expanding what she believes a female is. Thus, the first three chambers of sex/gender exist on a spectrum. Even aspect 3 exists on a spectrum—some lesbian and gay people are bi-sexual (bridging sexual orientations), while some are overtly gay or lesbian, not bi-sexual. Everything we can say about sex and gender must include the gender spectrum if we are to be accurate, which means there are "bridge brains"—females and males who bridge the genders. Scientists estimate that between 10 and 20 percent of individuals have "bridge brains," brain-exceptions that prove both the existence of the gender spectrum and prove the rule of sex-on-the-brain.

"She" then, includes four aspects of sex and gender—anatomy, brain biology, sexual orientation, and gender spectrum. To answer, "What is a girl, who is a woman?" in ways most helpful to parenting and teaching girls, all four aspects must be integrated. We must realize that female and male are both binary *and* exist on a gender-brain spectrum. When my GI team and I show brain scans at our lectures and trainings, participants can see both the gender spectrum and the binary nature of sex/gender. They can see how well-differentiated male/female brains are, and how wonderfully subtle the brain spectrum is.

Time inadvertently proved the concept of "exceptions prove the rule" when its editors wrote: "In a new survey from LGBTQ advocacy organization GLAAD, conducted by Harris Poll: 20% of millennials say they are something other than strictly . . . cisgender."

Cisgender is the term used by some media and scholars for males and females who feel that their own gender identity matches the biological sex they were born into (aspect 1 and 2). The 1 in 5 millennials in the survey who saw themselves as other than cisgender provided interesting anecdotal data for understanding exceptions to self-conceptions of female and male (gender), but that still means that 4 out of 5 people know themselves as distinctly He and She (sex).

Did You Know?

There Is a Transgender Brain

As we noted, transgender brains are exceptions that prove the rule. Researchers now understand why from studying some of the approximately 0.3 to 0.7 percent of people worldwide who are born with an extreme bridge brain in a cross-sex body—e.g. a "male" brain (aspects 2 and 3) in a female body (aspect 1) or vice versa, a "female" brain in a male body/biology. Recent studies confirming this have emerged in the U.S., Spain, Austria, and the Netherlands.

Spanish psychobiologist Antonio Guillamon of the National University of Distance Education in Madrid and neuropsychologist Carme Junqué Plaja of the University of Barcelona are two leaders in this field. Using MRI scans, they studied the brains of 24 female-to-males and 18 male-to-females. In the MRIs, they found that a number of brain structures in the trans people were similar to the brains of their internally felt gender, not the sex associated with their sexual anatomy—the physiological anatomy they were born with. The female-to-male subjects, for instance, had relatively thin subcortical areas like most men, while male-to-female subjects tended to have thinner cortical regions in the right hemisphere, like the usual female brain. Such differences became more pronounced after treatment. "Trans people," Guillamon points out, "have a unique kind of brain." It is a modified male or female brain.

The term I use is "extreme bridge brain" to help explain a

16

trans person's brain—a brain that not only bridges the sexes, but also the genders. Researchers such as psychologist Sarah M. Burke of VU University Medical Center in Amsterdam and biologist Julie Bakker of the Netherlands Institute for Neuroscience have corroborated this concept. Using MRIs to examine 39 prepubertal and 41 adolescent boys and girls with gender dysphoria (the sense that their brains and bodies don't match), the researchers saw that the brains responded to androstadienone, a steroid with pheromone-like properties that causes a different smell-response in the hypothalamus of females and males.

Trans adolescents responded to an odor like peers of their internally experienced sex (male or female), so what the "male" brain experienced within the female body, and what the "female" brain experienced within the male body fit the idea of a transgender brain. This is important research because, as Baudewijntje Kreukels at VU University Medical Center points out, "sex differences in responding to odors cannot be influenced by training or environment."

As a culture, we will certainly learn more about exceptions to the rule with every advancing year and every new study. Because it is difficult to carry a disconnection between sex on the brain and sex on the body, both internally and culturally, trans people can suffer a great deal of hardship. As this brain and body are bullied and treated reprehensibly by others in the society, transgender people face a high depression and suicide rate. Hopefully, as brain science is brought even more completely into social arguments about sex and gender, it will assist us in understanding and supporting transgender individuals, and all exceptions to rules.

Gender Fluidity and Gender Science

The minds of girls, then, are expansive, always unique, quite amazing. Any girl can at any time make internal decisions about how to see all four aspects of sex and gender culturally. *Time* reporters focused on gender fluidity, especially among young people in the developed West, and saw how gender roles are changing in ways helpful to society and reflective of increasing economic and personal privilege. This is a good thing.

But it also reflects the fact that we have culturally experimented with wondering whether to throw sex and gender out the window altogether, conflating "gender roles" with "sex" and "gender," and forgetting that there are four chambers to this heart. This forgetfulness is not new. It existed in a different voice when I was the age of many of the millennial respondents to the *Time* survey. What we called the "androgyny" movement is now being called the gender fluidity movement—the feeling that any person can identify with both masculine and feminine aspects of oneself.

As a young person in the sixties and seventies, I was happy we had the new social movement. It helped us fight for female equality, gender equity, and a sense of a new, complex man new males wanted to be.

But once I had children, I and many others saw that androgyny wasn't the whole picture. Boys' and girls' play is different, we saw quickly. Girls' and boys' educational experiences are different. Many androgyny-seeking parents of the past two generations have told me, "I was thinking 'boy' and 'girl' were just social constructs until I had a boy and a girl. Once you have kids, the two sexes become obvious."

Like all social movements, and like the androgyny movement before it, the gender fluidity movement will be both useful and problematic. As the androgyny movement swept through the political "Big Three" (universities, government, and the media), it created arts, literature, theater, and film in new ways; it created expanded conversations; it helped women in the workplace; it helped women and men thrive together. But because it confused sex and gender, certain people in the Big Three forgot about the genome, XX/XY, sex on the brain, and "female" and "male." In the end, while expanding our horizons, it did the same thing the gender fluidity movement is doing now by convincing academics, government, and the media to pretend there are few or no relevant neural difference between females and males.

Moving Beyond Simplistic Ideas About Girls

When schools try for impossible neural androgyny, children suffer. In the 1980s and 90s, the academic world, then the public, then our governments and legislators altered our school cultures so that educators are not trained on how to specifically teach math, science, language, and good behavior most effectively to boys and girls. Yet our population of girls and boys is growing ever more complex, and our teachers enter school systems unprepared to deal with the learning brains of boys and girls. As a result, our children have teachers doing their best to try to adapt to natural He and She learners (girls and boys whose brains obviously learn differently), while these same teachers are told academically that He and She learners are an illusion.

As a result, school systems constantly over-punish males for normal male behavior and under-develop resilience in females who need, in many ways, a girl-specific approach to resilience and STEM learning (I will explore these areas specifically in later chapters). Children do not get the help they need as girls and boys and often have difficulty "adulting" (the millennial word for growing up). Businesses lose both female and male populations to under-achievement and workplace tension. Bullying and emotional overreaction control school and social media environments. Our culture bends dangerously in its culture wars toward under-nurturing its children, especially those girls and boys who are having difficulty already.

These children need us to understand them not just as people, but as females and males.

Not He or She but He *and* She

Gender expansion and gender role equality is a good thing, but trying to dissolve sex does not ultimately help us raise, teach, and mentor the minds of our girls. Our culture can and must find a middle ground as we define what and who a girl and woman is. With four "chambers" of the sex/gender heart in mind, I hope you can now look again, with a new "citizen science" eye, at these statements by the *Time* editors: "Facebook, with its 1 billion users, has about 60 options for users' gender. Dating app Tinder has about 40. Influential celebrities, such as Miley Cyrus (who spoke to *Time* for this article), have come out as everything from flexible in their gender to sexually fluid to "mostly straight."

I hope you can see now that the *Time* editors are referring to the second two aspects of sex/gender, not the first two, and they are confusing the *existence* of 60 options with the *prevalent use* of those options. Most people in the world still use she/female and he/male and that use does not harm LGBT people. As a citizen scientist concerned with child development, I hope you will scrutinize the *Time* issue and others like it that have come out throughout the public media (e.g. *National Geographic's* gender issue in May 2017) through the lens of the four aspects of sex/gender, not just the singular concept of gender fluidity.

Pulitzer Prize winning historian, Carl Degler, of Stanford University, recently published *In Search of Human Nature,* a fascinating book in which he points out that the idea of a biological root to human nature was universally accepted throughout human history. Only in the last hundred years did it "all but vanish from social thought." In the last few years, it is, he notes, "reappearing," in books such as the one you are reading, and in studies such as those conducted by Wendy Johnson of the University of Edinburgh, and her colleagues.

Their results, published in "Sex Differences in Variability in General Intelligence," have wisely confirmed the importance of studying sex and gender from the perspective of natural science. Ideological values, Johnson writes, "create emotionally charged climates pervading discussions of sex differences, making it difficult to evaluate scientific data objectively. Values are extremely important and appropriately form the basis of many actions and social contracts. But the laws of nature are not responsible to us or to our values and may not conform to them. It is important to understand the laws of nature as completely as possible within our circumstances in order to actualize our values as we intend."

This latter point is crucial: if we do not understand the laws of nature, we cannot fully actualize the values we have either been born into or developed in life. We may, for instance, highly value the equality of women and their freedom to choose who to be; we may value the delight in a girl's eyes when she learns something so completely her mind flashes with insight and joy; we may value helping girls define themselves first as girls, then as women. But none of these values will become effective practice without our understanding the nature of a girl, the nature of a woman.

If we have any doubt that this is true, we can look to the sciences of astronomy and physics to see both failed and successful collaborations between study of natural law and ideological values. When humanity held to "values" not grounded in natural law, the prevailing social doctrine was that the earth revolved around the sun. Because of these "values," we could only barely explore our own natural inventiveness. With the arrival of Copernicus, Newton, and others, we began to transcend ideological values and understand how nature actually worked. From there, we made leaps in social consciousness not by choosing natural law over values, but by combining natural laws and values realistically— adapting our values to fit who we are.

To enjoy the evolution of this kind of consciousness, check out a wonderful book by physicist Neil deGrasse Tyson, his recent bestseller, *Astrophysics for People in a Hurry*. In it, he presents the realism of a social thinker who is both a proponent of natural law theory and of various modernistic human values. Capturing the evolution of this way of being, he looks back a century. "Einstein's general theory of relativity, put forth in 1916, gives us our modern understanding of gravity, in which the presence of matter and energy curves the fabric of space and time surrounding it. In the 1920s, quantum mechanics would be discovered, providing our modern account of all that is small: molecules, atoms, and subatomic particles."

Tyson goes on to note that "these two understandings of nature are formally incompatible with one another, which set physicists off on a race to blend the theory of the small with the theory of the large into a single coherent theory of quantum gravity . . . but the clash between gravity and quantum mechanics poses no practical problem for the contemporary universe. Astrophysicists apply the tenets and tools of general relativity and quantum mechanics to very different classes of problems."

In these sentences is wisdom for those of us working in sex and gender issues. The question, "What is a girl, who is a woman?" is as profound a question as "What is a universe?" and "What is an atom?" Sex/gender questions are just as important to human development as atomic ones because the rearing, education, and success of the world's population depends on our answers. From these answers will grow our best practices, and from those practices will grow a resilient, empowered, successful, and emotionally profound adult who will shape our world for the good.

To answer the questions, however, we will need to think simultaneously in large terms like "laws of nature" and in smaller, molecular terms too, like, "How do I build more spatial intelligence in my daughter?" or "In what ways is my daughter an exception to the rule?" We can and must elevate our social conversation to consider all questions at once, just as both Einstein and Bohr could collectively and coherently affect contemporary technology and society in the positive by blending nature and values. Citizen science, I am saying, is as profoundly important—and capable of constantly evolving a binary and fluid philosophy—as physics.

When we fully understand the hidden nature of girls and women and boys and men (even while noting exceptions to the rules), we will discover, in the words of the poet Louise Bogan, "in concrete terms some reflection of the universal laws under which we live—which we must not only accept, but in some manner, forgive—as well as the fact of the human courage and faith necessary to that acceptance." At stake as we understand and develop the minds of girls is our courage and faith as a human society.

For ideological reasons, our culture is polarized in its answers to "What is a girl, who is a woman?" I hope the chapters of this book help you build a bridge between history and religion and natural science and social experiments. The minds of girls are a human treasure—they are absolutely amazing—and those minds are at stake.

Chapter 2

The Amazing Minds of Girls:
Three Minds in One!

> My candle burns at both ends;
> It will not last the night;
> But ah, my foes, and oh, my friends—
> It gives a lovely light!
>
> —Edna St. Vincent Millay, "First Fig"

I RECEIVED THIS EMAIL FROM CARRIE, a mother of four:

"Hello Michael, I'm writing to thank you for your nature-based theory. Your books have been like Bibles to me as I've raised two girls and two boys. In my husband's corporation, the leadership team used Leadership and the Sexes. *I previously worked for that company as an engineer, and I'm still in contact with the CEO, who happens to be a woman. She has two daughters just like I do, and our kids are friends. We spend a lot of time talking about your idea that the minds of girls are so busy so much of the time it is hard to turn them off! For girls and women both, this seem very true to us.*

"My youngest daughter, Sara, is a case in point, and my questions to you revolve mostly around her. She's a good kid at 12, she does her homework, helps with chores, most people like her. She loves soccer and she loves to read and she's constantly talking. Even her siblings, 13, 14, and 16 (girl, boy, boy) tell her to stop talking! I wasn't much of a talker as a kid—though I do recognize the quality she has of her brain never shutting off—but sometimes my husband can overwhelm me with talk talk talk and I have to beg him to stop.

"So, with this background in mind, I have some questions:

"Is this a genetic thing, this talking all the time? Did it pass from my husband to Sara? Or is it something we taught my daughter?

"Isn't it usually true that the woman talks more than the man? If so, since I am not much of a talker, am I a bridge brain?

23

"My daughter really likes math and plays video games with her brothers. Is this unusual for a girl? Is it a good thing or not so good?

"Sara's older sister has had some trouble with depression, which is being treated, and I worry a little about Sara too. I would like to get help from you on that, and I will write another email about that.

"My kids all have smart phones, which is something I'm thinking about changing, but I'm not sure how to change it. Sara seems to get even more wired and high strung when she is texting back and forth on her phone. We take the phones away an hour before bedtime. This is one of the calmest times for her. Do you think we should take the phones away earlier?

"And Michael, what should we do with my daughter to get her to understand how overwhelming it is to have to constantly listen to her talking about anything that's on her mind? We want to nurture her nature, as you say, but we don't want to nurture all the talking anymore! Please help us."

Given the number of topics here, I wrote a long email back to Carrie, and within a few weeks, our Gurian Institute team developed a coaching relationship with her and her family. As we got to know the family, we noticed many of the characteristics of the female brain I will discuss in this chapter. The question about the smart phone I will save for Chapter 8.

The Many Female Brains

Every human brain is many brains in one. We think of the brain as being able to create nearly endless functioning because it contains billions of cells that can activate and deactivate depending on the brain's own genetic template and its stimuli and triggers in its environment. The human brain is miraculous in its adaptability, plasticity, and capacity to learn and grow.

However, the human brain is also self-limiting. The genetics that handle the talent sets of Sara, her siblings, her parents, as well as your children and mine are, in some ways, pre-set. A child who is clearly great at math will have gotten some of that talent from her genes. A child who is a constant talker will also have gained some of that talent—and its potential to irritate family members—genetically. The "nature vs. nurture" argument regarding gender trait differences and certain talent sets worries some people when it comes down on the side of nature, but I will provide you with a different analysis.

Studying and Discussing the Science

To start down this road yourself, I hope you will gather your group and discuss how there really is a "natural girl" who is different from a "natural boy" because the first two aspects of sex/gender are different, even when exceptions are noted. Talk with one another about how each of you has already instinctively integrated gender-brain differences into child-rearing, marriage, and workplace interactions. Discuss the following comment by University of San Francisco neuroscientist Louann Brizendine, author of *The Female Brain* and *The Male Brain:* "The male and female brain are different in the ways they handle stress, communicate, learn, grow, and love."

Do you agree? How?

Go to the Notes and Resources section of this book, if you wish, where you and your teams can find research by the National Institute of Mental Health, the National Institute of Health, the Amen Clinics, Vanderbilt University, Rutgers University, and many others.

Look at this seminal study by accessing it on Google: Halpern, D.F., Benbow, C. P., Geary, D.C., Gur, R.C., Shibley Hyde, J., and Gernsbacher, M.A., "The Science of Sex Differences in Science and Mathematics." It makes up the August 2007 issue of *Psychological Science in the Public Interest* (Volume 8:1). This meta-study was a compromise approach to male/female brain difference research, and you can read it to increasingly arm yourself with deep knowledge of the female and male brains, as well as the political pulse of this work. And if you are a "science geek," you can access approximately 1,000 more studies and resources on the Research Reference List on www.michaelgurian.com. I've placed those studies and resources there to be immediately accessible to everyone because I believe each of us needs to become well-briefed on the science so that we can battle the DGP stereotypes in our communities.

Here is a summary from a 2016 study by Ruben and Raquel Gur of the University of Pennsylvania's Neuroimaging Unit that you can discuss in your group.

"In summary, behavioral measures linked to brain function indicate significant sex differences in performance that emerge early in development with domain variability that relates to brain maturation. Notably, our findings are in line with a robust literature documenting sex difference in laterality and behavior (e.g., Linn and Petersen 1985; Thomas and French 1985; Voyer et al., 1995; Halpern et al., 2007; Williams et al., 2008; Hines 2010; Moreno-Briseño et al., 2010). These findings support the notion that males and females have complementary neurocognitive abilities, with females being more generalists and outperforming males in memory and social cognition tasks and males being more specialists and performing better than females on spatial and motor tasks."

Did You Know?

Ten Key Nature-Based Differences

As you deepen your reading and research into the work of these scientists, you'll find that there are few if any parts of "male" and "female" that don't include differences in the male and female brain. Here are some differences that are pre-set chromosomally, before children are born, and appear in all races and cultures.

The Female Brain	The Male Brain
Up to 10 times more white matter activity	Up to 7 times more gray matter activity
Verbal centers on both sides of the brain	Verbal centers on the left side of the brain
More cross-brain activity for most tasks	More lateralized activity for most tasks
More connectivity of verbal centers to emotive	Less verbal-emotive connections
Fewer active spatial-visual centers in the brain	More active spatial-visual centers in the brain
Higher words-to-feelings ratio	Lower words-to-feelings ratio
More cingulate gyrus activity (up to 4 times)	More cerebellum activity/ larger cerebellum
Faster limbic to frontal lobe development	Slower limbic to frontal lobe development
Higher oxytocin/lower testosterone	Higher testosterone/lower oxytocin

| Oxytocin (bonding) rises when under stress | Testosterone rises when under stress |

These differences can affect:

- How trauma influences the behavior of girls and boys as girls are more predisposed toward overt depression and anxiety disorders than boys.
- The way girls and boys learn. Because girls tend to process so much information verbally, talking with them, and inviting them to talk can enhance their learning and memory achievement. We will explore this more deeply in Chapter 7.
- The way girls and boys grow, physically and social-emotionally. Girls are social-emotional creatures for whom physical appearance is a ground of much of their self-image. This will be a topic of Chapter 4.
- How environmental toxins affect girls. This will be the subject of Chapter 5.
- How females approach sexuality, love, and commitment in some ways differently than males. Girls are experiencing love and affection in some ways adolescent males are not, and this is important to teach them. Chapter 4 will discuss this.
- Differences in communication, discipline, self-discipline, motivation, conflict resolution. When we discuss resilience-building in Chapter 6, we will look carefully at this part of nurturing girls.
- Different approaches to bonding, attachment, and relationships with peers and adults. Even basic attachment can feel different to girls and boys, as we will explore throughout this book.

I love this explanation of internal differences in *The Female Brain,* from neuropsychologist Louann Brizendine.

"Common sense tells us that boys and girls behave differently. We see it every day at home, on the playground, and in classrooms. But what the culture hasn't told us is that the brain dictates these divergent behaviors. The impulses of children are so innate that they kick in even if we adults try to nudge them in another direction.

"One of my patients gave her three-and-a-half-year-old daughter many unisex toys, including a bright red fire truck instead of a doll. She walked into her daughter's room one afternoon to find her cuddling the truck in a baby blanket, rocking it back and forth saying, "Don't worry, little truckie, everything will be all right."

"This isn't socialization. This little girl didn't cuddle her 'truckie' because her environment molded her unisex brain. There is no unisex brain. She was born with a female brain, which came complete with its own impulses. Girls arrive already wired as girls, and boys arrive already wired as boys. Their brains are different by the time they're born, and their brains are what drive their impulses, values, and their very reality."

Since 2003, which is when genome mapping became feasible, parents and professionals have been able to think in terms of mapping some of a child's gene expression. We can have courageous conversations with science to back us up.

Gene expression is the way a child will express in her life the genes she has been born with. Nothing is set in stone, everything is constantly adapting; but even with that caveat in mind, it is liberating to focus our energies as a parent on nurturing the child's nature. My book *Nurture the Nature* (2007) helps you use genome research to try to figure out some of your child's nature (core personality and inborn assets). *The Minds of Girls* helps you continue that quest in your daughter's life.

In this chapter and the next, I will use the miracle of the human brain as my baseline for exploring the themes Carrie has laid out for us, themes that can help you develop a map of your daughter's brain. Here are some topics and strategies we will explore:

1. The mind of a girl is three minds in one—verbal, spatial, and quantitative—with the verbal mind sometimes dominating one or both of the others. Understanding this biological trend in the female brain can immensely help us parent, educate, and mentor girls from birth onward.

2. The female brain relies heavily on white matter activity (spread throughout the brain) for its relational and intellectual work, which can often make that brain feel like it is "never turned

off," especially in comparison to a man's brain. When I show PET and SPECT scans at my lectures and the audiences can see the capacity of the male brain to almost completely shut off when needed, there is often a sigh of envy from women.

3. As in everything we have said already about the brain and everything we will say, female patterns in verbal, spatial, quantitative, and white matter activity are not stereotypes. In all these areas of focus, there are exceptions, and those exceptions both buck the rule and prove the rule.

4. The female brain is more prone to overt depression and to certain kinds of anxiety, e.g. perfectionism, than the male brain. Some of this tendency is genetic—involving brain differences—while most of it also involves hormonal and/ or environmental triggering. All depression must be watched carefully and treated immediately.

In Chapter 3, I will spend more time on how to specifically protect the miraculous lives of girls by using all the assets we can, including genetics. Let's begin by exploring the linkage between genes, gene expression, and the developmental arc of the female brain itself.

Your Daughter's Verbal-Emotive Intelligence

Carrie mentioned my work in businesses and corporations captured in *Leadership and the Sexes*. One of the reasons I wrote that book and asked my colleague, Barbara Annis, to join me, involves the power that corporations can tap into when they decide to maximize their use of the female brain. When they do this, they tap into the power of *female verbal intelligence*. If we are to understand the minds of girls as parents and professionals, we must study this intelligence—a girl's ability to produce words—with an eye towards the ways in which it is a unique asset and (as Carrie was hinting) ways in which it needs mentoring from us if it is to fully thrive.

A brain fact: *The female brain produces and processes words on both sides of the brain and connects those words to memory, sensorial, and emotive centers in the mid-brain on both sides, as well. The male brain produces words only or mainly on the left, and for some male brains, only or mainly in the front left part of the brain. Unlike females, males connect word centers to limbic, sensorial, memory, and emotive centers only or mainly on the left, especially the front left.*

29

Think about this for a minute. Doesn't it fit your life experience? Don't you notice more girls than boys producing more words about more varied sensorial and emotive phenomenon, i.e. how people feel? If you take a tape recorder around with you for a month, I think you'll see and feel this male/female difference up close.

Recent research shows that the cholinergic neurotransmitters in the female brain (chemicals that make human brains plastic) may be more fully developed and connected in girls than boys near or in the female brain's word centers. Conversely, some of the inhibitory chemicals (chemicals that inhibit or counteract the cholinergic neurotransmitters) more conspicuously develop to inhibit words-to-feelings connections in male brains than in female brains.

Females, then, have a biological and gene-based tendency to produce more words. Even when she is silent, your daughter is probably living in a wealth of words. Knowing this, however, does not mean every girl will talk more than every boy. In fact, a study at the University of Arizona, in which researchers provided a word-counter to college students showed that young women's spoken-word use was only slightly higher than the men's spoken-word use on any given day. Your own citizen science will show you that some guys talk a lot, like Sara's father, and some girls and women do not.

What the Arizona researchers did not count, however, was the "holy trinity" of word use: *reading, writing, and speaking*. It is in this aggregate trinity that girls use more words than boys, and this aggregate trend seems to hold true throughout the world. When researchers study all three aspects of word use in an experiment, they find that females may speak around the same amount as males, but girls and women read and write words more than males do in any given day. Halpern, Gur, Benbow, and many others, have proven this with brain scan research, laboratory experiments, and multi-cultural analysis. Benbow, for instance, studied more than a million children to determine her findings.

These scientists have also discovered a data-driven way to study female vs. male word use: math, science, and literacy scores in school-based tests. Particularly useful are the PISA-OECD tests of 15-year-olds in 72 industrialized countries. These tests show a math/science disadvantage in female aggregate scores of approximately 3 points and a literacy gap in males' scores of 10 points. American NAEP (National Assessment of Educational Progress) scores show similar results.

On these comprehensive tests, the literacy gap for males is three times as high as the math/science gap for females. There are always many reasons for a given finding, but one of those reasons is the female brain's advantage in word production and word use—especially on written tests of literacy.

In Chapter 7, we will focus on the math/science and STEM gap in order to help girls succeed better in these fields. On both the math/science and literacy fronts, I will argue that the word-use advantage in the female brain is clearly brain-based, and therefore all the solutions we develop to close literacy and STEM gaps must also be brain-based. As I have done throughout my career, I will again be arguing in this book that focusing on culture alone (e.g. "gender bias keeps girls and women out of certain careers") will not solve issues raised by gender gaps in core classes and core careers. Your daughter's verbal abilities—in reading, writing, and speaking—comprise an amazing quality of being.

At the same time, verbal, quantitative, and spatial intelligence can become unbalanced in any brain, female or male. In the female brain, verbal intelligence often takes center stage to such an extent that word production and word use may overpower and mitigate quantitative or spatial activity in the female brain. One reason is that the female brain's attention to myriad details around it, especially sensorial and emotive details, can distract it from certain other tasks.

Meanwhile, beautifully so, a lot of what is happening in your daughter's brain involves connectivity of word centers (the "verbal" aspect of the female brain) to production of "words-for-feelings" and "words-for-memories" (what scientists call "verbal-emotive functioning"). As your daughter meets the world around her—trees, wind, cars, colors, sounds, and emotions—she absorbs and processes a lot!

She will tend to have three advantages over the typical male:

- She will probably notice more sensory information around her (more colors, more sounds, more sights) than males because the female brain takes in more sensory information, on average, than the male brain.
- She may store more memories of what she sensed and noticed during her apprehension of a scene around her. She may thus have more access to "working memory" of what she sensed and experienced, especially regarding emotions, than a male might.
- She will tend to develop more word arrays for her feelings,

senses, and memories than might her brother or father who had exactly the same experience. Much of the "plasticity" of the female brain—its ability to adapt, survive, thrive—lies in the cells, synapses, and neurotransmitters connected to "working memory" and "emotive" word production.

You can track these differences in your own life, as Gail and I did in ours. We have recognized the sensorial advantage in the female brain, especially its ability to remember details more fully than the male, and its greater use of words for these experiences.

In 1986, just after Gail and I were married, we jumped on a plane for Ankara, Turkey, where we would live and work for the next two years. After getting our work visas, we traveled up into Europe with backpacks, visiting relatives as broke tourists. We had a lot of fun together but didn't realize, until these travels, that we were not very good travelers together. As a boy, I was accustomed to lots of travel from having lived in a new town or country every year or two. Gail had lived in Nebraska throughout her childhood and traveled very little. Now, as we changed countries or cities every few days, tension arose between us. I felt I was doing too much and wanted more help from Gail who felt that I was too active, moving too fast; she just wanted to sit and enjoy our time in new places. In Barcelona, Gail remembers, I said in frustration, "Gail, you are not the woman I married!" This was clearly a stupid thing to say, and I apologized, and Gail, thankfully, forgave me!

The point of the story is that I don't remember saying the words, nor the place, nor the time, nor the feeling-experience. Gail, however, remembers everything and can verbalize all the details whenever she recalls the episode—exactly where we sat in the restaurant ("near the window looking out toward an alley"), sounds and smells from the kitchen and exactly what we ate (polenta), the waiter's appearance ("thick dark hair and a long dark face with a goatee"), and even the color of the table cloth ("red background with tiny black squares"). And, of course, she remembers the words themselves and how they felt.

Gail's brain:

1. Took in more sensorial information than mine did in the moment.
2. Stored more of it in her long-term and then working memory;

and

3. Expresses and produces more words connected to her senses and emotions than I do.

I am known as a verbal guy, but Gail's female brain's advantage in this area is profound. You can prove it yourself in your home, travels, and workplace.

And in the female brain, stress can enhance this advantage. When the emotive center in the mid-brain, the amygdala, is stimulated by stressful emotion, more of the male brain's electricity, or neural processing, moves downward into the cerebellum (the "doing" center of the brain), as well as the brain stem, the spinal fluid, and then, through that conduit, into the physical body itself. Thus, boys physically process their emotions more than girls, resulting in more pacing, fidgeting, and physical anger. But in a girl's brain, more of the stress-processing moves upward into Broca's and Wernecke's areas, the word centers in the upper brain. This is one reason why the therapy profession, as it now generally exists (in which patients/clients sit down in an office for fifty minutes), favors the female brain. This systemic issue accounts for many therapists keeping more female clients than male. Sitting still and remembering emotional life verbally is not a strength of the male brain, but it is a strength of the female.

When I talked with Carrie on the phone, she corroborated brain difference in her family, telling me that even her very talkative husband was more like the boys in his quick stress-release techniques, including rough housing with the boys or letting out a quick loud burst of sound to release his anger or irritation, then letting it go. Carrie, who thought of herself as a bridge brain, noticed that when it came to emotive material, even she spent more time "talking things through" than her sons or husband. "After a few minutes, they're done," she smiled. "But the girls and I can keep going."

This may sound like it contradicts her email in which she said her husband was the talker and she was not, but remember, now we're digging down into a certain kind of conversation, one that involves emotional memory, senses, and feelings as they are experienced. In general, the minds of girls will spend more time in this territory than the minds of boys.

Courageous Conversation

When Should "Good Listening" Become "Let's Stop Talking About How You Feel and Solve This Problem?"

The verbal-emotive intelligence difference, like all differences, can have an advantage and disadvantage for the brain experiencing it. Carrie was asking about strategies to deal with the disadvantage—the brain that just never stops talking. Many girls and women have asked me about the other side of the coin: how to get males to fully understand the verbal-emotive female brain as an advantage. Many males get overwhelmed by female discussion of feeling and don't see how pro-social and useful it is.

If we care about nurturing and advancing the minds of girls, we will need to carry on courageous conversations about both sides of this coin.

Regarding the advantage, the female brain's facility with words is one of the reasons that males/fathers must learn to "listen" when girls and women talk—listen for at least a few minutes before moving to problem-solving. The female brain is revealing itself in words, especially words-for-feelings and words-for-memories. Identity and self, internal world and experience, are coming through as she talks. We need to listen! If we cut off this expression too early to try to problem-solve, we may prematurely stop the flow of that brain's word production before we've validated and valued the emotive content. In stopping a girl's verbal flow too early, we can miss a great deal of what our daughter, wife, partner, or co-worker is saying, feeling, and "being." Best would be to listen, hear, and then respond.

At the same time, new research also shows that too many words, including too many words-for-feelings can impede good mental health. Daniel Amen calls some of the negative thoughts in girls' minds "ANTs" (anxious negative thoughts). Because the female brain is more prone than the male to ruminate on emotive content, that brain can often get lost in that content. As Carrie and her family have intuited, there comes a time when Sara must stop talking about it!

How do we find a balance with girls? I suggest trying out two strategies to both value a girl's words *and* help her to self-regulate them.

- Don't interrupt until you have heard the real emotional "point" she is making. You will know you've heard it by its repetition in her long speech. She will talk for a few minutes about various tangents on what she is thinking, feeling, and remembering, and you might even glaze over with the flood of words, but keep listening. As you nod your head and say, "uh huh" to validate and value her feelings and self-development, also store away the key phrases that she repeated. Get ready to use them with her.

- Once she starts repeating one or more of these key phrases a second and third time, your interruption and insertion of yourself will generally do no harm. In fact, it will help her toward greater empowerment. You can say, "Okay, I need to stop you, you're saying a lot there, let me see if I understood what you were feeling . . ." Once you stop her flow, you can repeat back to her the key phrases and "points" she was making. You needn't repeat it back perfectly. You can rephrase, then ask her if you "got it."

She may say, "No, I meant . . ." even if you did get it right, because she wants to keep talking! You can listen for a bit again, but then stop her as needed to say, "I really do think I got that."

Depending on how emotionally charged she still is, you may have now come to a point when you can begin a problem-solving process with her, one that leads to impulse control, self-regulation, maturity, and resilience. Even if she wants to keep talking, you may need to be courageous about saying, "No more now. You've talked this out. It's time to do something about this."

Here is real dialogue Carrie reported a few months into my relationship with her and Sara.

Carrie: "Okay, I think I got it. You felt really bad when Emily seemed to be whispering about you to Felicia during lunch. That was the thing that really made you mad."

Sara: "Well, yes, but . . ." Now Sara listed other things and then returned to repeating how mad she was about the other two girls whispering together without her inside their group.

Carrie heard the repetition again and felt certain she was "hearing" her daughter completely so she said, "Okay, let me stop you there. I really do get it. You're saying . . ." She repeated the key phrases back. "Is that right?"

Sara: "Yes, I felt . . ." And she began to detail the same feelings again.

Carrie (interrupting): "I get that, I really do, and I would have felt bad too, but did you ask them what they were whispering to each other? Maybe it wasn't about you? Did you find out if it really had anything to do with you?"

Sara: "No, I didn't ask them, but I know it did because . . ."

Carrie let her talk only a bit more and then interrupted again. "You have to talk to them. You're going crazy in your head. You have to go talk with them."

About this discussion Carrie reported, "I'm noticing with Sara that sometimes she will wind down herself and just feel better from having talked about something, but other times I have to be the adult and help her wind down by letting her know I really do understand what she is saying. If I repeat back to her what she's saying, she feels better, and so I feel better too. Then we can get into problem-solving. Now that I'm understanding, I don't have to just let her talk forever to build her self-esteem and her voice. I'm looking at some of these other strategies for dealing with her issues. I think she is not reacting to things as much as she used to. I'm going to study this further."

Carrie's courageous conversation with her daughter was one that benefited both mother and daughter. The daughter gained impulse control and learned good strategies from the mother, and the mother found parenting the daughter to be healthier and easier.

I believe Carrie did well here. If her daughter had been autistic or had a brain issue that created the need for a constant barrage of words, then we would be saying something different about her. But given that Sara had no such condition, a good rule of thumb is: if everyone in a family is becoming irritated by a plethora of words, then the plethora of words may be dysfunctional in some way and may need a change of plan.

Greater Verbal Intelligence Can Mitigate Spatial and Quantitative Intelligence

Neuroscientists like Diane Halpern, Ruben and Raquel Gur, Camilla Benbow, David Geary, and Louann Brizendine have verified the advantages we just discussed in female verbal-emotive intelligence. Similarly, they have found advantages for the male brain in visuospatial intelligence, including "the ability to maintain a visual image while simultaneously deciding what it would look like if it were viewed from another perspective, moved to another location, moved through space at various speeds, or physically altered in some way." In this kind of thinking, male brains, on average, have an advantage, and that advantage appears, in some cases, in quantitative processing (math), though this advantage should be approached with some subtlety. Let's remember: girls and women test out similar to boys and men in "numerical processing," which is the kind of processing that would be used in bookkeeping and accounting. The male advantage in overall quantitative processing occurs at the highest levels of testing (genius levels or just below that).

Why? In both quantitative and spatial processing, the male brain localizes more activity for these quantitative functions, especially in some areas in which the female brain has not developed its quantitative or visuospatial centers but, instead, had built word centers. This fact is a key to the mystery of these brain differences. As Ruben Gur has put it, "Some of the parts of the brain women would need for these functions are used up with verbal centers." Louann Brizendine has called this a reality of the female brain. People who are stuck in the DGP disagree with this ideologically, but the science to back it up is robust. For a further elaboration on this, reference the study I noted earlier by Halpern, Gur, Benbow, et.al., "The Truth About Sex Differences in Mathematics and Science."

Because the human brain has billions of neurons, we don't have to think of it as "finite." We can think of its potential as endless. Because we know that certain parts of the brain and certain functions are "neuroplastic," we can, as neuroscientist Daniel Amen has put it, "change our brains" through personal focus and new environments. When, for instance, our memory centers don't feel to us like they are working well enough for us to function in our environment, we can commit to doing Sudoku an hour a day so that we can develop new cells in our hippocampus, our memory center, thus improving our memory system. Similarly, when we want to learn a new language, we study the new language and our brains create connections between cells in Broca's and Wernecke's areas that reflect our new language learning.

Neuroplasticity is a crucial part of modern brain science and it is true that a smart humanity is one that believes the potential of each brain is endless. But . . . and this is a big but . . . this idealism doesn't mean every brain is plastic in the way we might imagine it should be. *For each brain function we improve, we may mitigate another function.* This is the case with verbal functioning, spatial functioning, and their sibling, quantitative functioning. If a brain is great at one or more things, it may not be as great at some other things because the human brain, to some extent, specializes. If a brain is highly verbal-emotive, it may not be as quantitative or visuospatial. If it is highly quantitative or visuospatial, it might not be as highly verbal-emotive. While approximately 1 in 5-7 people are "exceptions," as scientists like Simon Baron-Cohen and Daniel Amen have noted, our brains do specialize to such an extent that, by college age, we can start seeing quite well who we are. By our mid-to-late-twenties, when myelination and other brain development completes, we will see even more clearly who we can become—and not become.

Will we "forgive" this aspect of natural law, or will we despise it?

Before we decide, let's study it.

Scientists have done just that, by digging deeply into K – 12, college admissions, and graduate admissions testing.

As we noted earlier, in the NAEP test scores, "females scored higher, on average, in all racial or ethnic groups and across all ages, in reading, writing and civics." But males scored higher in quantitative areas. This continued through the SATs, GREs, and GMAT tests used for admission to business school in which "males score higher across all racial/ethnic groups, with the largest differences in quantitative areas."

Digging even deeper, researchers found, "there were no sex differences for GRE math problems when solutions required multiple algorithmic steps (i.e. differences were not due to the ability to hold information in working memory), but the usual male advantage was found with math problems that had multiple possible solution paths." The more completely the quantitative or spatial task relied on spatial or quantitative multi-tasking, the more advantage the male brain tended to have; the more completely the task relied on other kinds of multi-tasking, the more advantageous was the female brain.

What is happening here? The visuospatial advantage in the male brain, as well as memory-processing differences in the female and male brain, improve male scores on certain kinds of tests that revolve around spatial multi-tasking. This kind of multi-tasking is the only kind of multi-tasking males show more proclivity for than females, on average. In other kinds of multi-tasking, females do better—as they do on the kind of verbal functioning that does not just use a particular spatial or "math" center of the brain, but spreads neural activity out all over the brain.

The Amazing White Matter Brain

This idea of "specializing" brain activity into certain areas of the brain is a crucial one. A lot of the kind of brain activity one needs to do well in certain spatial and math tasks is "gray matter focus." The variable multi-tasking that females often dominate utilizes more "white matter activity." Gray matter occurs in "splotches" in the brain—localized areas of brain activity. White matter occurs among the myelin, so it spreads throughout the brain.

Especially when it comes to thinking about problems, processing issues, raising new questions, and organizing complex emotive activity, the female brain relies more heavily than the male on white matter activity than gray matter activity. This is a brain difference you can test out in your home, school, and community.

Study who in your family tends to organize disparate details from various areas of focus better (on average). You will see more females with this advantage, just as you see more women in complex multi-tasking jobs. Even as early as 7 or 9 years old, it becomes clear that female brains organize their many different folders for school more assiduously than males (on average); that they care more about the ten different colored tabs for each class or extracurricular subject; that they tend to show more organization in homework than males, keep their rooms more organized . . . the list is endless. There are always exceptions, but the rule is lived out by everyone raising children.

Now, to dive into the other kind of multi-tasking, give five boys and five girls a set of light bowling pins and ask them to learn how to juggle. The males will tend to more quickly and more completely master this physical-spatial juggling task than the females. Meanwhile, if you ask these same children to keep five or more emotive details in their working memory, the girls will tend to do better than the boys. You will be seeing, among other things, a difference between white matter activity and gray matter activity as you study the various kinds of multi-tasking.

University of Pennsylvania neuroscientist Ruben Gur was one of the first to use PET scans to discover that while girls and women have more gray matter than males, they rely more on white matter activity for tasks and relationships. Cambridge neuroscientist Simon Baron-Cohen joined Gur in the 1990s in exploring this difference, discovering that the female brain is generally more committed than the male to a variety of verbal-emotive functioning, including empathizing with others first and putting off certain kinds of systemic/logic-analysis in favor of this functioning. In other words, Baron-Cohen discovered that the female brain may put off doing abstract thinking so that it can account for feelings and facial and social cues. This became known as a "feeling" vs. "logic" difference, or "circular" vs. "linear" thinking difference.

In 2005, University of California-Irvine neuroscientist Richard Haier used fMRI scans to reveal exact numbers on white matter/gray matter activity differences. Haier discovered that, "In general, men have approximately 6.5 times the amount of gray matter related to general intelligence than women, and women have nearly 10 times the amount of white matter related to intelligence than men. Gray matter represents information processing centers in the brain, and white matter represents the networking of—or connections between—these processing centers."

Rex Jung, a University of New Mexico neuropsychologist, and co-author of the study, said, "this may help to explain why men tend to excel in tasks requiring more local processing (like mathematics), while women tend to excel at integrating and assimilating information from distributed gray-matter regions in the brain, such as required for language facility. These two very different neurological pathways and activity centers, however, result in equivalent overall performance on broad measures of cognitive ability, such as those found on intelligence tests."

This point is crucial. Brain difference research does not show women or men as more intelligent overall. Rather, as Haier confirmed, "These findings suggest that human evolution has created two different types of brains designed for equally intelligent behavior." The issue is not intelligence, but the internal choices and paths of attentiveness the brains make as people live out their lives.

To look at gray matter development in a brain, take some time on Google to read results from autopsies of Albert Einstein's brain. Researchers discovered a very dense and well-developed visuospatial gray matter area in the parietal lobe. From his brain, we can see him capable of spatial and theoretical multi-tasking regarding quantum physics and astronomy because his brain concentrated and localized brain activity into the areas of his brain that he needed most.

The "words-for-feelings" difference we discussed earlier is a case of "spreading out activity in the female brain." When I give lectures on the female and male brain, I show PET, fMRI, and SPECT scans of those brains. Audiences often feel what I felt when I first saw the scans—a sense of "Wow" at how differently the female and male brains process white matter and gray matter activity for language use. Unlike Einstein's brain which processed astronomy and physics in, mainly, one or two gray matter areas, when the female brain is processing words, it generally does so throughout the brain, moving the signaling to various word centers via white matter activity.

Study all this in your own life. Watch how girls will often connect dots in the brain that boys won't, especially regarding words, memories, and relationships. Women will often multi-task in ways men will not. Men might feel immense delight climbing up a hierarchy, whereas for a woman, the intricacies of relational life can feel like a profound victory. Goal-setting can feel different in a female and male brain, as can the development of purpose, meaning, and legacy. The call to invent and build things, and the way people construct teams to build and invent can feel different in the male and female brain. While you might instinctively try to help 12-year-old boys become better at multi-tasking their homework and school folders, you might realize that constant emotional multi-tasking is making your adolescent daughter anxious. Perhaps you instinctively try to help her find just one or two areas of focus for a while, so that she can calm her brain down.

Indeed, clinical research shows that the anxious feeling of "burning the candle at both ends" grows, in large part, from the constant white matter activity in the female brain. Daniel Amen, M.D., author of *Unleash the Power of the Female Brain,* recently wrote, "In the largest brain imaging study ever done, we compared the scans of 46,000 male and female brains using a study called SPECT, which looks at blood flow and activity patterns. Out of 80 areas tested, females were significantly more active in 70, which just explained my whole life—I have 5 sisters,

3 daughters and 14 nieces. These differences help us understand some of the unique strengths and vulnerabilities of the female brain and give us important clues on how to optimize it."

A Baby Girl Experiment

In my lectures, along with brain scans, I often show a video clip of babies pulling on strings. The clip reveals an experiment done famously at Rutgers University in the 1980s and then replicated in many other universities and countries.

Babies of six weeks to six months are placed in front of a screen with the ability to pull the string to receive the picture of a happy face. The children love doing it, but when the researchers disconnect the apparatus so the string-pulling leads to no happy face at all (a blank screen, for instance), the girl and boy babies respond differently. On average, the boy babies keep pulling the string longer than the girl babies, while the girl babies start to cry more quickly than the boys. The boy babies become upset too, but overall, the girl babies more quickly moved their brains into emotional reaction, from "I'm getting a good result pulling this string" to "I'm getting no result and something has to change." Because they are not capable yet of talking this out with anyone, they do the next best thing—they cry. Their parents and other nurturers are right there to hug them and make them feel better. This experiment has been replicated with a one in five exception rate.

As they watch this DVD clip, many people in the audience chuckle or nod their heads. It makes intuitive sense to them that girls' brains are moving faster and spreading out more internal information than boys' brains about lots of things at once. It also makes sense to them that boy babies are laser-focusing their internal cognition on the string-pulling and they will NOT be stopped—not until they finally realize they are powerless. Watching this difference together, my audience and I are sharing a moment of citizen science.

The Crossroads

Given the amount of scientific evidence available to us, I believe we stand at a crossroads in our ability to understand what is happening in the female brain. I believe we can now say with near certainty, as Ruben Gur and Louann Brizendine have explained, that when the female brain emphasizes verbal activity it will tend to mitigate visuospatial and/or quantitative activity. While, as we've noted, this fact does not mean girls aren't good at math, it does mean that we have to approach gender gaps in STEM differently than we currently are.

Try This

Improving Your Daughter's Spatial Intelligence

In Chapter 7, I will delve even more deeply into helping girls in STEM, STEAM, Math, Science, Coding, and Engineering. For now, let me give a few strategies you can use to make sure your daughters (who will often tend to utilize their verbal intelligence more than their spatial) keep developing their spatial intelligence from their earliest years of life.

- In preschool, try "girls only" day in the block corner, such that no boys are allowed to play in the girls' corner for various periods of time. This will allow the girls to build things with blocks and Legos without a few very spatial and aggressive boys knocking down the girl-built edifices and structures.
- Make sure your daughter spends daily time in natural settings. Unless the conditions are too hot or too cold for basic heath, keep this regimen going. The natural world is a non-verbal world in which spatial intelligence can be built organically and instinctively.
- Foster spatial play. Get on the floor and play with Legos, cars, even dolls that can move around. Throw balls back and forth with your girls. Teach your girls to juggle and let them get good at it, if they like that sport.
- Play lots of board games, do puzzles, do more that is hands-on than on-screen. Remember that pushing a button on an iPad creates a visual result, but it is not very kinesthetic or spatial at all, thus it is generally less useful for spatial intelligence than doing the task in the real world.
- Encourage girls to learn and play in single-sex groups and, even in elementary school, encourage single-

sex classrooms in math and science so that girls can flourish in these tasks without high-math boys overwhelming them.

- Starting in middle school and then high school, begin teaching girls (and boys) about the male and female brain so they can become aware of who they are, who they are becoming, and what areas of brain development they want to try to improve.
- Keep girls in sports for as long as they enjoy and/or perform well in the sport. This does not mean we need to push girls into the hyper-competitive soccer clubs or baseball leagues. The idea is to keep them doing spatial tasks, like kicking, throwing, and catching balls and objects because this builds the spatial brain.

Many Roads

In the human brain, neural roads and pathways try to connect with one another to build a mature adult. When the brain is still young, various pathways and areas of neural landscape exist somewhat separate from others. The brain is trying to grow and flourish by building up its internal sections and by connecting them with other sections. It is trying to nurture its own nature, express its own genes, adapt to its environment, and succeed and thrive in close relationship with others and its natural environments.

To become a student of the female brain is to hold a scale in each hand. On the one hand, we must weigh the miraculous qualities of that brain. In so doing, we can appreciate the rich gifts our girl has been given by genetics, nurture, and our culture. On the other hand, by understanding her brain and being, we will notice that our daughter (like our son) likely won't "have it all." This reality can confuse us because some social ideologies tend to claim that boys and men should have limits, but not girls and women.

This very protective instinct in us (one I felt when raising my daughters) has led to many good things for girls and women, including a toppling of patriarchal culture in the U.S., but it has also led to a fear of studying the female brain. Somehow, we have decided that for raising girls it is best to only talk about nurture and culture, not nature. But research shows that a well-nurtured female and male brain lead to the greatest success for our children. As your daughter, for instance, realizes that she is burning the candle at both ends, she can get help to decrease her brain's constant multi-tasking. Or, if your daughter notices that a candle is not yet burning in parts of her brain (like the spatial centers) that she wants to further explore, she can approach her own neural activity with evidence, wisdom, and new strategies that work

The science-based approach is the most empowering. It can build a whole self, which was Carrie's intention with her daughters. To use this approach, she and her family had to make some uncomfortable new changes, but they did make them, and Sara was all the better for it. That said, Sara did not suffer brain disorders like depression or anxiety, anorexia, bulimia, ADD (attention deficit disorder), OCD (obsessive compulsive disorder), or ASD (autism spectrum disorder).

In the next chapter, I will explore with you some new tools for understanding and treating the genetic roots of these disorders. Even if you do not have a daughter struggling with a brain disorder, I hope you will read the next chapter because it reveals a great deal more about the "nature" of our daughters—and new ways to use genome research and gene testing to help our daughters with difficulties they may face.

Chapter 3

Nurture their Nature:
Using the Science of Genetics to Help Girls Thrive

"Rapid advances in molecular biology have revealed the genetic and molecular bases of a number of sex-based differences in health and human disease, some of which are attributed to sexual genotype—XX in the female and XY in the male. Genes on the sex chromosomes can be expressed differently between males and females because of the presence of either single or double copies of the gene and because of the phenomena of different meiotic effects, X inactivation, and genetic imprinting."

—Institute of Medicine, Committee on Understanding the Biology of Sex and Gender Differences, National Academy of Sciences.

CARLY WAS 20 WHEN I MET HER. She came into my office well-groomed and clothed, and she wore a smile I learned, quite quickly, was a mask she wore to cover her pain. From a conversation with her parents a week ago, I knew she had taken enough sleeping pills to kill herself three weeks earlier.

"We never saw this coming," her mother, a chemical engineer, told me with watering eyes. "We have a good home. She and her two brothers had happy childhoods, she seemed to succeed in school, she's a good kid, we kept her off too much screen time, we kept her outside—she loves horses—and she never said anything about depression. We're racking our brains to figure this out."

Carly's father agreed. "Carly had every asset growing up, but we missed something. Clearly we missed a lot." Her father, a lawyer, sat in the chair in my office seeming emotionless, although it was clear how desperate he was for help, too. Overall, I sensed that Carly's distress had come into the family below the surface, as a surprise, and I was ready to meet a young woman in distress.

I studied this 20-year-old carefully now. Carly wore somewhat faded jeans with white threads showing at the knees, red pumps, a thin red sweater, and red fingernail polish. She used makeup on her face, but not much of it. Everything about her matched—color, smile, bouncy step, firm handshake.

"I'm okay," she said as she sat down. "I got some Prozac at the Health Center and I'm fine."

Setting my yellow pad on my knee, pen poised, I invited her to, "Tell me everything you want to tell me. Pretend your parents haven't said anything to me. Tell me what you need me to know."

Carly crossed her legs, breathed in, and told me the story of a girl who had, she felt, lacked confidence all through childhood. "My parents didn't know it, but I was fighting feelings of sadness all the time."

"When did this begin?" I asked.

"Around fifteen maybe," she said. "But before that too."

She finally felt her inadequacies catch up to her, especially in her computer science classes.

"It's mainly guys, and I feel out of place. I'm the kind of girl who's always trying to do everything, please everyone, and take care of everyone. I'm such a 'girl,' huh?" she grinned sheepishly. "I was stupid, I guess. But I see what's going on and I'm okay now."

She clearly did see a great deal, but she admitted as we talked that there was more to see. As we worked together, she opened up further and talked about her family and history and the dark months at college that led to her loneliness and depression. Hers was the story of a person, a child, a human being—but also, very importantly, a girl and woman. I respected her perspective and so we worked well together over the next few months as she became more self-reflective and confident.

In our counseling sessions, her family explored with her the stressors and tensions she experienced. When I learned that this family had depression and anxiety in its genetic line (grandmother, uncle, and aunt) I suggested that Carly get some genetic testing. Carly became intrigued with the idea of understanding the gene map she had gained at conception. This genetics discussion sounded a bit odd to Carly's mom at first, but then the family became interested. They followed through on some of the suggestions of this chapter to gradually see Carly as a person, female, girl, woman, and . . . genome. From that perspective, solutions revealed themselves. Solutions, and new growth for Carly.

The Female Genome

When I wrote *The Wonder of Girls* in the early 2000s, we were building knowledge of "the female genome," and how it can be differentiated from the male. As the authors of *Exploring the Biological Contributions to Human Health: Does Sex Matter?* wrote in 2001, "The hallmark of human biology is variation, and much of the observed variation both within and between the sexes is encoded within the human genome."

The authors further explored variation by stating that, "At the DNA level, an estimated 1 of every 1,300 bases on the autosomes (non-sex-determining chromosomes) differs between any two individuals. In other words, the genomes of individuals may differ at some 4 to 6 million base positions. Some of these differences will lead to gene products that are functionally distinct, for example, receptors that differ in their affinity or rate of turnover, enzymes that differ in their steady-state levels, and genes that differ in their degree of hormone responsiveness . . ."

Because hormones like testosterone and estrogen are sex-specific, variations in genomic material include the sex component and "the precise composition and functioning of thousands of proteins will differ between any two individuals."

Even before the genome map was revealed in 2003, we already knew that:

1. Every individual's genes comprise that individual's baseline experience for interaction with his/her environment; and
2. These genes include elements of sex and gender in their chromosome markers.

But even with that knowledge in tow, we did not yet have a *map* of the human genome, so a lot of what we "knew" was supposition. When we leaped forward with the mapping of the human genome, we found ourselves in somewhat new territory, especially those of us who are nature-based in our theory and practice. Now, we realized, we might be able to help parents, educators, professionals, and children—not only by talking about their relationships with others, and their potential attachment and trauma issues, but also by integrating genomic analysis into our assistance with brain disorders.

When I wrote *Nurture the Nature* in 2007, I had developed a seven-stage model for bringing the science of genetics into a parent-friendly format. I developed tools included in the book for understanding genetically templated personality, temperament, and talent sets. Now, ten years later, the genetics revolution is even more well-developed. The quiet revolution in the medical sciences can also be a revolution in parenting and—for young people like Carly who struggle with depression, anxiety, and other disorders—a form of self-discovery. We now have tools available to us as parents and professionals by which to target interventions to our own daughter (these tools exist for our sons too, as detailed in *Saving Our Sons*).

The Journey Toward Carly's Genome

Carly's treatment was effective in large part because, once we learned her gene map, we could target a treatment plan for her. Three things she discussed early on inspired me to suggest genetic testing for Carly:

1. Her experience with medication;
2. The probability that she had adolescent-onset depression; and
3. Her sense of feeling inadequate "in a man's world" (i.e. computer science).

I'll discuss the first two immediately, and the third toward the end of the chapter.

As I worked with Carly, I learned that she had gradually begun to feel depressed in adolescence, especially during and around menses. While she initially told me her medication was working, she later confessed that it hadn't worked as well as she initially reported but didn't want to disappoint her parents. These were the first two reasons I suggested genetic tests.

One set of tests was handled through a local psychologist who utilizes the blood-based studies of the Walsh Institute in Chicago. The tests revealed genetic vulnerabilities in the way Carly processed gluten and dairy. Dairy, it turned out, was an environmental toxin for this young woman because her DNA, and thus her cells, took it in as a poison, triggering a number of internal reactive responses that were associated with depression and anxiety. Gluten, too, was poisonous for her. While she did not have Celiac disease, she was sensitive enough to experience difficulties when she ate gluten, especially when combined with dairy.

Once she saw these results, a lightbulb went off in her head. "Yes," she said, "I do crave pizza and milk together, which people find weird."

Then she wondered, "If I'm allergic to these things, why would I crave them?"

We discussed the complexities of this cellular biology, that our cells often crave what is not good for them, and Carly made the decision to forego gluten, dairy, and sugar—cold turkey.

Within three weeks of instituting these environmental and nutritional changes, Carly felt better. She did end up eating sugar again, especially chocolate which she loved, but she also found that when she stopped eating gluten and dairy, her craving for other sugars decreased.

"I just feel a lot better," she said, very relieved.

Her genetic tests also resulted in changes to her medication. Because her psychologist at the college had prescribed medication without doing a genetic test, medicating Carly was somewhat "hit and miss." Unfortunately, her first medication wasn't doing what she needed it to do, so she asked a new psychologist to order genetic testing that might reveal the best medications for her gene map. He refused, claiming genetic testing was "junk science" and did no good. Carly made the decision to move to a new psychiatrist who did order the tests.

Once the tests came back, it was clear that Carly's original medication did not have a high probability of working well with her individual genes, but the Wellbutrin class of medications did. With this information in mind, Carly's new psychiatrist switched her meds, and that too helped her a great deal.

Within a month, Carly was feeling much better. She reported that she wasn't "just *hoping* to feel better because I don't want to worry my parents so much, but actually feeling *better*." Carly and her parents (indeed, her whole support system) felt relieved and newly inspired by her happier, improved life. Carly began to ponder the future, including when and where to finish off her college education.

Epigenetics and Our Daughters

Epigenetics is the study of changes in organisms caused by modification of gene expression. Like the field of genetics, it is now available to you as a citizen scientist. You can now peer into your own and your children's genes as if peering into the seat of the heart and soul.

Because the science of epigenetics and an array of science-based genetic testing mechanisms can deepen your ability to nurture the nature of your daughters, I want to spend this chapter exploring it with you. Whether you have a daughter in distress or just want to learn more about genes and the female body and brain, you may be able to study and use this material in your home or other environment right away.

Did You Know?

The Genetics of Procrastination

Two "P's" are often a part of counseling with girls: perfectionism and procrastination. Both are partially determined by genetic vulnerabilities on a girl's genome, internally and externally triggered during gene expression (life). Later, I will look at perfectionism; for now, let's focus on procrastination.

In working with Carly, I heard her describe her own procrastination frequently. During one session early in our counseling, she said, "I always wait until the last minute on stuff and it stresses me out, but I can't stop myself. Somehow, I did well in high school and school in general, so I don't think my parents or I worried about it, but in college it didn't work. I mean, my grades were okay, but I was always stressed out and had to hide it."

I asked her to try to explore this stress and worry more specifically by remembering a moment of procrastination. She recalled an assignment in her computer science class a few weeks before.

"I felt like there was a fear in my gut all the time," she described while her previous anxiety was mirrored by the lines of her face and her hands clenched together. "I read somewhere, in National Geographic I think, that all the spiders in the world could eat up all the human beings in the world. It freaked me out. I would sit at my desk with an assignment right in front of me, but I wouldn't do it because I would think about spiders eating up human beings—myself, my family, everyone—and I'd go off into some fear thing like I would screw up, like it wouldn't be good enough no matter what. Then I'd get back to the spiders chewing on everyone and I'd look down at the coding sequence I was supposed to work on and it just becomes so scary, so weird, and I can't stand it. So usually I get my phone out and play a game on it or get some food or just get up and go do something else to get away from whatever the assignment is until finally I know I just have to do it or I'll really get a bad grade. Somehow, I do it, but it's always at the last minute and not as good as it could be."

Carly, I came to see, experienced some neuroses, a fear of failure, and impulsivity—three aspects of procrastination. Understanding this, I felt it stood to reason that her genetic code might align with these elements, and because Carly enjoyed science, I gave her a study to read. This study requires a lay person to really stretch into scientific language, but it is a nice way of advancing your "citizen science" on procrastination. The study, "Genetic and Environmental Associations Between Procrastination and Internalizing/Externalizing Psychopathology," looked at 764 young adult twins (right around Carly's age).

The study's authors concluded that, "procrastination was positively correlated with both internalizing and externalizing latent variables and that these correlations were driven by shared genetic influences. Moreover, the association between procrastination and internalizing was accounted for by fear of failure and neuroticism, whereas the association between procrastination and externalizing was primarily explained by impulsivity."

The authors are revealing that in procrastinators there is a chicken/egg effect in which the person's fears and neuroses can seem to "cause" the behavior, while the genes that stimulate the behavior can also cause the fears and neuroses. Furthermore, the internal chromosomal stimulus for the behavior happens more through fear of failure and neuroses, while impulsivity stimulates it externally.

The study was one of the first to show that individual differences in procrastination are "primarily due to genetic influences, suggesting that a common set of genetic risk factors predispose individuals to engage in procrastination and experience psychopathology symptoms, but that the environmental influences on procrastination are largely independent of those that influence psychopathology." This finding deepens available research on the links between behaviors like procrastination and the genes that cause the internalized and externalized feelings and behaviors. The use of twins was a great way for the researchers to study both genetics and environment. Procrastination is one of those traits that is much more "nature" than "nurture and culture."

Carly read the study and we talked about it. She saw almost immediately that the study's authors shined a lens into her life by providing insight into her own genetics. As her family read the study, they too gained awareness of Carly's psyche from a nature-based perspective. Understanding that much of Carly's distress came from genetic vulnerabilities didn't mean the family now thought Carly's environment (nurture and culture) didn't matter, but for Carly and her family, the genetic takeaways brought immense *relief.* Carly's parents had convinced themselves that there must have been flaws in their parenting that were tragically at fault for what their children felt or experienced. Their own anxiety about Carly's suicide attempt kept growing as they tried to figure out how they could have "created" their daughter's procrastination, depression, anxiety, and self-violence. Learning about genetics and doing gene testing helped the whole family see probabilities on Carly's genes.

Carly and her family understood that her vulnerabilities emerged in adolescence due to the stresses of:

1. early menses, which affected Carly's stress and sex hormonal system and thus her cellular activity;
2. normal adolescent struggles in her high school years, which combined with her elevated stress hormone levels, triggered various internal vulnerabilities; and
3. being away from home (at college), which contributed to

feelings of loneliness and the partial loss of her family support system.

The family realized that gradually, over a period of years, Carly's internally and externally-triggered genetic vulnerabilities led to gradual destruction of self-confidence, then overt depression, and then attempted suicide. As Carly and her parents understood all of this, Carly learned the genetic vulnerabilities that would become both a battle and inspiration for her throughout the rest of her life. She and her family discussed them, gaining insights and strategies for development of new self-confidence. Specifically, Carly worked on her fear of failure and her procrastination. These insights led her to begin using techniques for managing both her procrastination and her depression.

One technique I helped Carly to engage in was journaling. She recorded on paper, then in her computer, the moment her dark visions (spiders eating humans) appeared in her mind. She also recorded the moments her fear of failure emerged. Gradually, her journaling moved to the Notes app in her phone. A week into her journaling, I suggested she expand to track the impulsivity (the impulse, for instance, to move away from her homework or task and play a game on her phone). Each week we came back together to discuss her "study" of her own procrastination and fears. Within three weeks of tracking her neuroses and impulses, Carly began picking one thing to change per week.

"I think I'll start with the fear of failure," she said early in the process. "When I feel it, I'll snap my fingers to get myself out of it. Then I'll get back to work."

After she tried this technique a few times, we discussed the results. Every few weeks, we added a new technique or element of study. Meanwhile, Carly stayed on what were life-saving medications and, equally empowering I believe, she did not eat the foods that triggered her genetic vulnerabilities for depression and anxiety.

I also worked with her parents to help them read Carly's needs and tells stories of their own "failures" so that Carly could constantly hear the message that things didn't have to be done perfectly. She didn't have to put off doing important things because of her fears of failing or being imperfect.

Gradually, Carly's "dark visions" diminished considerably. When they did come, they did not intimidate or engulf her. She had gained more self-awareness, as well as improved her "externalizing factors" via diet and medication so that she controlled her visions and lived a new, empowered life.

From One Case to Many: Replacing the DGP with Gender Science

Throughout this book you will find me very consciously pleading with our new generation of parents to delve into science for good parenting and to avoid social constructs of girls (and boys) that don't have decades of rich science behind them.

Carly and her parents represent the potential sea change in parenting, educating, and mentoring girls. This family decided to combine nature, nurture, and culture in their parenting and support system, thus joining a new science-based social movement in the child development sphere. Gail and I joined this movement as we learned about genetics while raising our daughters. Gabrielle was 13 and Davita 10 when the gene map become public in 2003. As we studied it from a parent's perspective—and to increase our own self-awareness as adults—we became increasingly suspicious of the Dominant Gender Paradigm's approach to girls' distresses. We were working with clients, too, and saw far more going on in our female clients than "shifting gender roles" or "patriarchal oppression."

Carly's case is an illustration of the DGP's influence on her self-assessment. When she talked early on with her parents and me about her computer coding classes, she said, "It's depressing to feel so alone there, mainly me and another girl the only girls, the rest guys and the guys always watching me to see if I measure up. It makes me anxious. I worry all the time. I think that classroom environment is why I became so depressed."

For the first month of our time together, she and her family insisted that the "male-dominated environment in computer science classes" was at least partly to blame for Carly's suicide attempt.

Listening to Carly, I had no doubt her feelings of aloneness were accurate, and I supported her in exploring them since a person's feeling of belonging or not belonging can absolutely impact stress hormone levels. But I heard her saying that the male-driven environment *caused* her depression and anxiety, so I tried to help her work through, then out of, that unlikely idea. Linking her depression, anxiety, and procrastination to this culture-paradigm, I argued, would paralyze her in the future by keeping her focused on something that was not causal, and thus distract her from what did cause her issues.

In fact, her comments about the males in her computer classes was the third reason I suggested genetic testing to her and her family; I wanted to help her and her parents discover and address *causation*. Carly's (and her family's) focus on the DGP paradigm was a normal starting point, especially in today's cultural and popular conversations. Every parent of a girl today is, I believe, a de facto student of nature, nurture, and culture, and thus learns the DGP because it is the easiest discernible source of female distress in the popular culture. Carly came into counseling from a college environment and was fluent in DGP language.

"It's a male-dominated world that crushes my confidence," she said. "Computer science is a place where white male privilege (and some Asian male privilege) runs the show."

There was some insight to be had there, but as part of her support system, I wanted her to go deeper into herself because I could see that she was a young woman who had a lot of assets—well-resourced and not oppressed. Culture analysis, I knew, could only get her so far. So, I asked her to consider that the DGP-inspired culture-conversation is generally about gender norms and gender stereotypes, but that depression and anxiety come from a different place. While each of the DGP constructs is worth studying, few of its culture-constructs about masculine oppression of females and female victimization via stereotypes can scientifically help young women who have brain disorders.

Over the months of our counseling together, Carly and I discussed this subject many times. I've summarized some of our later conversations below:

> Me: You came into my office thinking your issues in college came from undiscovered childhood trauma or an anti-female culture at school. Do you still think so?
> Carly: Hmmm . . . I think my parents and I didn't discuss certain things, like how hard I had to work in high school not to seem sad. But no, I don't think my childhood had a lot to do with things like my procrastination, or even the depression. I get now that the genes they come from were and are a big deal.
> Me: So, how will you approach your computer science classes when you go back to school?
> Carly: Well, I think computer science is still a very male world, but I don't think that's an attack on *me* anymore. It makes me kind of sad that I will have to change some things about myself

to succeed in that world, like I will have to stop feeling like such a failure, but I can't blame the guys for being competitive.
Me: What about the changes you've made—gluten, dairy, Wellbutrin. Will you stick with those changes?
Carly: I don't ever want to go back to how I felt before. Now that I know about my genes and what triggers them, I don't want to go back. I'm whole now, I make sense. This is who I want to be.

I saw Carly's mother last year in the grocery store and she told me Carly is now working in the public relations industry and has, in her mother's words, "turned out very well." Proud Mom told me, "Since we saw you, all of us have done the genetic testing. Some of it worked for us and some didn't, but all in all, it was really life-changing."

Carly and the family are doing well, I believe, because all of us—her treatment team, her family and mentors, and Carly herself—re-aligned her life (and to some extent, the whole family's life) toward what was most successfully *natural* to Carly's genome. Carly paused from college-stress to take six months to construct an internal "map" for her own nature and subtly shift her life to *nurture that nature*. She decided that discovering herself as a fully-realized person (nature, nurture, and culture) gave her the best chance to grow into a self-confident, whole woman, and it looks like she has done just that.

Mapping *Your* Daughter's Genome

The sciences of epigenetics and genetics are constantly in flux. There is a lot we still don't know, but we know a lot more than we did even when I was raising my daughters, and as parents and professionals, you can become a citizen scientist who gains insight into your daughter's internal map of being in real time. While her genes (and ours) are not a pre-determined destiny, they do possess an initial template for who we are and will be.

Without asking for gene testing, you can still figure out a great deal about your daughter's genome. In fact, I'm guessing you already have. Isn't one of your children innately good at math and another not so good? Or perhaps one started reading at four and loves books while another started at six and may prefer a more physical life. And perhaps one is naturally more "emotional" while another is less verbal-emotive and more "logical."

You raised these kids the same way in the same place, but they are different because talent, personality, temperament, and gender are mapped in their genes. Each of your children possesses DNA that commingles adenine, cytosine, guanine, and thymine in combinations that repeat one or two or thousands of times. The exact repetitions on each genome are largely responsible for talent sets, personalities, temperaments, neuroses, as well as specific physiological and mental diseases/disorders like cancer, heart disease, obesity, female-type ADD/ADHD, schizophrenia, bipolarity, depression, anxiety disorders, etc.

If you have an autistic child, you will likely be very aware of this already. Scientists have identified more than 65 genes, including MECP2, that each play their parts in causing an autism spectrum disorder (ASD). In 2007, biologist Michael Wigler of Cold Spring Harbor Laboratory and geneticist Jonathan Sebat of UC San Diego discovered that, "*De novo* mutations linked to ASD in the form of copy-number variants— alterations in chromosomes that involve the deletion or duplication of whole chunks of DNA—can affect multiple genes."

These *de novo* mutations on the genes give the ASD brain low-density social-emotional pathway development (the hallmark of ASD) via mutations triggered pre-birth by as little as a single-nucleotide variant on the child's DNA. This single variant can be so powerful it can raise the child's risk of ASD by 20 to 80 times. Wigler and his colleagues know of no children with these variants who don't have ASD.

Mapping My Own Daughters' Genomes

Not just with my clients, but with my own daughters, Gabrielle and Davita, I have used gene maps. Before gene mapping was available, I kept a journal of their traits and what I perceived to be their vulnerabilities. Both girls (now women) share sex/gender traits but also clearly came into the world with different gene expression of personality traits. Gail and I raised them the same way and neither of them experienced abuse trauma, significant disease, or malnutrition. They had a "normal" childhood (as normal as any childhood is!) without significant environmental differences between them. Nonetheless, they are different people, and I wanted to understand how to nurture their nature, so I "tracked" their personalities and vulnerabilities as best I could. You can make this map for your own children by journaling what you observe—and what others observe—in your children's behavior and needs.

Among the differences between our daughters, Gail and I observed that:

- Gabrielle tends to observe first and speak second, while Davita is more likely to argue first and then do more observing.
- Davita tends to be more sensitive than Gabrielle to other peoples' opinions of her or of her ideas.
- Davita ruminates somewhat more than Gabrielle with more agitation associated with the rumination. Gabrielle's ruminations remain more internalized than externalized.
- Davita uses more "steel" in her interactions with others, while Gabrielle uses more "silk."
- Both girls did well in school, but Davita had dyslexia which affected her educational journey. It also inspired significant resilience and adaptation in her and her family.
- Both girls played soccer, but Davita was, overall, the more physical child. We used to call her "Tigger" because, like the character in Winnie the Pooh, she bounced up and down continually! Not surprisingly, she is now an accomplished climber and is pondering a career in physical therapy.
- Gabrielle was more interested in the ins and outs of certain ideas and social commitments. While she enjoys a physical life, she spends much more of her time bent into a computer or a book. Not surprisingly, she is now in law school where she is focusing on food and consumer protection law.

As you journal your children's genetically inspired traits, talk about them with your support system and with your children once they are old enough to become self-aware. Self-awareness of genetic predispositions helps them prepare for the big world and marshal internal forces for survival and thriving. Also talk with your children about the family lineage that gifted them with their genome.

When the Gurian family discusses these things, we take verbal stabs at connecting with inheritance. "Oh, yeah, that's like Mom," or "I'm like Dad in that way," or "I think my father was like that, Gabrielle, and you inherited some of that from those genes." This discussion can lead to an ongoing, lifelong "study" of genes in the family lines. If your child or children are adopted, anything you can learn about their biological parents will be helpful to understanding potential disease or disorders, as well as personality traits, assets, and vulnerabilities. *Nurture the Nature* contains numerous tools to help both biological and adoptive parents to complete personality and trait assessments. And with any child, no matter how little or much you know about genetic lineage, observation and journaling, as well as conversation and community connection, can lead to externally helpful "genetic testing."

For internally accessible gene testing, you will likely need a professional to help you.

Try This

Use Genetic Testing for Your Daughter (and Yourself) When Appropriate

Marta, 13, was a quiet, studious adolescent who did not initially respond to talk therapy as her parents and I hoped she would. No matter what we said or what new family practices were instituted, Marta remained consistently depressed and continued to self-cut. She was seeing a psychiatrist who had prescribed Zoloft, but it was not having the needed effect. I asked the family to go online to study epigenetics as citizen scientists. The family took my information and spent a great deal of time online. Within two weeks, they scheduled a series of visits for Marta with a naturopath who helped the family—through trial and error with eating habits—to discover that Marta's "gut-brain" was awry, thereby triggering genetic vulnerabilities.

"Gut-brain connection" is a term representing the chemical and cellular reactions that transpire between our digestive system (in the gut) and our neurochemistry in the brain. Both Marta and Carly had difficulties in the gut-brain connection because of food allergies. Once this discovery was finally made, Marta's mom, Janice, remembered that her grandmother had needed significant dietary and nutritional changes when she was going through menopause. Janice telephoned the grandmother and learned that Grandma Joan had cut out sugar and artificial sweeteners in the 1990s. For Grandma

Joan, certain foods were clearly neurotoxic (poisonous to genes associated with the stomach cells), and that predisposition was now affecting the mind of her granddaughter.

As Marta's family delved deeper into the genetic tests (aided by their psychiatrist), they learned that Marta was a person who under-methylated folate, most likely because of mutations in her MTHFR gene. This meant she didn't metabolize or absorb one of the body's essential B vitamins in an adequate way. This genetic issue led to a great deal of mood difficulty for her, and the family's psychiatrist suggested a prescription for folic acid, including Deplin® capsules. Marta's mood, behavior, and daily life improved.

"She is a different person," Marta's mother told me with tears in her eyes. "She is less depressed and doing better in school."

In Chapter 5 and throughout the Notes and References, you will find even more specific material on gene testing. Certain corporations and workplaces are now offering this testing to their employees, but even if you don't work for such a company, these tests are getting easier to do every year. The tests generally fall into two categories: blood tests, such as those used by the Walsh Institute, and spit or swab tests. Generally, it is best to have a medical professional order and interpret the tests as the technical language of the results is often complex.

Looking Through a Food-Based Lens

In my clinical practice, I suggest these tests for any girl who is under any kind of duress. That duress may lead to a suicide attempt as it did with Carly, or it may be less overtly dangerous but nevertheless worrisome, like when a child feels anxious, sad, lethargic, or is physiologically at risk for something like obesity. Costs are generally not prohibitive, and should continue to come down as we lobby health insurers to allow them. In Marta's case, it was both her physical situation (she was 30+ pounds overweight) and her mental health that initially triggered me to suggest gene testing to her parents.

When her genetic tests came back, the psychiatrist, her family, and Marta herself could see that she was prone to process what she ate and drank in ways that could harm her. She had vulnerabilities on three genes: DRD2 (an "eating behavior" gene), MC4R (an "appetite" gene), and FTO (a "body fat" gene). Her psychiatrist suggested several changes to her diet and lifestyle, including no more pop, smaller meals with less unhealthy carbohydrates, no more refined sugar and flour, no more artificial sweeteners, and much more exercise.

As with the interplay of genes and environment in your daughter's life, Marta's interplay was complex. The obesity genetics were not the only vulnerabilities that were being triggered in her. Her genes for folate methylation also increased negative outcomes for her. This kind of scenario can similarly apply to a girl who develops anorexia nervosa, bulimia, or other eating disorders.

In 2016, scientists in the U.S. and Austria completed an international whole-genome analysis which showed that eating disorders such as anorexia are associated with genetic anomalies on chromosome 12. The study included 220 researchers analyzing genetic material of 3,500 anorexics from around the world, and the results were compared with a control group of 11,000 people who did not have anorexia. Through this comparison, they located the chromosome 12 gene locus. They also confirmed correlation with other disorders, such as Type 1 diabetes, autoimmune disorders, insulin metabolism disorders, and even neuroticism and schizophrenia.

Child and adolescent psychiatrist Karwautz, who headed the Austrian team, concluded that, "Such studies form a basis for providing patients and their relatives with a logical and realistic explanation for this persistent disorder, which is the third commonest disorder in this adolescent age group. Prevention programs will also benefit from these new findings."

The study, which you can access online, is Cynthia M. Bulik et al. "Significant Locus and Metabolic Genetic Correlations Revealed in Genome-Wide Association Study of Anorexia Nervosa," *American Journal of Psychiatry*, 2017.

Courageous Conversation

Question: Is Genetic Testing a Good Diagnostic Tool for My Daughter and If So, How Do I Access It?

Even though I believe gene testing and epigenetics are becoming essential for good parenting, genetic testing can be controversial. I hope you will have a courageous conversation in your family about whether to use the tests and how.

There are potential disadvantages to gene testing.

First, the tests may not end up helping with the issue the patient is dealing with right now. Perhaps the gene cluster in question can be isolated, but that knowledge may not lead to immediate help with a treatment plan. The gene test might show a proclivity for a certain medication to work but, for reasons unknown, that medication might not end up helping as hoped. Additionally, other factors unknown to the gene testing might impede assistance for the problem.

Second, you might learn your own or your child's genetic vulnerabilities and become anxious about them. I know I am prone to die one day of some form of heart disease or stroke. Knowing this can be a blessing in that I can now set up a diet and exercise plan that should best postpone this demise, but knowing my own genetic anomalies or vulnerabilities can be frightening. For a child or adolescent, it can be especially anxiety-producing. While you might assuage your daughter by saying, "Remember, these genetic vulnerabilities may never get triggered in your life, don't worry," the child may remain frightened.

So, before engaging in genetic testing, it is important that you research it, Google it deeply, talk with your physician or psychiatric resource, and talk with your family about it. A new book by journalist Bonnie Rochman, *The Gene Machine,* gives a fascinating take on the history of genetics research, including the present-day revolution in genetic testing. Ms. Rochman's book poses the important question: "We now have a user's manual available to us for the construction and operation of humans, but how should we use it?"

Given that scientists believe they have now learned how to fix a defective gene in a human embryo, this is one of the most important questions of our time.

How You Might Access Gene Testing in Your Area

Gail and I were recently asked by someone in Phoenix for a way to do genetic testing for their child who had developed some confusing mental health issues. With Gail's permission, I'm printing her response because it provides a nitty-gritty approach to how to get the testing where you are, if you choose to do it.

"There are various kinds of genetic testing. The company 23andMe looks at DNA and risks for diseases and possible abnormalities among other things. The 23andMe test can be ordered by an individual, and a parent can order for a child. You can access 23andMe online. The test results will need to be read by a physician or other qualified professional. My daughter had this done and found it very helpful.

"Alpha Genomics, which we use in our office, is more designed to look at how each individual metabolizes medication and what medications might be best for them. That test has to be ordered by a physician or psychiatrist who has diagnosed and sees that client/patient regularly. I talked to the Alpha Genomics rep here in Washington State to see if there were resources in Phoenix I could suggest to you. He said to tell your physician, pediatrician, or psychiatrist that the family would like to do this testing and ask that professional if they've heard of Alpha Genomics or another similar company. Some medical professionals have not caught up to genetic testing so s/he may not know about it. If they will order the test, the rep said it is available locally from Alpha Genomics in Phoenix. He said if there is any question, you or the physician could call the Phoenix reps and they would see what they could do to set up the testing if the doctor doesn't currently have that resource available.

"I also checked online for you and there is a company in Phoenix called the Genetics Company that appears to do genetic testing. I'm not sure what they offer, but it might be worth giving them a call. They may be able to provide the type of genetic testing that would best serve your children. If not, I would guess they could recommend other services."

Nature's Daughter

As you and the professional interpret genomic information, you will be using a powerful tool for understanding the nature-based map your daughter (or son) has brought into this world. Cultural factors like gender stereotypes can have some effect on girls (and we'll look closely at them in Chapter 7), and gender norms and gender roles can also affect some girls' health, but these are not what cause the most painful distresses your daughter can fall into. They do not *cause* the depression, anxiety, eating disorders, self-cutting, or other clinical conditions you might be facing with your daughter. Gender stereotypes had little to do with Carly's depression. Gender norms in which males dominated her computer science classes did not cause her to attempt suicide.

We must deepen our culture-conversation courageously if we are going to heal the hearts of our daughters. Genome research can help us go deeper, but I admit I've heard some people say, "Studying genetics is what Hitler's people did. How can you want to pursue it?"

There is fear that studying genetics will become somehow an experiment of genetic determinism, where babies may be killed before birth because they are genetically wanting. My answer to the question lies in my own past. I am Jewish and lost most of my living relatives to extermination by the Nazis. Thus, I have been sensitive all my life to negative potentialities from the pretense that one genetic line might be superior to another.

Clearly, what I've shared with you about genetic research in this chapter has nothing to do with eugenics or racial superiority. My purpose is to help update parenting, educational, academic, governmental, and media systems to fit the new sciences. When people ask me how I can go down the "genetics" road, I tell them that for parents specifically, science-based tools are generally better than loose culture-based tools.

We are tasked as adults with nurturing nature's daughters. Genes are not everything but, to me, not to nurture a girl's nature because of certain cultural obsessions will distract us from ensuring that our girls thrive. While each culture-concept or ideological fear may have some merit in some situations, few areas of focus lead to as much direct success for the Carly's and Marta's of the world than those strategies and interventions that grow from looking into the minute details of the female genome.

PART II

NURTURE

Chapter 4

The Truth about Girl Drama: Protecting the Emotional Lives of Girls

"Relationships are one of the greatest classrooms for girls."

—Rachel Simmons, *Odd Girl Out*

ON YOUTUBE, TAKE A MOMENT to search for "Dove Commercials," and watch some of the ways the female brain experiences its own emotional life. A particularly powerful commercial involves women who are asked to sit for an artist.

"Describe your face," the artist instructs a woman kindly.

As she describes herself, he draws what she describes.

Afterward, they look together at the drawing. The woman shrugs somewhat, confirming the accuracy of the likeness while also feeling some disappointment that her face seems more wrinkled and less attractive than she would have hoped.

Now the artist asks a second woman to describe this first woman's face. He draws the exact same face he drew before, but this time in a likeness the female observer, not the female subject, has suggested.

When his new drawing is finished, the subject of the drawing looks a second time at "herself" on canvas. She compares this second drawing to the first drawing that was based on her own verbalized self-image.

To her surprise, she discovers that another woman observing her sees a more beautiful face than she herself did. Observing this video clip, we feel empathy for her, and we can see how her eyes water at these results.

These Dove commercials provide content for citizen science we can all use in conversations with your own daughters. As you and your daughters watch them, you may be inspired to share your own stories of adolescence and adulthood. Even as a man who did not experience female adolescence, I was able to feel useful to Gabrielle and Davita as we watched the commercials and talked about them. Gail certainly used them even more intimately and usefully.

These commercials introduce some of the subjects of this chapter, including something you have already deduced—that your daughter will spend a lot of time in front of a mirror measuring herself worthy or unworthy, engaged in internal dramas, and often finding her face and body wanting. Even when she projects high self-esteem to you and the world ("I don't care what people think, I'm beautiful just the way I am!") she'll still compare herself to others as her growing brain spends the better part of ten adolescent years finding her place in the world. Behind her mirrored physical deductions will be mental, spiritual, and emotional ones.

All this she will use as data with which to both encourage and attack other girls around her. Sometimes quite impulsively, she will attempt to befriend and, later, ostracize another girl because of facial cues that girl has sent her way. She will judge other girls wanting based on physical and facial cues that become immersed for her in social and peer influence. Enjoying a girlfriend's company—even merging her own spirit and soul with this other girl—your daughter may, a few weeks later, pick a terrible fight, perhaps breaking off relations altogether. To be nature's daughter is often to become sorrow's daughter. Relations may remain strained and distant forever onward, or perhaps your daughter will reunite a few weeks later with this girl, the friendship repaired. Sorrow can quickly become new joy.

Girl Drama as a Developmental Resource

Numerous powerful books and articles have been written about what is now called "girl drama," including *Queen Bees and Wannabees* by Rosalind Wiseman, which grounded the *Mean Girls* movie, and *Odd Girl Out* by Rachel Simmons, which led to the formation of empowerment organizations like Girls, Inc. I won't repeat their insights here. Instead, I will take a brain-based approach to girl drama that I hope you will find fresh and helpful as it is grounded in the idea that girl drama (except when it slips into bullying or violence, including crimes on cyberspace) is an important part of female development.

Did You Know?

The Truth About Girl Drama

"Girl drama is good for girls." Does that sentence seem surprising? It often does at the beginning of a presentation or in a counseling session, but within a few minutes of explaining why, I begin to see heads nodding. The same lightbulbs go off for audiences that went off in my own head as Gail and I raised our daughters. By integrating brain research into our parenting, we learned that girl drama is nature's way of:

1. Building emotional boundaries in girls and women —boundaries that will become essential parts of their ability to love and be loved.
2. Strengthening and toughening girls' psyches— making them more resilient—and thus enabling them to face adversity later.
3. Building healthy competitive abilities and helping girls make internal decisions about what is worth competing for.
4. Teaching them who to trust and how to trust without losing or erasing oneself.
5. Training them to become less negatively impulsive and more positively altruistic (i.e. helping them learn healthy self-regulation).
6. Helping their psyches develop true, not false, self-esteem and self-image.
7. Teaching the brain to avoid excessive selfishness and narcissism.
8. Revealing to girls the limits of freedom while empowering them to push into and, sometimes, beyond those limits.

In short, girl drama matures a girl from childhood to adulthood. If we help our girls through it successfully, girl drama is one of nature's best teaching and growth tools—truly a "classroom" for girls.

Nevertheless, the pain girls feel from these interactions often frighten us, and thus it is also natural for us to try to protect our girls from the dramas. In Chapter 6, I'll focus specifically on resilience-building in girls, so I will save insights on that for later. Right now, let's focus on the many other ways to use girl drama as a nurturing asset—a teaching tool in your family. Primarily, I will help you to show your daughters the science of girl drama and thus use it to build healthy self-image, self-esteem, and self-worth.

As my own daughters understood what their brains, biochemistry, and psyches were doing throughout their dramas, they were better able to grow up well and more quickly. They made many mistakes (as did I) in their process, but self-understanding was a key to success so I've set up each section of this chapter to be girl-friendly. You can show the sections to your daughter and talk with her about each element so that her self-awareness can aid in her maturation.

But before we go on, let me give this caveat: nothing I say in this chapter is meant to trump your own intuition of *danger*. While I will treat girl drama as a useful human function, if you think your daughter's drama has gone into something dangerous, your immediate intervention will transcend anything I teach here. Some girl drama can originate in and end in mental health issues such as depression and anxiety, and treating those must come before anything else.

Courageous Conversation

Is My Daughter Anxious or Depressed?

Even though our ancestors faced far harsher conditions than our children generally do, more of our daughters are clinically depressed and anxious today than their ancestors. Why? There are three primary reasons for this trend:

- Environmental neurotoxins triggering genetic vulnerabilities in girls (the subject of Chapter 5);
- Traumas to the brain including abuse and, in some cases, poverty, which can trigger mental health vulnerabilities in girls;

- Significant isolation, rejection, abandonment, or neglect, which can trigger depression, bullying, and many other issues.

2017 saw an unprecedented increase in female suicide rates, but all suicide rates in the U.S. have been increasing steadily for the last fifteen years. Most female-completed suicides take place post-adolescence, but attempted-suicide rates for girls are still high in adolescence. Overall, increasing numbers of girls are so depressed as to use pills, knives, guns, and ropes to end their own lives.

This recent trend of increased emotional distress in our daughters is a primary reason I wrote this book. Even if your own daughter does not become depressed, you will likely know a girl who is. As my team travels from community to community, we bring a science-based perspective to assist in courageous conversations.

A powerful article in *The Atlantic* in 2013 can make for foundational reading by parents and children: "Depression is a Disease of Civilization" by Stephen Llardi. Through a simple Google search, you can access Llardi's article, as well as the powerful TED Talk on the same subject. Like mine, Llardi's perspective is nature-based.

Another valuable addition to your community and home conversation is a study recently published in the journal *Translational Psychiatry*. The researchers interviewed more than 100,000 children participating in the National Survey of Drug Use and Health from 2009 to 2014 (the NSDUH is an annual survey of a representative sample of the U.S. population). The interviews found "that depression in many children appears to start as early as age 11. By the time they hit age 17, 13.6 percent of boys and a staggering 36.1 percent of girls have been or are depressed. These numbers are significantly higher than previous estimates. Understanding the risk of depression is critically important because of the close link between depressive episodes and serious issues with school, relationships and suicide."

As if these statistics weren't grave enough, new research reported in *Counseling Today* reveals that, "Anxiety disorders are the most common mental illness in the United States, affecting 18 percent of the adult population, or more than 40 million people, according to the National Institutes of Health. Among adolescents the prevalence is even higher: 25 percent of youth ages 13 to 18 live with some type of anxiety disorder."

Our country is especially prone to creating these disorders in our children. I believe by the end of this book, the many reasons for this neural pressure on our children will be clarified, and you'll have tools in place to protect your daughters. If, as you are reading these pages, you are concerned about whether your daughter is depressed or anxious or struggling with any brain disorder, such as anorexia or bulimia, please move toward psychiatric assessment and counseling immediately. While 5 years old is generally too soon to give a correct diagnosis (with some exceptions), 10 years old may not be.

To determine if your daughter is anxious, look for:
- racing thoughts
- irrational fear
- excessive rumination (constantly thinking about emotional slights or other worries)
- seeing too many negative possibilities in nearly every situation
- insomnia
- racing heart
- sweaty palms
- upset stomach
- headaches

If you are seeing at least three of these symptoms in your child in worrisome quantity or quality, it may be very important that you seek insight from a mental health professional.

The Power of Negativity Bias

People who are anxious operate out of self-damaging "negativity bias." Negativity is a normal survival response, locked into our limbic systems by millions of years of survival. Indeed, it is partially responsible for the fact that we are still around. Our senses perceive the world as it is, then certain parts of the brain (e.g., the *cingulate gyrus, basal ganglia,* and *caudate nucleus*) process our sensory apprehensions so that our bodies will act and move toward survival. The limbic brain signals upward to the executive decision-making parts of the brain (the *prefrontal and orbitofrontal cortices,* for instance) so that new, good decisions can be made—healthy reactions to the world's pressures.

If your daughter is overly anxious or suffers from a clinically-diagnosed anxiety disorder, however, her survival/negativity bias is likely working overtime, hyper-active, hyper-vigilant and reactive. She likely carries DNA markers for this vulnerability. Trauma may have been a factor in triggering her anxiety. Prolonged anxiety (constant negatively bias) can trigger other genetic vulnerabilities such as anorexia, bulimia, obsessive-compulsive disorder, and obesity.

Negativity bias also plays a part in depression, which is one reason that depressed girls feel anxious, and anxious girls often feel depressed.

To ascertain whether your daughter might be depressed, look for:

- excessive rumination (constantly thinking about the same negative thoughts)
- constant feelings of guilt
- constant feelings of sadness
- headaches
- constant overreaction
- lethargy
- insomnia
- suicide attempts

Anxiety and depression can be treated effectively and those treatments can often have positive effects on parents who may struggle with anxiety and/or depression themselves without even realizing it. If you are one of these parents, your courage will be an asset to your child. Any adult who has battled with a mental illness can share strategies for success in dealing with the condition. For us adults, that courage and that sharing can become a powerful part of our own purpose and life-work.

The Neurochemistry of Healthy Girl Drama

While girl drama and female emotional life can become toxic and even include mental illness, much or most girl drama will not fit this category. It will be "normal," though often painful. It falls into a developmentally normal category because the human brain—especially the female brain—is set up structurally and biochemically to build emotional intelligence on the path we've recently renamed girl drama.

The following are some of the nature-based factors involved in normal and useful girl drama:

- Female brain function utilizes high levels of the neurochemical *oxytocin* which can create both useful and painful "psychological merging" in female friendships and relationships.
- The female brain activates blood flow in certain specific areas that impact girl drama including "rumination loops" in and through the *cingulate gyrus,* and "white matter activity" that leads to female-specific emotional distress.
- Girls nurture and acculturate in *gossip* and *ostracism* patterns in which they experiment with *conformity* and *non-conformity* in both healthy and unhealthy socialization.
- The sensory life of the female brain (accessing the world through the five senses) relies heavily on reading *facial cues* and *physical attractiveness* which play a large part in female self-esteem development.

In all these elements, we will notice not only similarities with males but also some distinct and instructive differences. Talking to girls about these differences can be very engaging for them, and a positive way of helping them see themselves and their own behavior more clearly. Again, please show your daughters these sections if you feel they are old enough to understand them. I've written this science to stimulate courageous conversation.

Oxytocin and "Merging"

When my daughters were growing up, and beginning early in pre-school, they formed dyad and triad groupings with friends (friendship groups of twos and threes). In one of them, Davita, Anna, and Brittany became inseparable, doing homework together, playing together on the playground, having sleepovers. They combed each other's hair, tried on each other's clothes, and shared their most intimate lives. Then something happened. Brittany said something to Anna that Davita saw from across the room. Certain that the conversation was about a flaw in her, Davita reacted negatively, first by ruminating on it (thinking and brooding on it), then by seeming depressed, then by becoming angry at the other two girls, then by trying to make up with Anna but not Brittany. Throughout the next week, the friendship became strained. Anna and Brittany ostracized Davita, which caused her terrible pain, then a week later, Davita and Anna somehow got bonded again, but Brittany was left out.

Oxytocin, a powerful neurochemical, and polymorphisms on the OXTR gene (the oxytocin receptor gene), was very important factors in the drama of this triad. Oxytocin and the OXTR gene, in part, control:

- social behaviors linked to attachment and bonding;
- female brain development and structural activity;
- pro-social activity, including gossip, ostracism, and conforming and nonconforming behavior;
- facial and affect recognition, including one's sense of attractiveness;
- empathy behavior (including the dark side of empathy, to be discussed in a moment); and
- development of self-esteem and self-worth.

Males do all this, but female cells—in body and brain—possess more oxytocin than do male cells and brain. More oxytocin floods girls than boys because there is more oxytocin reception in female gene expression.

When females feel stress, the stress hormone (cortisol) rises and triggers a rise in the bonding chemical, oxytocin. Females under stress are thus more likely to "tend and befriend" than are males under stress. Because a cortisol rise in males stimulates a rise in testosterone (the aggression chemical), males are more likely to experience "fight or flight."

Nature appears to have set human beings up in this somewhat binary way in order to ensure varied strategies for handling stress. While one group (females) might seek deepened emotional bonds with others in the community, another group (males) might increase their protective aggression or withdraw from the fight in order to allow others to bond.

Davita and her friends were living out the female OXTR/oxytocin journey. One very specific way involves the reading of facial cues and other sensorial gestures. Higher oxytocin in female biochemistry is one reason females generally read facial and social cues better than men, *and* why they read more into facial cues than a man might. Davita read Anna's and Brittany's facial cues and body language better than her friend Jimmy might have, but also read more into them than was there. This is a crucial point we must make with our daughters.

Early autism research discovered a link between functions in the OXTR gene and autism, helping all of us to realize the importance of social cues in the human brain. Autistic kids do not read social and facial cues as well as non-autistic kids in part because of discrepancies in oxytocin/OXTR functioning. More males than females are on the Autism/ASD spectrum, in part, because males generate less oxytocin. Even females on the ASD spectrum tend to read facial and social cues somewhat better than males on the spectrum because female biochemistry and cellular biology includes the significant role oxytocin plays in maternal functioning.

Oxytocin, then, occupies a significant place in female gene expression and thus sits at the heart of female friendships, girl-bullying, and normal girl drama. As Davita, Anna, and Brittany bonded, they "merged" their personalities, joining selves and psyches (as a mother might with a child) to such an extent they combed one another's hair and wore one another's clothing. This felt joyful, as very little separated them from one another. Their brains, if scanned, would show constant bonding chemistry in full flow, thus they were constantly picking up facial and other social cues to bolster the bond and increase the good feeling of oxytocin flow and surges of the brain's reward chemical, dopamine.

But the human brain can't stay very long in this kind of merging. Even a parent and child must become psychologically separate to become mature human beings. Even two lovers, immersed in one another sexually and socially at first, must develop into separate, independent beings if they are to successfully marry and live adult lives. There is an inherent and useful fragility to the immersion of the three girls' brains in their complex friendship; the conflict they started was painful but helped each girl's self to breathe, to grow, and to expand autonomously. The Three became One, but then returned to healthy separation of Each.

Davita, Anna, and Brittany learned about boundaries, love, friendship, respect, independence, and self-growth through the drama.

Your girls, too, will likely live this journey, experimenting with attachment and boundaries in preschool to learn its abilities and limits. Then, as your daughter moves through elementary school and toward puberty, her brain may feel even more experiential pressure both to bond and to remain a separate self with adequate boundaries. When the hormones of pre-puberty begin around nine or ten, her brain will be washed with whole new biochemical wonders (and potential pains), and now begins a new phase of bonding/merging and separation/boundaries. Most of this will be normal and useful, while some of it will become bullying and may even become relational violence. Fortunately, you and your daughter's mentors, teachers, and friends will be there to protect her from the violence, and help her manage and recognize the dramatic growth that is possible for her in each stage of her journey.

Gabrielle, at 15, provided our family with an example of girl-girl friendship that bordered, we felt, on danger. As she became bonded with her classmate, Amy, the two of them became inseparable. It was very sweet at first, and seemed like a bond that shined brightly for them both. They became so merged, however, that Gabrielle and Amy would text back and forth (cell phones had just begun their power during that time) and become agitated if they did not hear back from one another right away. "Where's Amy? Why isn't she responding?" Gabrielle wondered, agitated, worried, her emotions and self so "one" with Amy's that even time became a burden, withholding contact and connection as if to hurt Gabrielle. When Amy finally did text back, Gabrielle's sense of relief was palpable.

A few months into this friendship, luckily, something happened between the girls that activated Gabrielle's need to set boundaries and separate herself from Amy so that she could take the next step in her maturation. Between the girls now there was immense drama for many weeks, painful to both. But the separation was needed, and Gabrielle saw its need. Gail, I, her godmother Pam, and others in our community helped her to take this next step in life, and after this drama, the two girls were never close friends again. Gail and I felt very happy for Gabrielle. We felt that Amy was not a healthy influence on her and we discussed this with her. Fortunately, Gabrielle came to this realization internally, and gained strength from the end of this friendship that has helped her to be strong throughout her adulthood.

Could either Davita or Gabrielle have fully grown up—fully developed healthy emotional and psychological boundaries—if they had not gone through the dramas of their childhoods and adulthoods? No, they could not. The dramas were painful, the oxytocin and OXTR genetics wreaked some havoc, but there was a great deal of joy for all these girls along the way, and in the end, the goal of childhood—maturation—was reached. Again, it is crucial to note that severe trauma caused by bullying, cyberbullying, or violence can harm maturation. But most girl drama is not that, and so it should be studied and even utilized for growth.

The Female Brain, the Cingulate Gyrus, and Rumination Loops

Because we hoped to shape our daughters into citizen scientists, we discussed oxytocin/merging with them each time a drama occurred. When they were early adolescents, we suggested they read *The Tending Instinct* by Shelley Taylor, *Women's Moods* by Deborah Sichel, and *The Wonder of Girls*. Later, when they were adults, Louann Brizendine's *The Female Brain* was published, and the girls and I discussed those books. Now, in working with families, I also suggest Leonard Sax' *Girls on the Edge* for more nature-based information on how the female brain and biochemistry affect female development. Our girls also read Rosalind Wiseman's *Queen Bees and Wannabes* and *Odd Girl Out* by Rachel Simmons, as well as other school-based anti-bullying curricula, some of which integrated well into the brain-based information we gave them. Sometimes, they would hear from a bullying expert online or at school that girl drama was not normal and was dangerous—that it was an attack on female development created by a toxic society that turned girls on each other in order to keep them from power. We checked these concepts with them, too, so that they could decide for themselves what they thought. Generally, more nature-based in their approach, they disagreed with this extreme view.

One of the things we often discussed around our dinner table was girls' and women's tendency to *ruminate*. Davita, for instance, noticed that while guys loved their friends and bonded quite deeply, they did not tend to take things as personally in their friendship as the girls did. Yes, they merged selves, but they also tended to remain more separate. As we discussed this, I suggested she watch how much or how little the boys, compared to the girls, were reading facial or social cues.

Both Gabrielle and Davita noticed that for most males another guy rolling his eyes would likely not merit a destruction of bonds—in fact, it might be part of a one-upping social bonding mechanism. While some males, they noticed, are more sensitive than others and read more cues, Brizendine's, Taylor's, Sichel's, and my own research was confirmed in my daughters' school environments. Males tended to make friends without as much emphasis on merging mechanisms like wearing one another's clothing, or grooming the other person's hair, or thinking (ruminating) constantly about what other people thought of them. This latter element led to many years of discussion.

"Why do we have to ruminate so much?" Gabrielle asked at the dinner table one night in vast frustration. "I wish I could just get these thousand thoughts out of my head!"

She knew the answer by then from our discussions and her research, but she also felt the internal pressure of neurochemistry, brain structure, and blood flow filling up certain parts of the brain with "rumination loops" that were difficult to quiet. Rumination (running over the same thoughts and emotions again and again) is a mid-brain/upper-brain collaboration in all human beings. Like negativity bias, it is a survival mechanism in which signals are sent from the mid-brain upward to the frontal lobe then back down to the mid-brain, repeatedly "looping" the brain structures together.

The female brain is more prone to rumination loops for a number of reasons. One is the female brain's tendency toward feeling and thinking via high levels of white matter processing (connecting "dots" from various parts of the brain). Another is the highly active attention/focus center, the *cingulate gyrus* or *anterior cingulate cortex*. SPECT scans at the Amen Clinics have revealed that this part of the female brain is larger than in the male brain, and up to four times more active. As this focus center loops to an emotional or memory center in the brain, it attends to a facial cue or feeling constantly, looping attention to the distress it feels. This kind of rumination feels like "constant worrying" and is one of the reasons many women spend so much of their lives in low-grade (if not clinical) anxiety, and are more prone to overt depression. As they run something over in their minds for hours, days, or longer, they elevate stress hormone levels and heart rate. They can, literally, ruminate themselves into illness.

Remember that rumination, like negativity bias and merging, are all survival mechanisms. They are not flaws or failures. They present every girl and every parent with joy and growth as your daughter ruminates and merges, and also with challenges as she ruminates too much for good health and merges too much for the development of autonomy. Compounding the joy and the challenge, the activity in another part of the brain, the *insula,* is different in female and male brains. Daniel Goleman in *Emotional Intelligence* explains.

"Neuroscientists tell us one key to empathy is a region of the brain called the insula, which senses signals from our whole body. When we're empathizing with someone, our brain mimics what that person feels, and the insula reads that pattern and tells us what that feeling is. Here's where women differ from men. If the other person is upset, or the emotions are disturbing, women's brains tend to stay with those feelings. But men's brains do something else: they sense the feelings for a moment, then tune out of the emotions and switch to other brain areas that try to solve the problem that's creating the disturbance."

Goleman notes that one reason girls get into long rumination loops more than boys is that their mirror neurons stay active a long time. They keep processing their empathy for others and their empathy for themselves much longer than boys or men.

A mom told me the following story after a talk I gave on the minds of girls:

I have four girls and one boy. When we go on trips, my son, 10, who is fourth in birth order, tries his best to keep up with all the emotions around him, and he does pretty well—his sisters have trained him! But it's obvious what you said about the insula. He just doesn't empathize like his sisters do, and when they ruminate and talk about stuff or become "dramatic," he tries to problem solve as quickly as possible.

My husband and I have had this argument many times too. Before the girls came, he would just move to problem-solving mode immediately when I shared emotions with him. Gradually, as he had more and more daughters, he has had to get better at just listening and empathizing, but neither my son nor my husband can listen and mirror like my girls can.

And by the way, I should note, I'm the "hard-ass" in the family. I'm more prone to tell the girls to toughen up and stop whining. I'm more of the disciplinarian. But this 'insula' difference is so clear! The girls and I feel something and it lasts longer in us. We ruminate and talk and ruminate again. I can see it as both a blessing and a curse."

It is indeed both. Because of the female brain's ability to retain mirror neurons for so long, girls and women are often amazing in their empathic responses. One of the primary reasons we will likely never see as many male as female kindergarten teachers is this insula/rumination combination in the female brain. Empathy in males and females is done differently, and the more intensely vulnerable the individual, the more likely there will be female brains nearby trying to empathize. Similarly, because the female brain is so constantly attentive to details of emotion via its rumination loops, girls and women sense and feel much more than males, on average. This is a blessing.

Women and girls feel it as a "curse" too. To help your daughters with the negative side of it, identify rumination loops in your daughter by watching for:

- repetitive thinking about certain relational issues or experiences even when the experiences are long over
- a sense in your daughter that life-outcomes are not ever controllable, no matter what she does
- thinking in which she has constructed an abstract worst-case scenario (and worries about its presence constantly) when, in fact, no such scenario may exist
- constant thinking about memories of past events that worry her in the context of the present event
- repetitive focus on herself and how she might be harmed when no harm may have occurred

When Davita kept processing the facial cues sent out by Anna and Brittany, she was ruminating excessively by playing out an internal script in which the other girls were gossiping about her and ostracizing her. Much of this was abstract in her mind and connected to past events, not the present one. As she found herself doing many of the things on the list I just gave, we pointed this out and tried to help her understand that she:

1. needed to put the rumination in perspective (i.e. she had not been harmed by what the other two girls had done, so she really didn't need to stress out about it so much), and;
2. she needed to go talk to the girls about how she felt.

She didn't necessarily take our advice at 5, but we were constantly near her to give her this message again and again. Gradually she took control of her rumination loops and matured into a young woman with good boundaries, strong self-regulation and self-awareness, and the ability to both empathize and emotionally problem-solve. Gabrielle voiced the core concept in our parenting approach after she was an adult.

"We always had to be self-aware in our family," she said. "Sometimes all this talk about our brains and being female was overkill, but it did help me to get a grip on growing up faster, and understanding who I was and who I could become."

Often, I am asked for the best trick or tip for ending girl drama and rumination. There is no trick or tip better than to remember that it's normal for the female brain so we shouldn't change it. Rather, our job is to keep helping our daughters become self-aware "scientists" of their own internal processes so that they can gradually master them into adulthood.

Gossip and Ostracism

As we do that, and no matter where our daughter is raised, she will no doubt experience some ostracism in her life—feeling left out. She will also most likely be both a gossiper and a target of gossip. I received this email from a couple in California:

Our daughter, Deena, 14, is always the target of gossip. She became so depressed about this last year that we took her to a counselor. Now she is taking Zoloft and things have gotten better, but we are thinking about changing schools or homeschooling.

We read "The Wonder of Girls" last year and it helped us to understand how she was reacting, but now we have a question: do some girls just attract gossip? If so, why?

We think of Deena as a pretty normal girl. She does her homework, she dresses in the uniform all the girls wear at her school (a Catholic school), she tries to get along with people, but somehow she doesn't make friends very well, and she seems to frustrate her friends too.

We don't understand what she's doing wrong and we can't figure out how to help her become better at avoiding the gossip and the ostracism.

After speaking with both parents, I learned that Deena's father had been exactly this way as an adolescent. He had alienated people in high school, and he had been the target of bullying until he grew big enough and courageous enough to fight back. When we spoke, he called high school, "my dark time." I asked him what he did to navigate through this dark time.

"I learned to just ignore it," he replied. "My brother and I were twins and I did most stuff with him or on my own, not with other people."

I asked him when things changed for him.

"By about the time I went to college," he said. "I grew out of being such an asshole to other people and other people seemed to like me in college."

When I asked him what triggered the positive change, he couldn't think of anything specific.

"I think I just finally figured out that the way I was acting with people wasn't working."

In working with Deena over a period of four months, I found out that she, like my own daughters, ruminated about gossip and ostracism, and probably even created some of the gossip and ostracism herself. From social media, I could see that her peers called her "fragile," "nasty," "sad." Social media made gossip about her feel even more intense because it lasted in cyberspace. While Deena was an only child without access to a safe sibling with whom to bond and weather the storm of adolescence, she did have a father who had experienced her pain, so I suggested she and the father talk a great deal more about his experiences at her age.

A year later, I learned in a follow-up conversation that Deena and her father did indeed become closer as he talked with her about the mistakes she was making in her social groups. She had also found a girlfriend by then who was perhaps an equivalent of a sister. Deena was being gossiped about and ostracized less in school. But in the intervening year, I learned that relationships were still drama-filled and painful for her as she still ruminated over small slights and overreacted to other girls' (and boys') comments or facial expressions. She took things personally and got her buttons pushed by peers. Change throughout the year was incremental (as much good change is), not sudden. In my time working with her, I helped her see that she had some of the same genetic personality markers her father had, and his life was evidence that painful adolescence would give way to maturity and positive growth.

Try This

Rather Than Intervening, Teach

As the family worked with Deena, both Mom and Dad practiced "teaching" rather than "intervention." When they saw that Deena had formed a rumination loop about something another girl did, they knew Deena would likely say something mean or self-deprecating to the other girl, thus creating tension and ostracization. So, they interrupted their daughter's ruminations by pointing out what she was doing internally ("You're ruminating!") and asking her to list everything she was ruminating about.

They did not, however, try to rescue her or otherwise intervene in or manage her actual relationships by calling other parents or trying to force play dates or relationships. They trusted Deena to keep working things out, both inside her own brain and, gradually, via friendships. As they helped her become self-aware, Deena kept making mistakes, but she also kept getting better at controlling her impulses to say things to others that would create their negative reactions.

The success of this process of trusting courageous conversation rather than constant intervention has been confirmed by recent studies of both younger and teen girls. In a 2017 study at Brown University's Warren Alpert Medical School, researcher Laura Stroud worked with middle school girls and found that, "Girls whose parents give them strategies for solving social problems—by suggesting they join a school club to meet peers with similar interests, for example—have stronger friendships."

Studies at the Laurel School Center for Research on Girls in Shaker, Ohio confirm, as Lisa Damour, the study lead, put it, "Teens who are able to ask for and receive support and problem-solving help from their mothers at age 13 tend to be more independent and better educated at 25." Michael Simon, a school counselor in New Orleans, summed up the research by stating, "The number one mistake parents make when their kid is in distress is to jump in and solve it."

If you have a girl who is constantly ruminating about anything, including her social rejection, research shows that *teaching* girls about rumination loop via *conversation* may be better than *intervening* in the girl's relationships through other means. In fact, a new study called *Looking on the Dark Side: Rumination and Cognitive-Bias Modification,* conducted by scientists at Trinity University and Hebrew University, confirmed the usefulness of non-interventionist teaching.

Researchers studied rumination behavior in young adults and found that as the subjects became increasingly aware of the dark side of their rumination loops—including awareness of their own part in negative outcomes via assistance from parents and others in helping them understand the rumination—they were gradually able to alter their behavior and quiet the rumination activity. As parents and mentors helped a girl stop her constant rumination by increasing her awareness of her own internal process, she became more empowered to stop the excessive rumination herself.

The following is an example of a "teaching" conversation between Deena and her father.

Dad: "I can tell you're brooding and ruminating. What happened?"

Silence.

Dad: "Come on, we agreed you would tell me when you got dark. Tell me what you're thinking about."

After more silence and prodding, finally Deena started talking about a teacher, Mrs. Kelie, and another student, Latrisha. Deena confessed that she had been ruminating a lot lately about how Mrs. Kelie didn't like her the way she liked the other student.

Dad: "What proof do you have of that?"

Deena remembered two or three other instances in which Mrs. Kelie paid positive attention to Latrisha.

Dad: "What about the times she has encouraged *you*? Do you remember some of those times?"

After frowning and saying no, Deena did. She remembered more than one.

Dad: "Tell me about those."

Deena talked about those times aloud.

Dad: "So, maybe yesterday was just Latrisha's 'moment' with Mrs. Kelie. You've had yours and you will again, but maybe this was Latrisha's. That's okay, right?"

Deena agreed sullenly and still ruminated for the rest of the evening —but much less, she told me many days later when we discussed this conversation in our counseling session. By the time she fell asleep that night, she remembered, she no longer felt that the incident with Mrs. Kelie and Latrisha was harmful to her.

Fortunately, unlike other ruminative times, she had not created a subversive or overt conflict with either Mrs. Kelie or Latrisha this time, and so she did not face new gossip or ostracism. This was a moment of growth for her, as in the past she had often created conflicts in response to her rumination and ended up ostracized because of them.

The Role of Gossip and Ostracism in Female Maturation

David Geary, at the University of Missouri, has been studying the role of social rejection in female stress levels for decades. While all children can suffer terribly from being rejected socially, girls tend to feel this rejection somewhat differently than boys. In his meta-study, *Evolution of Sex Differences in Trait- and Age-Specific Vulnerabilities,* Geary reveals that female stress hormone levels tend to rise more and stay higher than male when the person is rejected socially. Male stress hormones tend to rise more and stay higher from status-related social evaluations—being judged as low-status—whereas females generate more emotional reactivity, including constant rumination, when they are socially rejected.

A powerful new study, which you can access online, *Gossip and Ostracism Promote Cooperation in Groups* by researchers at Stanford University and the University of California-Berkeley, provides insight into both the pain and functionality of gossip and ostracism. In the study, you'll find an in-depth assessment of what your own daughters are going through.

The researchers studied social exclusion via the spreading of reputational information among participants. Previous research had shown that when people gossip to exclude others, they are generally doing it to promote more cooperation and less egoism. In other words, they are targeting someone they consider "not good enough" so that that person can become "better for the group." Often, they are wrong, but this is the intention.

The new study confirmed previous research that participants' gossip focused on the ways they didn't think a target was cooperating well enough. This could sound like, "She thinks she's so cool, but she's not" or "She dresses like a slut" or "She thinks she's better than us." All these assessments, shared through gossip, can ostracize a person until that person "does better" at joining the group. Indeed, the people who were gossiped about and ostracized generally tried to alter their behavior so that they would be perceived as more cooperative and could get re-accepted into the group. A key word here is "conformity." Gossip and ostracism are often about group conformity, which makes them both good and bad for girls.

The brain plays a part in all of this, of course. The study corroborated findings revealed by an international research team in the U.S. and England that used fMRI scans to look at what parts of the brain are involved in conforming and non-conforming behavior. The researchers showed the importance of the *ventral striatum*, an important mechanism in the mid-brain. When there is a threat of punishment in a group like the threat of gossip, this part of the brain works hard to re-orient that person toward conformity because ostracism is not only painful, but potentially dangerous evolutionarily (isolated humans don't survive long in the wild), and our brains know it.

Deena knew it as well. She tried to "make friends" and be a part of the group, but kept failing at this function. Her *ventral striatum* was working hard but with limited success for a few years until she quieted her own reactivity and finally succeeded in making and keeping friends. One way I helped Deena understand this process was through film.

I asked her to watch two movies, *Mean Girls* and *Wish Upon*, and we discussed them afterwards. *Mean Girls* provided many conversation-points well known culturally now for discussing gossip and ostracism. It also showed various problem-solving strategies. The lesser known film, *Wish Upon*, helped too. This film is about a girl who is so much the target of gossip, she takes revenge on the perpetrators via a lethal Chinese wishing box. From the box, a "demon" rewards her angry impulsiveness by harming not only the kids who have hurt her, but other innocent people as well. The movie is a kind of morality play on how an adolescent girl's vengeful impulsiveness can wreak havoc on not only the bullies, but also herself. Deena found this movie somewhat "campy," but the film also inspired healthy and courageous conversation about the incidents in her life that felt like bullying.

Preventing and Treating Bullying

Bullying, by definition, is traumatic. It goes beyond normal teasing behavior, gossip, ostracism, or other interactions that we have discussed in this chapter. The FBI estimates that between 13% and 25% of American children are bullied or are bullies. To be considered bullying, an action must become not just painful but traumatic. By trauma we mean that the victim has experienced extreme stress that invades her ability to cope with daily life and function in the social systems in which she is a member. Trauma creates more than normal discomfort, fear, anxiety, or mood swings. It is a deeper pain that can have lasting effects on the brain and often comes from repeated bullying behavior in a social group.

A great deal of the trauma can be measured by stress hormone levels. During a stressful time, the body and brain experience a rise in cortisol and adrenalin levels. This is normal and useful, but when experiencing trauma, the stress hormone levels remain too high for too long. This constant wash of cortisol affects mood, mental health, memory, cognitive functioning, emotional stability, and can cause suicide or other violent behavior.

Your daughter may have been bullied if she:

- experiences an unexpected drop in grades or school performance
- becomes excessively moody for more than a few days
- becomes depressed for more than a few days
- becomes very anxious for more than a few days
- becomes angry and acts out
- "acts in"—turning her feelings on herself by becoming immensely self-critical
- cuts herself or otherwise mutilates herself (check for changes in clothing in which she covers her body up much more than she previously did)
- avoids talking about bullying or a certain person or friendship group when you ask.

If your daughter is bullied, you do not need to be alone in helping her through it. Counselors in her school and in private agencies can become your allies. A powerful and helpful book is *The Bully, the Bullied, and the Not-So-Innocent Bystander* by Barbara Coloroso. Girls, Inc. and many other similar organizations can provide you with tips and tools through their websites. I have provided resource links for you in the endnotes of this chapter.

As you help your daughter to deal with her trauma, it can be helpful to tell her your own stories of having been bullied. Your own childhood problem-solving is useful to your daughter, even when she tells you that you can't understand "her world." In some ways, she may be right, but in most ways this pushback from her is a defense mechanism. If she won't talk with you about her pain and its treatment, it is crucial you help her find someone who will understand. She needs to know she is respected, heard, understood, valued, and empowered.

Meanwhile, your daughter may at times be a bully herself. This too requires careful attention. A mom sent me this heartfelt email:

I learned that my daughter and three friends caused someone to lose her job. It took me a long time to really believe it, but it is clear to me that my daughter bullied an adult and even some of her own friends.

The story is, my daughter and two friends shoplifted and got caught. The female security person went to the restroom with the three girls and made them take the items out of their pockets. When the police came later, my daughter reported that the security guard had touched her in an inappropriate and uncomfortable way, "keeping her hands on my private parts for too long." Her two friends confirmed that the guard did this to them too.

The guard was suspended and later lost her job. A month later, one of my daughter's friends confessed that the girls had been angry at the security guard and so they made up the story. When I confronted my daughter, she said, yes, she had had the idea to make up the story. Both my husband and I are stunned. We raised a better girl than this. We feel terrible.

I spoke to this family and learned that the parents were going through a bitter divorce. Their daughter was basically a good kid who acted out in a bad way. She was grounded for two months, but the parents were put in a damaging situation since telling the department store managers and police about the false accusation could result in prosecution of the daughter or a civil suit.

The mom told me on the phone, "I hope other people will get helped by our experience, even if anonymously. Our own kids do bad things and we won't really change the world unless we figure that out and hold them responsible."

I'm So Ugly, I'm So Fat

Davita recently turned me on to the band Arcade Fire. One of their latest songs, *Creature Comfort,* tells of a girl standing at a mirror "waiting for feedback" and asking God to "make me famous, or if not, just make it painless." The girl is depressed and in the bathtub "with pills in her hand."

Beyond my empathy for the girl depicted in the song, I also heard in it a powerful reminder of the collaboration in the female brain between a girl's self-judgments at a mirror and her potential feelings of anxiousness and sadness about her face, her body, and her relative attractiveness. "I'm so ugly, I'm so fat," can feel, in the minds of girls, like "I'm worthless." Remember the women in the Dove commercial: they misjudged their own beauty.

While boys can feel this way, perhaps you've noticed that boys don't generally spend as much time in front of the mirror. They judge their own bodies and faces quite a bit during adolescence, but thoughts of suicide because they are overweight or don't have a lovely face do not generally plague boys like they do girls.

Nature is at work here, in a way every parent can study as a citizen scientist and discuss with your family and community. As you study this, decide:

- What will I say to my daughter about her body?
- What will I say about her face, her beauty, her attractiveness?
- How will I handle her potential love of make-up and other cosmetics?
- What about tattoos? What is the right age to let her get one?
- How will I navigate the fact that, for my daughter, much of her identity will be studied in a mirror?
- Will Mom and Dad (and other mentors) be gender-specific in their approaches to a girl's growth in this area, leaning toward saying different things and approaching a girl's questions about herself differently?

As cultures become more and more competitive, females increasingly focus on personal attractiveness as a competitive strategy. In non-competitive villages in remote areas, females are less engaged in this strategy; in larger cities and larger cultures, they are more involved in it. Especially in our capitalist and democratic society, girls' and women's appearance is a powerful asset and girls know it. They also feel a sensual pleasure at being and feeling attractive.

In our courageous conversations, the Dove commercials can be a huge help and "Why?" is the crucial word for discussion.

- Why do you think you look at your own body so much?
- Why do you think it is so important to you that your face looks beautiful?
- Why are you spending so much money on cosmetics (or begging us to spend it)?
- Why do you want to get a tattoo?
- Why is so much of your identity wrapped up in your own beauty?

As girls engage with adults in self-awareness, they absorb our values and build their own values strongly. We can admire our daughter's beauty without over-emphasizing cosmetics. We can allow tattoos only when they seem appropriate—for example, once a girl is working and can pay for a tattoo herself. Whatever your values are around physicality, I hope you'll discuss them a great deal with your girls.

I also hope your girls will hear you often give positive feedback: "You're gorgeous" or "Your haircut looks great" or "You are so beautiful." The verbalized compliment of beauty enters the brain and flashes a rush of dopamine (our brain's reward chemical) through it. You can look at decades of research about this process in a study titled, *The Dopamine D4 Receptor Gene (DRD4) Moderates Cultural Difference in Independent Versus Interdependent Social Orientation* by scientist Shinobu Kitayama and five others at the University of Michigan. It is written for a scholarly audience but can be read by laypeople, and even your daughters.

The Natural Girl

In female beauty assessments, dopamine matters and, as the study shows, some people are wired to be more prone to needing physical beauty assessments than others. Talk with your girls about this. Discuss the strengths and pitfalls of being beauty-focused. As our culture strives to get more girls and women involved in science careers, attaching science to emotional issues in this chapter, including issues of personal beauty, are a way of turning our homes into science labs, and getting our girls as infatuated with science as they are with their own faces and bodies.

While we protect our girls from danger and trauma, raising healthy, successful women means helping them be who they are—warts and dramas included. Oxytocin processing, the cingulate gyrus, reading facial cues, assessments of beauty, dopamine reception—all occupy their place in girls' lives as natural parts of female development.

Chapter 5

A Hidden Crisis:
Protecting Our Daughters from Neurotoxins

> "Everything hidden is meant to be revealed, and everything concealed shall be brought to light."
> —Gospel of Mark, 4:22

OVER A PERIOD OF FIVE YEARS, I polled parents, educators, mental health professionals, and leaders from both secular and religious organizations. I asked: "What are the most pressing issues facing the girls in your homes, schools, communities, and organizations?" I've repeated the question to my own lecture audiences and our Gurian Institute email lists and social media. More than 5,000 responses divide into these issues facing American girls:

- depression, anxiety, and other emotional-brain disorders
- heightened pressure to succeed at everything
- being unprepared for college and/or the workplace
- taking everything too personally, especially in workplaces
- the effects of technology in girls' lives, including social media pressures and increased time spent in front of screens of all types
- bullying, cyberbullying, girl drama, and relational violence
- the need for more female role models in science and engineering professions
- women undercutting other women
- assistance needed to help single mothers raising children on their own
- fathers often disconnected from daughters
- girls straying into bad behavior
- lack of faith-influence on girls lives
- the need for more girls' schools and girl-only classrooms
- physical abuse and/or witnessing domestic violence

- dysfunction in mother-daughter relationships
- women returning from wars in the Middle East severely damaged
- increasing aggression among girls, especially girls raised in poverty and in inner cities
- increasing number of females going into the criminal justice system and prison
- husbands, partners, and fathers who are unemployed or not looking for work, depressed, and unable to assist girls and women adequately
- fear of failure (and fear of success)
- racial tensions
- significant economic and inner city/rural social issues, including poverty and income inequality deepening between haves and have-nots
- the gender gap in some STEM and STEAM areas that end up keeping girls/women out of certain high-paying jobs
- the lack of women at the top of governments and corporations (the C-Suite and Leadership)
- male chauvinism, sexism, and misogyny, especially in domestic violence and rape against women where toxic masculinity and patriarchal gender-role pressure affects male/female relationships
- increasing rates of ADHD diagnoses, autism spectrum issues, and other brain disorders, including the new AMA diagnosis of "violence" as a disease
- substance abuse, drug use, gambling and sex addictions, alcoholism, opioid addiction
- lesbian and transgender girls targeted for their sexual orientation or gender identity
- mainstream culture tempting girls away from appropriate sexual behavior
- sexual abuse, sexual assault, and rape
- gender stereotypes and female role norms that keep women behind men.

I've listed these issues at the beginning of this chapter to set up a somewhat new way of looking at causation for many of them. That new approach to causation leads to new practical strategies for solving many of the issues. Here are stories from parents that imply the parent's sense of one kind of causation—I will show in a moment that there may also be a whole other set of causes.

"I have three daughters and two are doing well," a mom wrote, "but my third, 9, is having significant problems first with obesity and now we just received a diagnosis of sensory and reading disorders with mild ASD (autism spectrum disorder)."

Another mom wrote, "My daughter is having issues with bullying and her school is helping, but I don't think they realize how much pressure the girls are under to be exactly what the boys want. Emily gets angry all the time and I know she is depressed. She's only eleven."

A grandfather wrote, "We have been raising our daughter's two girls, 5 and 12, while their mother is in rehab. The 12-year-old was abused by one of our daughter's boyfriends and now she is acting out sexually. We aren't equipped to raise her, but we are trying."

A dad wrote, "We're trying to peel back the layers of what is going on with our daughter, 13. We have a good family with good values. Latrice gets lots of support and goes to a good school. But she cuts herself and she has been getting into marijuana and drugs. We have her in therapy and we ground her for the drug behavior, but it does no good."

A couple, Christians, wrote, "We have four boys and five girls, and they are all children of God and we love them. Two of them, though, have more troubles than the others. We believe God has given us these children to give us the opportunity to raise them in the light, but it is very difficult because both—our twins—suffer from OCD, though to different degrees."

And in a very long email, which I've excerpted here, a mom of a two-year-old wrote, "Malia is not even three yet, but my husband and I can tell something is going on. We love her more than life itself, but she can barely look us in the eyes and our pediatrician is already wondering about ASD. 'Why?' we asked him. 'How does this happen?' He said there could be many reasons, and asked us about our family, which is a good one. He asked about our parent-child attachment, which is good. Then he asked about what foods we eat, what we drink, all of that, and he talked about 'neurotoxins'. This was the first time we had ever heard that word. Now we are looking carefully at everything around us."

The Crisis of Environmental Neurotoxins

As I work with parents and collect data, I find something very clearly that can seem like an "outlier" concept in our contemporary social and political approach to helping girls. I find that the Dominant Gender Paradigm dominates our media and social media—the idea that gender role pressure causes most of girls' distresses—yet the actual *causes* of some distresses may not get addressed at all. In this chapter, I will present a "first cause" for many of your daughter's potential distresses and I hope you'll use this material as a way of deepening our culture's conversation about what most harms our girls.

I hope you'll join this effort personally and politically because I believe we have come to a time in our social history when we in the grassroots must compel the Big Three (academics, government, and the media) to see beyond some of our popular social constructs, including the overuse of the DGP's language. We have to all come together to see the deeper epidemic of neurotoxic threat. Our children's lives and health are at stake.

Did You Know?

The First Cause

Environmental neurotoxins are gene and cell disruptors your children absorb from the food, drink, lotions, plastics, paint, metal, toys, and other physical things around them. These neurotoxins attack the healthy gene expression of a child, causing mutations and exaggerated expressions that can become distress, depression, anxiety, rage, addiction, ASD, OCD, violence, suicide, self-cutting, and many (though certainly not all) of the elements listed in the survey responses.

Until the Industrial Revolution, our children ate and drank foods and beverages that were natural to their environment— what was grown around them. The natural ingestion fit, for the most part, the child's gene expression because the genetic makeup of foods and the girl's genetic makeup were both natural. While a particular girl could be allergic to a particular food or drink, a girl's life overall was a collaboration of nature, nurture, and culture.

Since the Industrial Revolution, and especially in the last fifty years, our children are ingesting artificial chemicals unnatural to their genetic template. These are synthetic toxins that can disrupt female gene expression and brain development. These synthetics can come in a food or drink or from lead in paint or pipes (as the beleaguered city of Flint, Michigan has discovered); inhaled air polluted by chemicals; or chemicals in plastics, fertilizer and cologne. Each or all of them can traumatize genetic templates and gene expression throughout the body and brain.

The science of these neurotoxins—*environmental toxicology*—crosses industrial and post-industrial cultures. In one set of studies reported in *Scientific American,* scientists analyzed 150 billion bits of genomic data from human tissues and cells from brain, heart, bone, and blood in multiple countries.

"Myriad control switches help to arbitrate how genes get expressed in different cells and tissues," Dina Fine Maron, who reported the research, wrote in 2015, "and those switches are often triggered by maternal diet, toxic exposures, and many other environmental factors. To begin to understand what drives these complex epigenetic effects, scientists . . . located the switches by analyzing specific chemical modifications on the DNA and the proteins that it wraps around. Then researchers took data comparing individuals who have specific biological traits with those who do not to see which traits are associated with which switches."

Health and maturity requires the switching on (or off) of certain proteins in certain cells and tissues. Unfortunately, if your daughter eats or imbibes neurotoxins found in plastics, fertilizer, foods, and beverages (often called "industrial toxins") the switches needed for full maturation of cells and brain tissue may either not turn on or get turned off. A new meta-study published in *The Lancet Neurology* revealed that a primary reason for brain disorders is "under-regulated industrial chemicals and pesticides, in addition to exposure to heavy metals" which directly invade gene expression and have become a "major factor in the dramatic rise of neurodevelopmental disorders in children."

Philippe Grandjean is the co-author of both the *Lancet* study and *Only One Chance: How Environmental Pollution Impairs Brain Development—and How to Protect the Brains of the Next Generation.* He told the *Huffington Post*, "The world is facing a 'silent pandemic' of 'chemical brain drain.' We have an ethical duty to protect the next generation, in particular, the next generation's brains."

Grandjean and study co-author Philip Landrigan note that since 2006, when they first published their results, things are getting even worse. The list of "confirmed developmental neurotoxins doubled in ten years. At the top of the list of culprits: pesticides." Pesticides, though helpful in keeping insects away from crops, are harmful to the brains of children, and they contaminate nearly everything our children eat and drink.

Plastic is another ubiquitous contaminant, and this material generally includes the estrogen-mimicking and potentially dangerous chemicals *plychlorinate biphenyla* and *bisphenol A.* This estrogen-mirroring sits at the heart of the neurochemical maturation issue for our daughters because it disrupts their endocrine systems, the systems on which much of their cellular and brain growth depends. Not every girl's gene expression will be negatively affected by these chemicals, however, millions of them will be, and your daughter may be among them. The interaction of the chemicals in food or fertilizer with her human cells may harm her at a hormonal and, therefore, cellular level. As the endocrine disrupting hormones attach to specific receptors in her body, they initiate a complex chain of events that impede cellular development and function. The endocrine disruptors will make fatter cows and larger, shinier lettuce, thereby making greater financial profit for companies selling them, but, unfortunately, the same chemicals keep many of our girls' neural switches off when they should be on, and on when they should be off.

Think of each hormone inside each cell as an artist at work—a sculptor who chisels at a blob of rock to create a Rodin statue. Natural gene expression, excited and assisted in a natural environment, is that chiseling, that sculpting, that art. Endocrine disruptors interfere with the artistic process because the disrupter can erase a natural function in some moments, and in other moments alter an action of cells completely. As the disruptor attaches to its unique receptor, it launches a different set of events in body and brain than what was naturally intended for this girl. We don't end up with Rodin's *The Thinker*—we end up with a statue without an arm, knee, feet, hands, eyes, or other essential parts of the body.

The disruptors and toxins don't just attack your child—they attacked you and your reproductive partner before your child was born, affecting sperm motility in dad and reproductive cells in mom's ovaries. Many brain disorders such as autism, anorexia/bulimia, and ADD/ADHD are linked back to these neurotoxin/sperm and egg issues. Depression, too, can be linked to these issues.

A very useful book detailing the science of neurotoxic effects on early puberty in girls is Leonard Sax's *Girls on the Edge*. Sax analyzes the effects of chemicals in plastics, tuna, dairy, body and hair lotions, and many other foods, drinks, and intimate products that can lead to obesity and early puberty. My intention in the chapter is not to repeat his book or my earlier books but to extend the research on environmental toxicology for you from early puberty into cognitive and emotional disorders so that you can continue improving your protection of your daughter.

Gail and I, as well as many clients we work with, did this during our daughters' upbringings. It was not easy (nor inexpensive), but we put this kind of protection very high on our list because we were immersed in the research on neurotoxins and understood how important it was to our daughters' personal health and social wellness.

The Five Horsemen

Neurotoxins, especially in the U.S., have become such a severe detriment to our children's health that scientist David Geary, author of *Evolution of Sex Differences in Trait- and Age-Specific Vulnerabilities* (2016), added "man-made toxins" to his list of major causative factors in human distress. Geary called previously studied "natural stressors" (disease, famine, war, and death) "the four horsemen of the apocalypse." Recently, he added environmental neurotoxins as the "fifth" apocalyptic horsemen in our genes.

I mentioned "in the U.S." because Europe and Canada are way ahead of the U.S. in dealing with these toxins. Though their own laws do not yet go far enough, many European countries and Canada ban many of the dangerous and ubiquitous chemical agents. As you deepen your knowledge of these neurotoxins, I hope you'll join with others in your community to battle for legislative and corporate changes.

Watch for:

- Poisons in pesticides and fertilizer like chlorpyrifos that directly impede fetal and infant brain development (a panel of U.S. scientists contracted to study this chemical by the federal government suggested its ban because its negative effects on brain development begin so early and resist treatment).

- Endocrine disruptors in food, drink, and lotions that affect estrogen, testosterone, and other biochemistry when taken in by children and adults (multiple studies listed in the endnotes to this chapter will provide you with grist for your own citizen science). These affect the hormonal systems of girls and thus all of your daughter's cells. As Reproductive Biologist Joanna Ellington has pointed out, "Female hormonal biology is complex, sensitive, and affects the rest of female life."

- Chemicals in medications like acetaminophen taken by mothers during pregnancy that can create mutations in the fetus and lead to later behavioral and cognitive problems in the child (this research was published in 2016 in the journal JAMA Pediatrics).

- BPA (Bisphenol-A) and Phthalates in plastics, noted earlier, that can "poison" your children, especially when they drink from plastic bottles that have become hot (the chemicals "leak" into the beverage from the heated bottle).

- Sugar itself which can be a poison to our cells if eaten in excess (a powerful book on this subject is *The Case Against Sugar* by Gary Taubes in 2017).

- Even products that we may want our adolescents to use (such as birth control pills) can affect some genetic structures with depressive symptoms. A study published in 2016 that tracked more than one million women between 15 and 35 on hormonal birth control found a 40% increased risk of depression.

- Allergies and intolerances to normal foods (e.g. wheat, dairy, yeast, tomatoes, etc.).

- Even the bovine growth hormones in cows affect their meat and milk to a potentially deleterious effect, as Sax has pointed out in *Girls on the Edge*. While many of our children's genetic systems are resistant to the effects of these hormones, many are not.

David Klein, in the Obstetrics/Gynocology Department at the University of California San Francisco, is a consumer safety expert. His work can be very helpful in your own citizen science and your advocacy for social change in this area. Klein pointed out in August of 2017 the dual need for each legislature to: 1) label the poisons; and ultimately, 2) ban them.

But, of course, the profit motive for corporations is very strong. Sleights of hand occur as producers of products adapt to labeling laws by claiming *their* products comply or are poison-free, then produce another chemical that is poisonous. In 2012, Klein notes, the "Toxic Trio" (formaldehyde, toluene, dibutyl phthalate) that is found in nail polish was removed from the product, however, the 2012 California Environmental Protection Agency Report revealed that the substitute chemicals were equally toxic. Klein also noted that endocrine-disrupting chemicals like DES and BPA now show up in the epigenetics of grand-children. Three generations later, they are still turning genes off and on in negative ways.

Neurotoxins and Your Daughter's Genetic Code

In Chapter 3, we looked at your daughter's individual genetic code. If you happen to get some gene testing and see that code mapped out in the test results, you will not only see the initial map of her identity and nearly endless potential as a human being, but you may also see her genetic vulnerabilities. These are especially affected by environmental neurotoxins. The ways in which her cells and DNA (her genotype and phenotype) are vulnerable have a high likelihood of getting "picked on" by the neurotoxins. This begins in the womb where some mutations will have already occurred, and will continue throughout life until those neurotoxins are removed.

For instance, if your daughter has the obesity genetics we described in Chapter 3, environmental neurotoxins that mimic estrogen will likely trigger those genetic vulnerabilities in childhood or early adolescence. Her leptin levels may be inordinately high at 8, catalyzing early puberty and all of the changes (including weight gain) that can ensue. As she gains more body fat, she releases even more estrogen. By 12, perhaps, you may see her becoming overweight and/or obese, which will just keep the cycle of estrogen going. The hidden enemy may also affect her mood, relationships, and cognitive functioning as she may become anxious, depressed, or in some other way, "just not quite right." These issues in early adolescence can later increase her risk of further mental and physical disease or distress.

Studies over the last decade, like one published in *Pediatrics* in 2016, reveal that girls who start puberty early have a higher risk not only of depression and anxiety disorders, but risk-taking behavior, alcohol and drug use, smoking, and earlier-than-normal sexual activity that can lead to increased risk of sexually transmitted diseases. The study further found that these girls had a higher risk of Type 2 diabetes and breast cancer. The study's authors note that it is impossible to ever find a single cause of multiple elements but felt confident in tracing a great deal of causation to "longer lifetime exposure to estrogen." The endocrine disruptors in the test subjects' food, drink, fertilizer, lotions, plastics, and other environmental elements had affected these girls and women at a cellular level, not just in body but in brain.

Courageous Conversation

Will Parents, Legislators, and Businesses Come Together to Remove the First Cause?

A trend in America is to seek cultural or relational solutions to issues that may not be healed or treated through culture or relationship. For instance, our most active culture-based paradigm (what I have called the DGP) argues that gender stereotypes and traditional gender norms cause girls' distress. We are told that girls are sexualizing themselves early in our culture (i.e. trying to look like women at 13 or 14) primarily because they are so hungry for male attention that they are forced to mature early. This is a kind of cultural determinism for nature's developmental moments. While in some girls' cases there will be truth to this, the DGP is too thin to really deal with any developmental crisis, including early sexualizing of girls. Even early puberty, sexualizing behavior, face make-up, and the will to wear revealing blouses and short-shorts are much more connected to hormonal and cellular intrusions by neurotoxins than we have admitted. Sax, in *Girls on the Edge*, has made this case with overwhelming science. Similarly, depression, anxiety, and most other adolescent female distress are caused by neurotoxic threat much more than stereotype threat.

This is a crucial point for those of us who long to advocate politically and publicly for our daughters. We now have more than enough clinical evidence to support an epidemiological view of our daughters' lives, and I believe it is our duty to preach this science. Not to do so is to continue allowing corporations to put profit over children.

Fortunately, when we fully advocate for our children, things really do happen. Because of consumer and parent advocacy, state lawmakers in Minnesota and Connecticut have passed legislation banning BPA in plastics.

This leaves most states without protections, however, making it all the more important to take books and studies into businesses, legislatures, and every school and community.

Ultimately, we will need to expand our public dialogue about how to ensure health and wellness among our girls, replacing the DGP with a "systems biology" approach, one that focuses on three causes of our children's distress and one set of correlations. I am reviewing them here so that you can use this section in your conversations.

The First Cause: *Genetic factors, including environmental neurotoxins attacking our genes.* Neurotoxins such as lead and aluminum in homes, BPA in plastics, artificial sweeteners, red dye, and monosodium glutamate in food, and endocrine disruptors in fertilizer have been negatively affecting female gene expression over the last fifty years. This direct cause of female distress remains relatively hidden in our social literature, yet is wreaking havoc on female development and, thus, on our society as a whole.

The Second Cause: *Nurture-trauma received in neurotoxic amounts by girls between birth and young adulthood.* These traumas include physical and sexual abuse, poverty, repeatedly witnessing violence, repetitive and dangerous bullying, rape, family instability, and abandonment. Many of the distresses listed in the surveys are linked to significant and repeated trauma to brain development at some point in the girl's first decade and a half of life.

The Third Cause: *Under-nurture of essential components of female development by nuclear, extended, and communal families.* Lacking a science-based understanding of females (but abhorring past patriarchal paradigms) we have broken down neurodevelopmental scaffolding for girls. Often, girls are raised without fathers and become more aggressive and violent and/or more depressed and anxious. Without fully realizing how profoundly they need moms, dads, mentors, and communities of support, we have made their lives isolated and lonely (despite access to social media connection) which can cripple psychological health.

The Correlation: *Cultural stereotypes and gender norms.* Gender stereotypes are factors to pay attention to, but they do not cause brain disorders, addictions, and most female distress. Among the list of issues confronting girls at the chapter's opening, most are not caused by gender stereotypes. Helping our cultural conversation look beyond ideological correlations, and at the first cause especially, will take courageous conversation and the development of allies in your community, in the media, and in legislatures. It won't be easy, but we can do it together, and I believe we must. For fifty years we have attacked gender stereotypes—and they need attacking when they abound—but now we must convince the Big Three (academics, government, and the media) to save our daughters from the fifth horseman of the cellular apocalypse.

The Nature of Homosexuality

While the DGP approach to girls' distresses tends to dominate our mainstream media, there is another paradigm in our polarized culture that is also inadequate to help us care for and love certain vulnerable populations. As I argue that we use systems biology to see beyond the DGP ideologies, I hope you will also use a systems-biology approach to generate courageous conversation in religious communities around the science of homosexuality.

When I speak with religious organizations, someone will come up to me with curiosity and a sense of some confusion. This person has generally agreed with what I was saying about biology, science, sex, and gender in my talk, but is troubled by the implications for his or her understanding of homosexuality. "So, is being a lesbian *natural?*" the person will ask. "Are you really saying *that?*"

I respond in the affirmative. Being gay is not "caused" by a choice in the culture. Genetic and neuroscience research over the last forty years have proven that same-gender sexual orientation (homosexuality) is natural for approximately 5 to 10 percent of females and males. As we noted in Chapter 1, this sexual orientation is set before birth in the *sexually dimorphic nucleus* of the *anterior hypothalamus* of either gender (just like heterosexuality is) via chromosome markers such as the Xq28 marker, and in utero hormonal surges during gestation. Approximately 5 percent of dolphins, whales, gorillas, and lions are also wired this way. You can access the research in the Notes and References section of this book.

Despite the availability of this science, some religious leaders argue for LGBT conversion therapy. They point to lines in the Bible and Quran that they believe condemn homosexuality as unnatural, not created by God—an aberration to natural design. They accuse LGBT individuals of causing AIDS, corrupting families, and causing divorce. While I can't change a person's religious beliefs, I must challenge everyone who cares about children to look more deeply into the available science. LGBT women and men have provided essential services to humanity throughout history, and still do in nearly every walk of life. They are doctors, lawyers, artists, scientists, spouses, parents, and friends. They no more need to be forced to change their sexual orientation than a heterosexual person does.

Some religious people at conferences walk away from this short conversation angrily. Their views are so entrenched, they see mine as flawed and, in some cases, dangerous. They feel that I am bowing to cultural norms. To them, homosexuality is a choice, and a bad one. When I disagree about causation, I have had people tell me I am going to hell. Because my goal is to build bridges between diverse groups, I try to stay focused on long-term, courageous conversation based in science. I believe deeply in my work in churches and religious communities and I've spent much of my professional life working with individuals who don't see God the way I do.

Meanwhile, I hope we can all meet in a place where science carries wisdom and insight for us. We all believe in one thing for certain—that we will do anything we can to care for the health of our children.

Pursuing the New Plan

For your daughters, I hope you will apply a systems-biology or epidemiological approach to the list provided by our five-year survey. Look back at the chapter's beginning and review the list. Which of the issues do you think are sourced in cultural pressures like gender stereotypes and which in the three causes. And most pertinent to this chapter, which might be caused by *neurotoxins*?

Here are the five issues that I see fitting with the DGP correlation:

- girls feeling heightened pressure to succeed at everything
- the need for more female role models in science and engineering professions
- male chauvinism, sexism, misogyny, especially in domestic violence and rape against women where toxic masculinity and patriarchal gender-role pressure affects male/female relationships
- lesbian and transgender girls targeted for their sexual orientation or gender identity
- gender stereotypes and female role norms that keep women behind men.

Which issues did you list as issues most directly connected to gender stereotypes or cultural norms? More issues than I did? Less? As you reviewed the list, did you notice how many more issues on the list and in the anecdotes could not be caused by gender stereotypes?

I believe the other 23 out of the 28 are best studied via the Three Causes. Once we study them in those contexts, we can fix the mismatch between what girls need neurobiologically and genetically, and the training, information, and the systemic wisdom we receive in our culture, whether through social media or governmental alliances. Our first step in doing this politically is to realize that gender stereotypes can't *cause* depression and other significant distresses among girls because:

- gender stereotypes do not raise female cortisol (stress hormone) levels enough to invade cellular and neural development;
- they do not invade genotype coding; and
- they do not affect a girl's sex-hormonal systems.

Neurotoxins, however, just like abuse or attachment trauma, can affect DNA expression, sex hormonal systems, and stress hormone systems in enough quantity and quality to cause disorders. Gender stereotypes are easier to focus on in our cultural media and our nation's simplified politics, but we must see beyond the superficial. While continuing our courageous cultural conversations on gender stereotypes, we must add the three causes and especially the first cause to all conversations.

Fifty years ago, I would not have made this distinction. In the 1960s, I would have found gender stereotypes and abuse trauma as the paramount stressors on healthy female development. But times have changed. To continue solely or mainly emphasizing the DGP in our social debates is to keep making societal and primal choices that leave our legislators and business innovators to create laws and products that harm girls' biological development.

Try This

Protect Your Daughter from Proximate Neurotoxins

Proximate neurotoxins are those right around your child—in your kitchen and bathroom, in her bedroom, in your car, on her soccer field, in her school. While battling for changes in laws and profit motive in the larger culture, we have to protect our kids right now. Here are some ways to do that.
- Go organic. This is costly and can seem very intimidating, but it can be accomplished gradually. Gail and I did it by going organic one item at a time.

The first month of our process, we bought organic vegetables—lettuce, broccoli, cauliflower, etc. The second month, we moved to chicken. The third, to meat. The fourth, to fruit. We were young, without extra money or resources when we decided to go organic, so we had to do this very carefully. We ended up having to give up on extra lattes and we had to remove one of our date nights. We discussed with our girls the need to shop for less "impulse-clothing" purchases. Going organic became a high priority family activity and financial sacrifices were made by both the children and the adults.

- Investigate your house and other dwellings and buildings for radon, lead, asbestos, and other chemicals in amounts that might be harmful. Remember to investigate water sources by applying tests of water that you can acquire at a hardware store or online via specialty outlets.

- Avoid using plastic bottles. Don't microwave any food wrapped or held in plastic. During soccer games or any sport played in the heat, especially make sure your children are not hydrating via water or other power drinks housed in plastic bottles. Overall, move toward glass bottles and stainless steel thermoses as much as possible.

- Study bottles and other food containers to make sure you see that they are BPA and phthalate-free. If you don't see this label on a food container, lobby the business and even the legislature in your state to compel the business to put this kind of labeling on containers and packages.

- Do the same with cosmetics, facial products, shampoos and moisturizers, and body lotions. Make sure they are BPA and phthalate-free. You can go to helpful websites like www.cosmeticsdatabase.com to search for the product and see how it is rated for BPA and phthalate safety.

- If you are pregnant or preparing to have children, study everything you take in, including pain relievers, for potential neurotoxic effects on yourself and your fetus. Talk with pharmacists and go on Google to find articles and studies about acetaminophen and any other helpful drug that may also contain neurotoxins (this is important for both females and males).
- Protect your children as much as possible from junk food and excessive sugar. *Fast Food Nation* is a powerful book to read as a family. My daughter, Gabrielle, brought it into our home and we were all happy she did. This book may scare you and your children, and with good reason. Like going organic, you can gradually cut out one junk food every week or month until you have basically removed all junk food from your children's familial diet. While you won't be able to control what your children eat at friends' houses, you will be able to control their neural safety in your own home or car.
- Lobby other parents and the children's school to cut out tater tots, sugary drinks, soda, and other similar junk foods as much as possible. Many school boards and legislators have never heard of neurotoxins or, if they have, they just avoid dealing with them by calling the science about them "unresolved." Be wary of that feint in leadership and join with other parents to bring this chapter, or other similar research, to the attention of school leaders.
- Support websites like letsgogreen.biz that are helping us battle hidden neurotoxins. Get your kids involved in these websites. They are a great way to teach science to your girls and engage your daughters in self-protection. Later, when they are mothers, they will thank you for opening this scientific world to them.

One Family at a Time

As you put these practices into place, get genetic testing when possible, and when it is not available, do your own "genetic profile" of your child by polling your family members for inherited genetic vulnerabilities. There is a lot of genetic wisdom in your own family. You have "experts" all around you and you can become one too.

Here is a very practical way this process led to a better life for one girl, Eden, who was having difficulty in fourth grade. Her mom, from Ontario, California, wrote me seven emails I have condensed here.

"Eden was getting into trouble a lot at home and at school. She couldn't sit still, poked and prodded other kids, and just drove everyone crazy. She wasn't depressed or anxious or anything, so we didn't think about something in the mental health area, but we did wonder if she had ADHD. So, we made an appointment with her pediatrician. He met with us and decided to prescribe Ritalin. Eden had a bad reaction to the drug—headaches, nausea—so we took her off it and the bad behavior continued.

At this same time, we were reading your book Saving Our Sons because we have boys. In it you mention food allergies, and we thought about that for our hyperactive Eden. We thought, maybe this is a food allergy. We didn't have the resources to get genetic testing, but we did realize that we could survey all our family members. We learned that Eden's grandmother had stopped eating yeast at one point and felt much better. We did a lot of research on it and became, like you say, 'citizen scientists.' I think I can recite all the pro and con research about food allergies, and I often do! There was some argument in our family about whether to completely change our household diet, but we finally decided to do it.

"Getting Eden off yeast has been life-changing for all of us. We stopped eating pizza and we only eat yeast-free crackers, bread, and pasta. This has been great for me too. I have lost weight and feel much more energetic. Eden is no longer getting into so much trouble. She concentrates better, she is happier. 'I'm better, Mom,' she told me the other day. Even she can tell. And we can also tell when she 'sins' and eats pasta or pizza at a friend's house. She gets very fidgety and tired.

I know this food allergy thing can't work for everyone, but it has worked for our family."

As I got to know this family via correspondence, I learned that they were active in homeschooling. I had just learned that the Gurian Institute's school-based resources—*Boys and Girls Learn Differently* and *Strategies for Teaching Boys and Girls: Elementary and Secondary Levels* —were being used by homeschool teachers. I had only been aware of homeschooling through the media up until this point, but emails and correspondence from parents like Eden's began to alert me of that movement. I learned it was, to some extent, Christian-religious oriented, and so I thought many of those fundamentalist parents would dislike evolutionary biology.

I was wrong. Over the next few years I have been invited to speak at many homeschool conferences where I meet with these parents, not only through lecture formats, but personally at the Gurian Institute booth. I have learned that for these parents, the nature-based and systems-biology approach to raising boys and girls, including an emphasis on environmental toxicology, made perfect sense. When I asked why, many of them pointed to the Bible, especially Genesis where "God created both woman and man in his own image." Males and females are natural creatures, these parents are saying, including their genetic differences.

Whenever I speak in churches or Christian schools, I find this openness to biology. While some people in these communities do not approach LGBT issues biologically, and while some religious people do not utilize evolutionary biology, most are open to the overall neurobiological approach, as are most people in my secular audiences. This gives me hope that our society is living in a new and profound cultural moment. People from all walks of life are ready to go deeper into girls' lives than some of our culture paradigms allow. They are ready to re-think causation regarding girls' multiple stressors and distresses. Approaches from research in systems biology can work parallel to cultural and religious ideas.

Each of us can help it do so, and through that work, we will nurture and protect our daughters in our complex world.

Chapter 6

Raising Girls with Grit:
Building Resilience and Strength in Our Daughters

"In working with girls and women, my motto is: add insight to injury."
—Karen Salmonsen, Kids in the House Program on Raising Resilient Children

AT AN EDUCATORS' CONFERENCE where I was speaking about girls' development, the organizers had asked me to focus on what will help make girls most successful in the future—most resilient, most mature, most "gritty." Because they knew I had worked with Fortune 500 corporations, they also asked me to provide a message on what women most needed for improved leadership and empowerment in the workplace. During my lecture, I told a story about a time that Gabrielle (15 at the time) was headed out to a party wearing a very revealing top.

"That's not appropriate," I had told her. "You need to go change clothes."

Gabrielle argued, saying I was disempowering her.

I fired back, "You're putting yourself in danger and in a weakened, unempowered position with these clothes, especially because there will probably be alcohol at the party."

We argued some more and finally she changed clothes.

As my story ended, I asked the audience if they agreed or disagreed with what I had done. Most in the audience agreed, but a few women called out, "No!" Hearing their voices, I asked them to come to my book table after the keynote. "I love a good argument!" I said by way of invitation, and there were chuckles all around. An hour later, I was at the book table and two women, Marissa, 28, and Dana, 29, asked to discuss what I had done with Gabrielle. They taught at a girls' school in another state and Marissa began explaining their disagreement with my points.

"Dana and I just want you to know that we don't want to argue. We work in our school to build a cohesive, friendly, and non-aggressive community, so Dana and I don't want to argue with you. We want to *discuss* your points."

My face showed some surprise as I saw these women weakening, not strengthening, their position.

"Don't you use debate and argument in your classes?" I asked.

Marissa shook her head. "Some teachers do, but we really want to create cohesion for our girls."

At the repetition of this justification, my antennae were all the way up.

"If you're afraid to teach healthy argument to girls," I suggested, "aren't you passing fear and weakness into the girls?"

They shook their heads. "No," Dana said. "We're teaching them to insist on a comfortable environment where their voices will be heard."

"But since they generally can't control environments around them, how do you develop resilience and grit in them? How do you help them compete?"

We do just fine, their faces seemed to say, but I pressed.

"Come on, I can tell from your faces that you want to argue with me and I want you to know I am fine with that, so let's argue!" My tone was inviting, not offensive or harsh.

"No," Marissa insisted. "Arguments can hurt feelings and we want our girls to feel comfortable and accepted. That's why we *discuss*."

"Acceptance is great," I argued, "but you and I disagree on methodology. It seems to me that by holding the stance you're holding, you're feeding right into the very thing the tech and engineering corporations are asking us to stop doing with girls—raise them in a bubble. The workplace needs women to be able to argue and hold their own in a complex adult environment. The world needs resilience from girls. It needs them to have grit."

"Anyway," Dana said, pivoting us away from that point, "We really wanted to talk about your position on the way your daughter dressed. We don't see how you as a man have any right to tell a woman how to dress."

"Really? But I'm her father."

This did not matter to a fifteen-year-old, they insisted. Gabrielle was a young woman and should make her own decisions. If someone accosted her or was inappropriate with her at the party, it was their fault, not my daughter's. Thinking otherwise put me, Dana said, "in the same camp as guys who blame the way a victim dresses for a rape."

At this point, my daughter, Davita (then 22), came up to us (I was speaking in the city she lived in and she had come to pick me up for dinner together). After I gave her a hug, I introduced her to the two women and caught her up on our discussion.

To Dana, I said, "Again, I disagree with you. Rape is a crime, it's a violent act. If someone rapes my daughter, it will be a criminal matter targeting that person's mental illness and his violent act. It will not be about how my daughter is dressed, so no, of course not. I would not blame the victim."

"But still," Dana insisted, "You're taking away your daughter's independence and empowerment by telling her how to dress."

"I see what you're saying, but disagree," I said. "To me, as a dad teaching empowerment, it would be neglectful to let her go out of the house dressed in a way that would weaken her position and power. My job was to use all my assets to help her develop a strong and socially adept self and self-image. At 15, most of what she did was indeed done independent of me, but some things still needed my input. Given that she was in potential danger, and given that she was being inappropriate, I had to confront her. That confrontation was not domineering or overbearing, it was parental. In fact, if you asked Gabrielle now, from her perspective as a grown woman, I believe she would tell you that our debate on the issue created more resilience, grit, and maturity in her, not less."

Davita concurred. "Dana, come on. Why wouldn't he tell my sister she was dressed in a dangerous way? Are you saying that the girl has no responsibility for anything? She can do whatever she wants, no matter what? She can dress or say whatever she wants? Really?"

Marissa and Dana both said, Yes.

Davita disagreed with her contemporaries in ways she and I had discussed throughout her college life. A number of times, she found her university professors insisting that males alone had responsibility for heterosexual miscommunication—females were 100% absolved of any responsibility. "It's not likely Gabrielle would have been raped," Davita said, completing her thought, "but she sure wasn't in a strong position dressed like she was initially dressed."

The argument, by now, was in full swing. Marissa said she was appalled at our belief.

"How can you think it's a woman's responsibility to make sure guys at a party don't look at her breasts. It's the guys' responsibility not to look at her breasts! Come on! There is no way I would tell my daughter to change her clothing. She is in control of her self-image, not me—or you." She pointed at me. "I would empower her to make her own decision. He (pointing to me and speaking to Davita, now), he wants to disempower her, he is imposing his patriarchal dominance over her. This won't create grit. It is oppression."

Davita kept arguing, and for a few minutes I just stood back to watch the argument with joy. Then, when the three women brought me back into the conversation, I said, "Truly, I think we disagree at a primal level. You are talking about an ideological approach to an issue and mine and, I believe, Davita's is *nature-based*. In nature-based theory, sexuality sits at the core of self-image development in the brain. If a heterosexual fifteen-year-old girl is dressed in a sexually provocative way, a way that says, 'come have sex with me,' then gets drunk with a peer or older male, there is a biological likelihood that the limbic parts of those brains will do and say things the frontal cortices of both female and male may later regret.

"In other words, these children will be put in positions that will disempower them. So, to mentor or parent a girl in physical/social appropriateness and personal safety is absolutely empowering to her. It helps mature her into a healthy adult. It is always better to err on the side of caution when we are dealing with alcohol, drugs, and biology. I think you are erring on the side of protecting a girl's *potential incident of independence* while I am insisting on a *biological danger to empowerment*. To me, empowerment is more complex than I think you believe it is."

Marissa had become somewhat agitated. "I have to stop talking with you," she said, visibly shivering. "You are giving me a really uncomfortable feeling." She touched her stomach, rubbed it, and Dana agreed.

"Congratulations for speaking up, Marissa. I feel the same way." Looking directly at me now and pointing her finger at me, she said, "We teach our girls how important it is to speak up right away when someone makes them feel uncomfortable."

"I understand," I said, "and I'm glad you told me. But did you want me to change what I'm doing because you feel uncomfortable?"

"It's why I spoke up," Marissa said. "Of course, I want you to change."

I shrugged somewhat sadly. "I'm glad you told me you feel uncomfortable, but I disagree with two things you said right there. One, you put the onus on me for *your* discomfort. Your discomfort is something you ought to process internally—it's not my responsibility. You won't develop grit and resilience if you always put your discomfort on someone else. This is the very thing corporate leaders are wishing we would stop doing with millennials and younger kids," I continued. "By convincing them that other people should change for their every whim, we are teaching them to take things personally, blame other people for their feelings, and then create dramas, internal or external, around their blame and those feelings. Relationships gets paralyzed and people overreact to every little discomfort.

"And that's the second thing I disagree with. I think feeling discomfort is valuable for girls, very valuable. Being and feeling uncomfortable is an important stepping stone to maturity, resilience, and grit. When girls feel uncomfortable, they think, they feel, they respond, they self-empower. Except in cases of abuse and violence, feeling uncomfortable is how we learn and grow. The science on this is very clear."

Marissa told me I had hurt her feelings, and Dana said I had shown my true colors. "You're just another patronizing and disempowering man," she said.

We parted ways, and at dinner that evening, Davita and I debriefed this conversation. Davita said, "They're just teaching girls to be fragile little creatures. It's the exact opposite of what girls should learn."

I felt very proud of Davita and was still processing these conversations the next day as I began writing this chapter. Two differing social viewpoints on resilience and empowerment of girls could not have been clearer.

The Resilience Conundrum

What is resilience? What is grit? How can four adults who all care about girls so vastly disagree on how to help girls mature into strong women?

Angela Duckworth and James J. Gross, of the University of Pennsylvania and Stanford University respectively, published a fascinating meta-study in 2014, *Self-Control and Grit: Related but Separable Determinants of Success*. The study begins with the question, "Why are some people more successful than others?" According to the authors, "One obvious answer is talent. Another is opportunity. But even people who have comparable levels of talent and opportunity often enjoy strikingly different levels of success."

There are multiple factors, they note, in how people handle adversity, avoid overreaction and blame, and otherwise experience a mature set of responses to obstacles, work-loads, ethical challenges, and emotional interactions. Resilience, their studies show, needs more than just one approach to empowerment. Grit, a popular term for resilience, is passion and perseverance from the beginning of a challenge to the end. Resilience and grit are keys to maturity.

Are We Raising Gritty Girls?

New research shows increased numbers of children putting off adulthood by living in a kind of perpetual adolescence. As of 2015, "adult independence" had lost its place as the norm. The Pew Research Center recently presented data showing that, "For the first time in more than 130 years, adults ages 18 to 34 were slightly more likely to be living in their parents' home than they were living with a spouse or partner in their own home."

The newest U.S. Census Bureau data shows that not only are more young people living at home, fewer are marrying and partnering as early as they used to. 60% live alone or with roommates, while only 40% in that age group live with a spouse or partner. One of the primary markers of maturity (and one of the primary expressions of grit and resilience), living with a partner and starting a family has diminished considerably among young adults.

Maturation, in general, has slowed down.

At the heart of my and Davita's disagreement with Marissa and Dana was how to best help girls *mature into strong women*. Marissa and Dana believed that girls would naturally develop empowerment and resilience if they felt comfortable in the short-term. Davita and I argued that long-term empowerment and resilience should be the target of maturation influence, which must include some empowering discomfort during childhood (not abuse, of course, but discomfort). This debate has been argued for millennia, but lately I think Marissa's and Dana's view has won out a bit too much. While every responsible parent will agree that girls should be raised in safety and non-violence, some people want to protect girls and boys even from *discomfort*. In this chapter, I will flesh out an argument on behalf of "empowering discomfort," and help you and your parenting team expand resilience, grit, and maturity in your daughters.

Did You Know?

There Are Genetic Markers for Resilience

Some children already come into the world with greater innate ability to be resilient, others with less. Understanding this is crucial to an expanded and science-based approach to building grit in girls because you can have two children who are raised in the same household and neighborhood in the same way with the same joys and traumas, but one appears more inherently resilient than the other. Why?

Researchers at Duke University have discovered that some children have more activity in the OPRMI gene, causing them to be more naturally resilient than those with less activity in that gene. Researchers at Emory University have studied the GABA (Gamma-aminobutyric acid) neurotransmitter, as well as polymorphism in the GABA alpha-2 receptor gene. The Emory team found that people with a genotype for G protein signaling 2 (RGS2)—a protein that decreases G protein-coupled receptor signaling in the brain—who also experienced repeated trauma, were more likely to experience a lifetime of damaging behavior, especially if they don't receive therapy or other support. Those in the same circumstances without this genotype were less likely to do so.

Similarly, fewer single-nucleotide polymorphisms (SNPS) in the FK506 binding protein 5 (FKBP5) can affect resilience. If one of your daughters' DNA emphasizes these resilience polymorphisms, childhood trauma may affect her less negatively than her sibling who appears to have more polymorphisms and, thus, fewer genetic fail-safes for surviving and thriving after trauma. In the same way, if one child has one long and one short allele on her 5-HTT serotonin transporter gene, she may have more optimism and more resilience than her sibling who has two short alleles on 5-HTT.

Putting genetics together with gender, you can study your daughter's resilience "coding" from the inside out. This can help you target resilience-building to your various children.

In my counseling practice, even if the parents never ask for genetic testing for their kids, I ask them to look at their child's innate assets for resilience-development by looking carefully at their children, themselves, and others in their lineages.

As you think about your daughter and each person in her genetic lineage, you can say:

"Brianna's like me in…"

"She's like Dad in…"

"She's like Grandma in…"

"She's like Grandpa in…"

As you gain a deeper picture of your daughter's internal strengths and sensitivities, you can talk with your relatives about what strategies worked with them when their own nurturing systems—parents, schools, communities—were teaching them resilience and grit.

One of my clients, the mom of an 11-year-old, shared her family's story with me.

This exercise of exploring Latrice's genetics of resilience made me go back to all my living relatives to get advice. As you know, Latrice was having a lot of trouble with overreacting and being hyper-sensitive. Just about anything could set her off, make her feel bad. She had trouble making friends or keeping them, she would always create some sort of conflict, then feel bad about that. She was almost paralyzed with low self-esteem. Her father and I tried encouraging her all the time. "It's okay," we would say. "You're doing great." But Latrice just didn't seem to have any strength to her. Since I'm a Pilates instructor, the metaphor I kept using with her was, "You have to have strength in your core. You have to develop your core."

I know we were helping her a little, but we just weren't doing enough.

Then in counseling, you suggested Latrice might have "genetic coding for less innate resilience." I think those were your words. Harry and I thought about that and decided it made sense. We got genetic testing, but it didn't go deep enough to show these genetics to us. However, it did show genetics for anxiety and depression, which really worried us. We realized we had to figure out what was going on with Latrice and how to help her now, at 11, before she really suffered in adolescence.

So, long story short, this is when I sent an email to three relatives I knew of who seemed to be somewhat like Latrice—kind of sensitive, shy, overreacting. One of them was someone Harry and I had been estranged from for seven years. We had wanted to find a way to reconnect—this was Harry's father, Bert—but hadn't figured out how until this exercise, so I wrote him to ask how he had developed resilience and strength through his shyness.

Bert wrote back, wanting to know why we asked. I told him and he really got into the genetics of this. It gave him something to talk to Latrice and Harry about, and we invited him out to visit and he came. He and Latrice talked a long time about how shy he had been and how his dad called him a "weakling" and all of that. He shared with her how he had to physically fight back against a bully when he was a kid so he stopped being a victim; how he had to stop blaming other people and focus on just a few things he did right, just those, not to worry about other people's opinions. He told Latrice she had to just focus on her gifts, including her love of music.

It was very moving, the way Latrice processed everything. Harry and I had told her most of this stuff, but because her grandfather told her—or maybe she was just ready to hear it—she really got it, really felt it. When Bert left to go back home to Florida, she told me, "Mom, I'm such a kid—it's time for me to grow up."

Wow.

Life didn't suddenly become perfect for her, but of all the things we tried, this process of reaching out to her similar family members and relatives is the one I remember the most vividly.

Latrice is 14 now and she is much stronger.

The Art of Bi-Strategic Parenting

With the help of her family, Latrice developed her Emotional Intelligence (EI). Her nuclear and extended family helped her to do this, and she matured all the more for it, using her newfound intelligence to become more resilient, grittier.

Generally, EI (popularized by Daniel Goleman's best-selling book *Emotional Intelligence*) is "the composite set of capabilities that enable a person to manage himself/herself and others." An emotionally intelligent person is generally an emotionally mature person with the self-awareness, emotional understanding, and social expressiveness needed for good relations with others. This person can handle strong emotions from others and control her own strong emotions. She tends to solve personal and social problems with adeptness, and generally does so in a way that others hope to emulate.

Is there a single way to develop EI in a child? No, there are multiple ways. When Davita and I and Marissa and Dana were arguing about what is best for girls, we were each arguing for our own position. But in fact, all of the ways we noted were good ways to build resilience and strength in girls. In biological terms, the multiple ways start with *Bi-strategic Parenting*. "Bi-strategic" denotes two somewhat different ways of building grit in girls. Let's look at how you can activate both kinds of parenting with your daughters, then we'll look at *Multi-strategic Parenting*.

Both the bi-strategic and multi-strategic approaches were hinted at in the email about Latrice.

Female Emotional Intelligence (FEI) and Male Emotional Intelligence (MEI)

Women and men parent differently. This is intuitive to anyone with children. Even individuals in lesbian/gay couples parent somewhat differently, as children of these couples will attest. Of course, as with all brain differences, not every difference will apply to every child at every moment. Some girls and women at certain times might practice traits of male emotional intelligence (MEI) in certain situations, and boys and men similarly practice traits associated with female emotional intelligence (FEI). Think in aggregates and in long-term studies (multiple observations of multiple children over a period of weeks and months).

With all that in mind, take a moment to go back to the brain differences we explored in Chapter 2, then look at these additional brain differences. See how they fit with your research.

Female Brain/Body (FEI)	Male Brain/Body (MEI)
More nerve endings for feeling pain	Fewer nerve endings for feeling pain
More pain/pressure receptors in brain	Fewer pain/pressure receptors
More activity in insula (more direct empathy)	Less insula activity (less direct empathy)
Slower exit of blood flow from insula	Quicker exit of blood flow from insula

More rise in heart-rate during conflict	Less rise in heart-rate during conflict
More blood-oxytocin flooding under stress	More testosterone under stress
More cingulate gyrus (feeling-rumination) activity	Less cingulate gyrus (rumination) activity
More word centers connected to emotions	Fewer word centers connected to emotions
More amygdala activity upward to word centers	More amygdala activity downward to body
White matter emphasis (multiple emotions)	More gray matter activity (singular focus)
Less active cerebellum (physical/doing center)	More active cerebellum during processing

Because of these and other brain differences, moms and dads tend to build resilience and grit in children somewhat differently. Female emotional intelligence (FEI) is *more directly empathic of the feelings felt by the person in distress.* Male emotional intelligence (MEI) tends more toward nurturing and empathy-strategies that are *aggressive and challenging of personal limitations.*

Try This

Do an Initial Study of MEI and FEI Around You

Both approaches to empathy teach resilience, and an overemphasis of one without the other can deplete the development of resilience in children and adults. In your own citizen science, you can study the differences by asking boys and girls in your own school, neighborhood, play groups, and home about how their parents parent them. You can also study the two kinds of empathy and nurturing by finding a group of early adolescent girls and boys playing a sport together. Let's say they are playing flag football. Watch them until you notice a girl fall and skin her knee. While trying to hold back tears, she holds her knee and rocks back and forth in pain. Watch a girl teammate come over to touch his shoulder. "Are you okay?" the girl might ask in an empathic tone. For her, what's important now is the imperative of direct empathy—to give personal aid for the fallen child.

She's stimulated by a rush of the human bonding chemical *oxytocin* that flashes through her brain and body as she sees the fallen child.

Her *insula* activates immediately and remains very active as she creates *mirror neurons* for the girl's pain in her brain. She literally "feels her pain."

Her *cingulate gyrus* (the attention/focus part of the brain) fills up with glucose metabolic flow that compels her to think out how to help this hurt child feel better as quickly as possible.

If the fallen child can feel better, the helper who is now suffering in the mirror-insula, will also feel better. Her brain activates verbal/word centers in both hemispheres (asking questions, verbally interacting) to help her give care to, return comfort to, and raise the self-esteem of this fallen child.

Simultaneously, watch what the boys are doing. Fewer of them will generally stop the game to help the fallen child. One might, but the alphas probably will not unless they think the girl is very hurt. These male teammates might run past the fallen child, conclude she's not badly hurt and yell, "Get up, get up, stop crying! Come on, we need you!"

In comparison to the direct empathy the girl is giving, the males seem to have less empathy, less nurturing. Even as the words leave the alpha male's mouth, he rushes away toward the football! Rather than oxytocin, surges of *testosterone* (the aggression chemical) heighten in his bloodstream and cells. Meanwhile, his mind is mainly driven by the competitive, aggressive, and purposeful "cause" of the game—a cause and purpose that doesn't "stop" in his mind like it does, momentarily, in the girl's brain. The instant he decides the fallen child is not severely damaged, his brain moves blood flow away from the *insula* and his mirror neurons deplete. The aggression-success of game and goal (from which everyone, including the fallen girl, will get their high self-esteem) are far more important to him than a child's tears. I call the male strategy "aggression nurturance." It could also be called "challenge nurturance."

Is the male strategy for building emotional intelligence less nurturing than the female?

I would argue no. The male is empathic, but in a different way than the female. While the girl helps the fallen child feel *better as soon as possible*, the boy helps the fallen child *feel stronger as soon as possible*. This is a crucial difference between FEI and MEI.

Study this difference in multiple settings—at home, at school, in your neighborhood, even in your workplace. You may notice that the boy and girl make unconscious decisions about what resilience is and how to nurture it in others. Look for at least ten situations in which someone is hurt. You should find children need both FEI and MEI to become fully resilient. In our home, I tended toward more MEI and Gail toward more FEI.

When we talked about this as a family recently, Gabrielle said, "If we hadn't had Mom, we wouldn't have developed the sensitivity we have. If we hadn't had Dad, we wouldn't be as strong."

Bi-Strategic Parenting is Both Cooperative *and* Coercive

MEI is often called "coercive nurturance" and FEI is called "prosocial or cooperative nurturance." Patricia Hawley, at Texas Tech University, studied these two different kinds of parenting and noticed that contemporary parenting and socialization (in most schools, for instance) tends toward pro-social nurturance, the maternal or FEI model. That tendency is based in the contemporary social trend, she argues, of believing that "aggression is largely an outcome of a process of maladaptation to perturbations in a child's ecology—such as coercive parenting, economic disadvantage, or criminogenic urban ecology—that ultimately lead to dysfunction."

In this prevailing contemporary model, aggression is not seen as prosocial or adaptive except to grab power or status, or to fight wars or predators. Thus, Hawley notes the vast majority of children who fit our present American view of emotionally intelligent, "adaptive" children are female while the vast majority of children who are viewed as less emotionally intelligent, dysfunctional, or maladaptive are male.

Yet as Hawley studied resilience and success of both boys and girls over a period of decades, she discovered that both boys and girls become more adaptive adults when they are raised in environments that include bi-strategic training throughout childhood and adolescence via both "prosocial (cooperative)" *and* "coercive (aggressive)" strategies. The "bi-strategists," Hawley notes, become the combination of female/male that lead to the most success in later life.

"Part of their success," Hawley explains, "is due to the fact that they are high in aggression yet mitigate the costs of aggression by employing pro-sociality."

She discovered that these children begin to show their greater success as early as fifth grade. Even more stunning, Hawley discovered that differences in maturation show up for preschoolers. The more bi-strategic the preschoolers are, the more they "have an advanced understanding of moral expectations and the norms of the social group."

Hawley's findings and their corroboration among her colleagues beg us to reconsider our obsession with some popular constructs in child development, including our belief that aggression is inherently bad for preschoolers and schoolchildren while direct empathy, especially via verbal literacy in emotional expression (talking about feelings, "use your words") is inherently better. While both MEI and FEI go too far in some circumstances, it is generally MEI we try to squash in most of our child-rearing institutions today. As we systematically overreact, a uni-strategic approach to empathy (only the FEI) ends up backfiring on the self-confidence and resilience-development in children. The loss of a strong father in a household, for instance, robs both boys and girls of MEI, and both children tend to be less mature, less resilient, and less adaptable, as research has shown now for over 40 years.

Kathryn Kerns, a professor of psychological sciences at The Ohio State University, has studied children and adults to discover the ways in which bi-strategic parenting is useful to children's resilience and success. She has noticed that the more coercive MEI approach ("paternal nurturance" or "the father factor") helps build resilience in the following ways:

- *Teasing.* By teasing children more than moms tend to do, fathers compel more resilience later in life as long as the teasing does not become abusive or bullying. Teasing, like talking about feelings, is a bonding activity that compels pathways to develop between emotion and thinking centers. A lot of the neural pathways people have tended to believe can only be developed when children "talk about feelings" actually can develop through teasing behavior, and some of them can develop more quickly and permanently through this more "coercive" form of nurturance.

- *Revving kids up.* By throwing children up and down, startling them, for instance, and petrifying their moms, Dad is actually stimulating a wider range of emotions in the child's maturation than just sitting still would. The revving up and the physical fear factor is crucial for resilience-building in attention, focus, and emotion centers in the brain.

- *Ending eye contact sooner but meanwhile scanning the environment.* Moms tend to keep eye contact longer with children than Dads, while fathers tend to look out into the world more, compelling children to also look out into the world to measure themselves. Resilience-building needs both kinds of eye-contact—the gaze into an intimate other's eyes, and the gaze into the larger world in which the child will be tested.

- *Exploration and building.* Paternal nurturance tends to do more bonding through tasks, activities, building things, experimenting on things, and exploring. Kerns has noticed that this is nuanced, as moms are more likely to teach a child a skill by helping her follow the established or written rules while dads are more likely to "throw the kid out there" to see how she problem-solves herself. Both ways are powerful resilience-builders.

- *Compelling the rules of independence.* Active fathers tend to challenge their children to take on big tasks, including hard ones, and wait to praise till the task is complete, whereas moms tend to praise children more quickly for doing the minutiae of each task during each step in its process. Kern also noticed that dads will, more often than moms, pretend not to know how to build a toy either in full or at a crucial stage of the process so that the child is compelled to complete the building process herself. Not only does this build independence in the child, it also compels the child to realize one of the rules of resilience: "While parents might do a lot for me when I'm young, in real life I'll have to be independent and strong to succeed."

Can moms teach all these things too? Of course! But, generally, Mom does this teaching in a more maternal and less coercive way.

Courageous Conversation

Will We Help Males Do Their Part to Build Resilience in Girls?

I chose the email about Grandpa Bert and Latrice earlier in this chapter not to imply that women can't do what Bert did. Latrice's mom, as she noted, had told Latrice all the things Bert told her, but Latrice "heard" them from Bert. It was like the peanut butter jar—Mom, Dad, grandma, teachers, counselors, and female peers had already begun loosening the cap, then Bert came around and got the credit for opening it! In part, this was, as Latrice's mom said, about timing. Some of it, though, happened because Bert was male.

In the endnotes, I've provided resources by which you can study statistics on girls' and women's success rates—maturation, leadership success, and personal safety—through the lens of fathering and male training. Males are, in general, very good for girls, but we tend to devalue male input or be afraid of the more coercive way males build strong daughters.

A grandmother of a 15-year-old girl told me a wonderful story.

"Cara has always been small, shy, and non-athletic. We've worried about her self-esteem for fourteen years. Right near her fifteenth birthday she finally gave in to her older brother, 16, who was always goading her into running track. 'You run like crazy

130

when I'm chasing you. Just try it, for God's sake! Who cares if it's painful and you don't do well! Just do it!' She finally did sign up for track and she lost the first few races by such large margins that she cried, even sobbed in the car. But, you know, something happened to her; the losing inspired her.

"'I don't want to cry like that anymore,' she said to me. 'I want to do better.' She practiced and practiced and practiced and two months later she won her first race. Now she's 16 and loves track. She also loves winning. Her self-esteem is much higher. My worry about her being strong in the future has gone from about 8 out of 10 down to a 4."

Tears welled up in this grandmother's eyes as she told me the story. As we talked, I felt the leap in maturation her granddaughter experienced by being goaded by a brother and coached by males to succeed through and with her pain. In her brother's goading, and in the ordeal of the sport, she encountered a lot of MEI. The sport, for these males, was a beautiful ordeal.

Males often see life as a harsh quest in which a child must face ordeal after ordeal to build and show character, strength, and self-esteem. Males see the way to emotionally intelligent adulthood somewhat differently than females. How wonderful this male approach ended up being for this girl.

The Role of Multi-Strategic Parenting

Our children are desperate for the nurturing that nature offers, and even when dads over-protect daughters or are absent or non-existent in their lives, girls need and yearn for their care. Similarly, if mom is gone, much of their own psychological development will be seen by the girl through the lens of the lost mother.

In the last fifty years, we've tended to argue over whether a child can get enough nurturing through two parents (a traditional or alternative "nuclear" family unit) or even one, a single parent. In reality, while certain parts of a girl's body and brain will mature on their own or with one or two parents, the child may not fully mature into a gritty, strong woman without other healthy attachments and relationships. Some will be peer relationships and some will be extended family and mentors. These combine with parental relationships to form a *safe container for social-emotional growth.*

To get a handle on what we mean by "safe container" and "other healthy attachments," think of the word "tribe" in English or, even more subtle, the word "pueblo" in Spanish. "Pueblo" has no real equivalent in English—it is both place and people together in a state of being rooted in allegiances and common values. The Mexican pueblo, for instance, is traditionally comprised of mom, dad, and many other people who mentor the child.

This pueblo, in my best translation, is what I call the Three Family System.

1. *The First Family.* The nuclear unit: Mom and Dad, two Moms/ two Dads, a single parent, or some other configuration of individuals who have the primary food, shelter, clothing, and attachment responsibility for the child; protective responsibility against substantial childhood trauma; and the will to challenge the child toward the developmental milestones of independence and maturation.

2. *The Second Family.* The extended family and other closely attached individuals such as nannies, other child care providers, coaches, mentors, and friends who supplement the work of the primary parents and biological extended family in protecting the child from trauma and challenge the child to mature. Just like the first family, it's best if the second family includes coercive and pro-social mentors, i.e. both empathy and aggression nurturers.

3. *The Third Family.* This family is made up of institutions, groups of people and individuals who wrap around and scaffold the first two families, including teachers, school principals, school counselors, therapists, social service providers, faith communities, governmental agencies, organizations like Girl Scouts and Boy Scouts—all of whom help insure that the child is further protected and challenged to mature in autonomy, independence, purpose and success. Sometimes, people in the third family, like teachers, become second family members.

Most human children had more than a single parent or even two parents in the past, but many girls don't have this now. Some of our innovations in the last fifty years have been very good for our children, but in our new millennium the Three Family System is in dangerous flux. The "safe emotional container" that females need to work out and experience their maturation requires both elder women and men like Bert, but our kids often don't have them. What we used to call "the neighborhood" was a second family (pueblo-like), a maturing influence that could substitute for extended family members, but it has disappeared in many parts of our country. Faith communities used to provide safe containers by acting as both second and third family maturation influences, but many of these institutions are no longer part of the three-family system anymore. Coaches in sports teams have, fortunately, taken up some of the three-family slack, as have our daughters' friends' parents, but because much three-family influence is moving toward peers and social media contact, we are again faced with paralysis of maturation.

I hope you will take a month to study all the mentors and family members your daughter has, what they give her in terms of resilience building (and what they do not), and then create a plan for her multi-strategic three-family system. Gail and I did this as we decided to have children, targeting certain people, like our daughter's godmother, Pam Brown, for three-family-system duties. As our children grew up, some of their parenting was done by Pam and their godfather, Clancy.

When we focus on the three-family system and on bi-strategic parenting, we bring relief to ourselves because we no longer need to be the perfect parent. Our job becomes the providing of food, shelter, clothing, education, and a safe emotional container in which our daughters are influenced not by just one or two, but by another five or ten people nurturing our child's nature. We pursue bi-strategic and multi-strategic approaches for our children, and we focus on various strategies within those approaches that target resilience-building.

Nine Strategies for Teaching Resilience

As you explore the assets in your Three Family System, here are nine powerful strategies you can use for building gritty, strong, mature girls.

1. *Both free and organized play.* Some playtime every day should be free play in which, unless a child is in danger, adults do

not intervene. By free playing, a girl learns multiple assets of problem-solving in her own way.

2. If you have a shy child, focus on *shyness* with your three-family assets. Shy (introverted) children often become resilient adults with amazing leadership abilities. In most cases, this happens because they had mentors and peers in childhood to help them "come out of their shell." Without the mentor and the activity, she would be more isolated and less able to feel strong; because of the activities and the mentors, she leads. If your shy daughter is hiding from the world, get her in an activity like martial arts that exposes her to multiple mentors for resilience-building.

3. Use *movies* to teach girls resilience. Some recent ones are *47 Meters Down, Wonder Woman, Megan Leavey*, and *Beauty and the Beast*. After the movie, talk with the girl about the lessons of resilience. Let extended family members tell their own stories and elicit good conversations.

4. *Use books to teach resilience.* When girls are young, parents and elders can read books like *Eloise* to them and set time aside to cuddle and talk about strong girls. As girls get older, we can read *The Hunger Games* and talk with girls about what Katniss is learning.

5. *Help girls get dirty.* Nature itself is a place where girls learn resilience. Send your daughter outdoors, into the backyard, neighborhood, or park. For safety, send her out with a buddy. Trees, wind, life and death, manure, silage, rivers and oceans, mountains, levees and dams—they all provide potential places for problem-solving, growth, resilience development, and maturation.

6. Tell family stories of adults *standing up for themselves.* A mom came to me after a lecture and told me about her mother watching a *Law and Order: SVU* episode with her daughter. In it, a young woman who is scared of testifying about having been raped, gets up the courage after a woman in her sixties sits down with her and tells her the story of her own rape when she was in college. The mom who came up to me said when her own mother and daughter watched this episode, her mother started to cry and her daughter asked why. Her mother confessed to having experienced date rape in high school.

The two women and the girl talked together. "If not for that episode of that show," the mom told me, "I wouldn't have even known this happened to my mother. And my daughter wouldn't have known how strong my mother really is."

7. Help your daughter take *risks*. Parents will try—and often succeed—at helping girls take risks, but sometimes extended family members and third-family mentors and coaches can do it faster and better. Risks mean making mistakes and being imperfect, and resilience grows from the mistakes, the errors, the awkwardness of the game, sport, or other ordeal.

8. Consciously work on the issue of *entitlement*. Nowadays, grandparents are often relegated to, or have chosen, a position of "spoiling" their grandchildren. There is nothing wrong with that, but grandparents also have wisdom they want to give. Often that wisdom says, "I'll spoil her so you don't have to," or "She's spoiled enough already, let's put her to work." Our daughters need people in their lives who support us in curtailing the social condition commonly called "affluenza," a disorder not of the body but of the soul.

9. Put her to *work*. Whether "work" means doing chores or, once she is old enough, working outside the home, work-life leads to mentors. When they turned sixteen, both Gabrielle and Davita worked at a nursing home ten minutes away from our house. They worked as servers in the dining room. By working in this environment, they entered second and third-family systems and are, now, much stronger and more independent, mature, and resilient for it.

Using Celebrities as Family Members

A tenth potential three-family asset is *celebrities*. While raising our daughters, Gail and I tried to find models of resilience for them (both female and male) among the celebrities they discussed with us. Because my daughters are grown, some of the models of their time don't apply anymore. Here are contemporary models you can use (or people like them).

- In May 2017, the Wimbledon champion Gabine Muguruza told a reporter about playing against her idol, Venus Williams: "It's great to go out there and play somebody that you admire.

I knew she was going to make me suffer and fight for it." What a wonderful comment on resilience!

- In July 2017, the actress Olivia Wilde recounted struggling with the ordeal of doing her Broadway Show, *1984*. She broke her tailbone and split her upper lip. To a reporter she shrugged this off with, "It's an intense story and it involves a lot of intense participation . . . but it's great. I don't feel the pain until we're offstage anyway."
- The feminist comedian and actress Ari Gaynor was asked by Stephen Colbert in the summer of 2017 how she liked working with various male directors. One of those directors, Woody Allen, she described as very critical but, she said, "I was okay with it because when I did something right, it felt great to hear him say it."
- James Patterson told the story in the spring of 2017 of being bullied and slapped around as a kid. Finally, he hit back and wasn't bullied again.

Making Maturation, Not Comfort, Our Ultimate Goal

The poet Mary Oliver has written, "What blazes the trail is not necessarily pretty." Deena and Marissa, I believe, wanted their girls to avoid the mess. They wanted to save their girls from too much discomfort, they wanted things to be pretty, even though life is not necessarily pretty.

They had, I believe, an idealized view of female resilience-building. Science is not always pretty. Parenting is not always pretty. It can feel very awkward at times, and that is more than okay.

A favorite TV program during my girls' growing up was the Kyra Sedgwick LA police drama, *The Closer*. I recommend it to anyone raising resilient daughters. What I love most about it—beyond its powerful and captivating crime stories—is the way it shows multiple goals for female resilience-building. It does not get locked in a single ideological view, but realistically—and at times messily—shows female grit in the real world.

At the beginning of the series, Sedgwick's character, Brenda Johnson, enters the LA police force as deputy chief, having previously worked for the CIA and Atlanta PD. Her presence as a woman and a strong personality-type angers people who were not promoted into her position. Creating even more tension, all the detectives working under her except one, Lt. Daniels, are male. While few of these males are sexist, all of them put her through the paces and judge her mercilessly. Some even try to undercut her work.

Surviving and thriving in this workplace required a lot of resilience from Chief Johnson. As the series unfolds, we learn that she was raised by a gentle (though very strong) mother and harsh (though loving) military father. These two people constitute a perfect example of bi-strategic parenting. From this grit-development, and from many previous years in law enforcement, Brenda knew she had to prove herself worthy of the respect of her team. She did not feel entitled to that respect without earning it. Messily, but with perseverance and a great deal of emotional intelligence, she did prove herself throughout the first season. By the series finale seven years later, Brenda and her squad grew not only to respect one another, but also to love one another.

Chief Brenda Johnson was, during our daughters' upbringings, an amazing TV asset for teaching resilience and organizational reality to our daughters. Episode 7 of Season One provides an example. In this episode, Brenda talks in her squad room with the team, listing qualities of autism (the present murder case revolves around an autistic boy). As she is talking, Lieutenant Flynn, a detective who dislikes her presence in the squad during year 1, says sarcastically, "Does he have a Georgia accent?" Flynn is obviously trying to put the Deputy Chief in her place. His sarcasm is not cruel, but quite challenging.

Brenda ignores it.

After we watched this episode, our family talked about how condescending Flynn was. We discussed, too, why Brenda ignored the slight. Our daughters saw that she did not take the comment personally, but rather went about her tasks of detection and leadership. "I will prove myself to this group of men who are already set in their ways," she is clearly thinking, and as our daughters noticed, by the end of Season 1, even Flynn became one of her major allies.

Consider using *The Closer* strategically in your family. Especially because of its constant subtext of female/male relationships, it provides constant and multi-faceted visions of the relationships between the sexes. It is a bit too gruesome and "adult" for very young children, but if you watch a few episodes yourself, you may feel comfortable showing it to many ages of girls. To me, the essence of its power is its constant message that 'discomfort' is crucial to building resilience. In fact, navigating "the mess" is a foundation of women's power.

PART III

CULTURE

Chapter 7

STEM, STEAM, Math and Science: Teaching Girls the Way Girls Learn

> "If you are sitting on a tack, the treatment is not two Advil every three to four hours. The treatment for "tack sitting" is "tack removal." Search for the root and treat the cause rather than the symptoms. If you are sitting on two tacks, removing one tack does not eliminate 50 percent of the symptoms. Complex conditions are 'complex.' To be effective address all the underlying causes for resolution."
>
> — Dr. Sidney Baker, Integrative Medicine Pioneer

WHEN *LEADERSHIP AND THE SEXES* WAS PUBLISHED in 2008, two of my editors and I were asked to visit Google Headquarters in Mountainview, California. That book, published by Jossey-Bass/John Wiley, grew from my work as a gender trainer and consultant in small and large businesses, including Fortune 500 corporations. Barbara Annis, also a corporate trainer and business consultant, joined me on the book. Between us, we had more than forty years of experience in the field. The visit to Google involved a lunch with an executive team and then a lecture I would give to some Google employees.

At lunch, an executive mentioned the very public issue Google (and nearly every other tech company) has had with 1) far more males than females choosing and remaining in tech careers like coding and engineering, and 2) more females than males stepping off the corporate climb before reaching the highest leadership levels and the C-suite.

"You're a gender science guy," the executive said. "What's your take on why this is going on? We are spending a lot of money to attract young women into these very specific fields and levels and believe deeply in this cause." As we talked, we discussed the controversy that erupted a few months before in Boston when the president of Harvard, Larry Summers, suggested there were multiple reasons for females not doing as well as men in certain tech fields. He called for a multi-disciplinary approach to the issue, including the use of gender neuroscience. Summers was castigated for suggesting this, and ultimately lost his job for various reasons, including this controversy. I asked the executive what he thought of Summer's comments about gender and brain science.

The executive responded, "I don't think Summers was the villain people made him out to be, but maybe he could have said things differently."

Nodding my agreement, I pressed further in.

"But do you think he was right, that there might be some other issues at work here than corporate sexism? Other issues involving the male and female brain, for instance?"

He thought about this silently for a moment and then said, "I think there's got to be more going on with our male/female ratios than just sexism. Some of us are very intrigued by the brain research, and that's why we invited you here. But we've got to be very careful. There are differing opinions in our organization, and people are very strong in their opinions."

Having seen this conundrum in other tech companies, I said, "So, not to be too blunt, but you're saying that your tech company, which is science-based in its research and technology, has to be careful about being science-based in its *gender* issues." He pondered this irony but didn't say anything else right then, so I pushed harder. "Would you be willing to say that brain differences between females and males *ought* to occupy more of our social conversation both inside and outside our tech corporations than they currently do?"

He paused and showed an affirmation in his eyes, but then he said, "Look, it can worry too many people and too many people overreact to it so I will have to say no."

"It's a minefield, then," I said reflectively.

"It's a minefield," he agreed.

Our lunch ended and I gave my talk to various employees. Afterwards, my editors and I and a small team met for a few minutes to say goodbye. An executive team member who had not spoken earlier said, "I would like to see changes made in the early pipeline—in the way children are taught from birth to five. Along the lines of your gendered brain theory, I think we have to at least try to make changes early in girls' development if we are going to be able to longitudinally discover whether a fifty-fifty goal for females and males in coding and other similar jobs is realistic."

My editors and I said our goodbyes and left Google headquarters intrigued by the wonderful facility and touched by the difficulty this tech company was having instituting gender science as a foundation to internal processes. One of my editors, Alan Rinzler, said aloud what all of us were feeling as we got in our cab to head back to San Francisco: "I think there is a lot going on here and a lot of interest in gender science, but it sure does seem to be a minefield."

We drove away from Mountain View with a sense of things to come.

The Minefield

Because a decade has passed since that conversation, I can't say for sure that each word in my rendering is correct, but I can certify its key concepts, including the "minefield" we sensed (and which I've discussed in the context of boys' development in *Saving Our Sons*). This intellectual minefield plagues our assistance to girls and women. It is cruel, dangerous, and in some ways, built on an illusion that I hope, in the early chapters of this book, you have seen through. The illusion is the DGP idea that talking about the female brain and the male brain is such a binary operation as to ultimately harm girls and women.

This fear is unwarranted, as our Gurian Institute team has proven over the last twenty years. In fact, just the opposite. As teachers, parents, and mentors receive science-based training in male/female brain differences—then gender differentiate their instruction and attachment as needed—girls perform better in test scores, grades, behavior, and motivation. For statistics proving the healthy and effective power of nature-based gender theory, please check www.gurianinstitute.com/success or *Leadership and the Sexes*. To get a glimpse of a more recent version of the minefield at Google, please check out http://www.gurianinstitute.com/blog--newsletter/archives/08-2017.

A Science-Based Approach to Girls and Math/Science.

In this chapter, I will pass through the minefield to focus on science-based theory and practice that have been proven to close gender gaps. Meanwhile, to parent or teach girls today is to be invited into the minefield; thus, the strategies and changes I want you to try in this chapter will be difficult to expand nationally without a groundswell in the grassroots that calls on schools, colleges, communities, and legislators to fund research and provide solutions that are brain-based.

The DGP has control of this part of our social dialogue—the girls-and-STEM part. To fully help our daughters, we must push beyond the DGP idea in our academic world, government, and the media that corporate sexism and individual gender stereotypes are the primary reasons tech and certain STEM fields don't employ as many women as men. If we do not, we simply will not close the STEM gender gap to the extent that it can close.

Courageous Conversations

What Do We Gain by Avoiding the Obvious!

As you begin this chapter, I hope you will consider gathering your family or study group together to talk about two things: first, the gender-brain differences we explored in part one of this book (I will explore them further in a few moments); and, second, the experiences your daughters have had in math, science, and related classes and fields.

As you come together, ask: "Do you think girls and boys often have different experiences in math and science classes at school?"

Most people will say or sense that "Yes" is a good answer, but they may need help in clarifying the feeling.

To help stimulate deeper discussion, ask each person to give specific and concrete examples of different experiences their kids have had—successes, difficulties, good teachers, bad teachers, problems, solutions.

Angela, a mother of three, who was an engineer before taking time off to raise her kids, told me about her courageous community conversation.

We had some very young parents in the group and the rest of us had older kids. We even had a couple college students in the group. It was quite a discussion in the beginning because a couple of the young parents with newborns and the two college students were like, "No way, there aren't any differences between boys and girls, that's just old sexist thinking," while the rest of us who had older kids knew that differences can affect things, especially in school. I said, "Hey, I'm a female chemical engineer, and there aren't many of us, but even I know there are differences between the brains of girls and boys." I carried a little bit of weight because of my profession.

At the end of this conversation, one mom said something generational about this. "I think the young people who are saying the differences don't exist or don't matter can only say that because they're young. I don't think there's hardly anyone in the world who has raised both boys and girls who would say their minds really work the same way. And if you've had kids in the school system for any length of time, you've seen a lot of girls struggling in math."

You can imagine how these comments offended the younger people. They accused the woman of being ageist and disrespectful of their opinion. The woman did apologize for how she said it, but she was right in a way—there was a 'youth situation' in the conversation by which only the young people without much experience were saying what they were saying. Those of us who had multiple kids of both sexes all agreed—the brain differences really matter, especially in things like math and science.

I connected with Angela by phone and told her I was writing this book. We talked for more than an hour and I learned a great deal from her. "I personally know I am what you call a *bridge brain*," she told me. "My brain is very spatial-mechanical—it thinks a lot more like a guy's brain when it comes to my work—and this helped me in STEM classes as a kid. But two of my daughters don't have brains like mine. Those classes are very hard for them. Most of their teachers just didn't understand how to teach them so that they'll learn math the way I—and a lot of the guys—learn it instinctively. To me, as an engineer, this is one of the biggest problems in our schools. Math is taught the way that male brains—and some male-type brains like mine—learn it. Some boys and even more girls are left out in the cold."

Isn't it time to grapple with this truth? In nearly every school, community, or corporation I visit, individuals at every level—from line workers to executives—feel quite sure boys and girls learn differently. The brain scans my colleagues and I show—scans I showed at Google in 2008—only confirms a belief many people have already gained empirically by being parents. Angela's plea that teachers be trained in how the male and female brain learn math and science is a bottom line I will support in this chapter. To help you study it, and to help you move the needle for your girls in STEM, here are ideas to discuss in your courageous and educational conversations:

- The word "now" is key. While nearly all contemporary sociological research points to "stereotype threat," "sexism," and "gender stereotypes" as the primary (or only) reason girls struggle in certain STEM areas, and while there is no doubt (as we will confirm in this chapter) that those things do matter, sexism is not what it was fifty years ago. Nowadays, women and girls are generally, and especially in developed and post-industrial cultures, in a different place than they were years ago when we first began to study the STEM gender gap. Today, there are larger issues at play than sexism.
- Our STEM conversation regarding gender is tacitly grounded on the idea that a 50/50 ratio in each STEM (and other) profession will be our best cultural indicator of gender equality. I will challenge that assumption in this and later chapters by asserting that it is not likely we will ever get 50% females in mechanical engineering, just as it is unlikely we will get 50% males teaching kindergarten or elementary school. Our new STEM conversation needs to start from a realistic basis—a point which will allow us to invest in science-based training for girls and boys, and teachers and corporate leaders.
- Pew Research and other polls show that more than 60% of women would like to stop working outside the home or work part-time when they have children. Meanwhile, these polls show that 70% of men expect to work full-time outside the home once children come. There is no indication that these numbers will change much, especially with new research showing that the wealthier a culture becomes, the more its women want to take time off to raise their children. Given

this reality (one that a wealthy culture can celebrate) and even despite the fact that the number of stay-at-home dads is increasing, we will never have 50% stay-at-home dads. Male/female brain differences—while not the only factor involved in these percentages—are a key factor in life and family-development for males, females, and everyone on the gender spectrum. In STEM and child care especially, they much more deeply affect education and career choice than do gender stereotypes.

- Brain differences account for a huge share of the girls/women STEM gap. As we discussed in Part I, our brains are different from conception and during in utero development. Not to take this into account ensures that the best STEM education our girls need and deserve—especially in T (technology), E (engineering) and M (math)—will not be provided in many of their schools. The Google executive was right—from birth onward, we must do a better job teaching STEM, STEAM, math, and science to all children, especially to girls in the first ten to fifteen years of life. Most of this chapter will suggest needed changes to math/science education in our schools and homes.

- Neurobiological differences also account for a huge share of issues women are experiencing in male-driven fields like chemical engineering, mechanical engineering, coding, etc. To attract more women for longer periods of time in these fields, and to advance more of those women higher in corporations, our culture and its businesses will need to understand how the female brain experiences these workplaces, and then alter the workplaces accordingly so that they're attractive to women.

Talk about a minefield!

Listening to Our Daughters

Perhaps the most prevalent story the Gurian Institute's team has heard from middle and high school girls in STEM-related classes is: "The teacher didn't explain it in a way I could understand. I just don't get it!" This lament was captured in an interaction with one of my daughter's friends, Alicia, 16, just before we sat down to dinner.

"How's school going, Alicia?" I asked.

"Fine," she shrugged.

"What are you taking this year?"

"English, Choir, Social Studies, Math, Physics, and Art."

"Any of the classes really move you?"

A long response followed regarding her love of literature, art, and music subjects.

"Not so much the Math and Physics, then?" I asked.

"No," she shook her head immediately.

"Not fun, huh?" I prompted.

She breathed in deeply and responded in detail! "I mean, I was pretty decent in math up through middle school, but now it's getting a lot harder and I can't really understand it. Luckily my brother is a year ahead of me and he had the same teacher, so he explains things better to me and helps me and I can do enough extra credit to at least get a B in the class. That's as good as I'll ever get.

"But in Physics, it's the teacher. I mean, Mr. Peters is such an asshole, excuse me, I'm sorry, but he is. He gets mad at me and Theresa when we don't understand. Like, we'll stay after class and tell him we don't understand it at all, and he just keeps saying the same explanation every time, but we don't understand it. And he just gets mad and yells, 'I explained that already, weren't you listening!' like I'm stupid and didn't listen, but I did listen and he doesn't explain it.

"Luckily, Theresa is really strong. She'll tell him he should explain it better, but oh my God, he gets mad and he tells her she's not thinking hard enough. 'That's lazy thinking,' he says. That's one of his favorites, 'that's lazy thinking.' I try not to say anything so he doesn't look at me like I'm stupid, but the problem is I don't understand the answer he wants, and he won't explain it so I go home and try to do the homework and I don't get it right and I do bad on the tests. Luckily, he lets us take all the tests over again for extra credit, and thank God, because if not for extra credit I would get a D or F. But the problem isn't us. I mean, Theresa is super smart and she's got A's in all her classes, but not in Physics, and she's not the only one . . ."

Alicia would have continued for another ten minutes, but dinner was ready so I interrupted her and asked some data questions as we moved to the kitchen table.

"How many kids are in your class?"

"27 or 28, I think."

"And how many are getting D's or F's or low C's?"

"Maybe 10 or 11."

"How many kids are getting A's?"

She pondered this. "I'm not sure, but not a lot. Maybe 5 or 6."

"So, more kids are getting C's or worse."

She nodded.

"And when a lot of you kids get the C's, it's because you are doing extra credit?"

She nodded.

"How many girls are getting A's, and how many boys?"

"About the same, maybe 3 or 4 each."

"And how many of these kids are getting the A's without doing extra credit?"

She saw the direction of my question and paused before answering. "I think there are a couple boys, maybe three. And there's this one girl, Ally, who doesn't have to do any extra credit. It's mostly the boys, though. Most of us girls are doing the extra credit to get our grades up."

I had heard similar comments from my daughters about their experiences in some math and science classes. Similarly, in many of the schools in which my team and I have worked, a major focus of our observation and feedback sessions revolves around STEM classes. Unfortunately, Alicia's pathway to a C represents the essence of difficulty for many of our daughters in math/science education.

Did You Know?

The Teacher Training Dilemma

Kathy Stevens, mentioned in the Preface, taught math and music before becoming the director of a non-profit, The Women's Resource Agency, and then the executive director of the Gurian Institute. One of her most profound observations about her teaching profession has been confirmed by twenty years of in-school research.

"Teachers of middle and high school," she said, "generally consider themselves to be content experts. They know math, physics, science, etc., and their job is to instruct students in math or physics through a good curriculum for that subject. What they (we, since I was a teacher for a long time) often don't get is that, for girls, the social-emotional stuff is just as important as the curriculum. How the teacher relates to the girl matters a lot. How he or she explains things means something."

In the twenty years that I have been working in the schools and gathering data, I have seen this vision confirmed. The teachers are good people and they love their subject, but few or none received teacher training in male/female brain difference. Once they get into the classroom and have been there a while, they often sense there is something negative going on with some of the boys and many of the girls in the math or science classroom. But unless the school undergoes significant systemic self-analysis, the staff doesn't have to alter teaching methods significantly because "math, physics, chemistry . . . these are just what they are, they're not subjective like English or social studies."

Meanwhile, in English and social studies, the girls are excelling, on average, far beyond many or most of the boys, so the math/science learning and social-emotional dilemmas can stay hidden. Mr. Peters is a case in point. I don't believe he is malicious at all, but he doesn't realize that he is teaching physics to the "math-smart" brains (often more boys than girls) in his classroom, leaving a lot of the girls to fail. Meanwhile, because pervasive grade failure is not something any teacher wants, he provides a way for a lot of girls and some boys to close the grade-gap in the class—by giving students extra credit assignments that will offset bad test grades. Girls and boys who would probably get D's and F's can thus get C's, and in some cases, B's or A's.

The lingering problems in this system were captured poignantly in Alicia's frustration. She told me she "hates" math and "will never understand" physics. Like so many other girls, she thought and sometimes made comments like:

"Boys are better than girls at that stuff and everyone knows it."

"Mr. Peters is a terrible teacher!"

"I can't wait to get to college and just take the classes I want to take."

While Alicia may not be destined for an engineering career, and while she made peace with that, the educational system she grew up in committed some sins of omission—it let this girl down. After planting her in the middle of a beautiful grassy field that should have given her ample opportunity to explore science and mathematical mystery, it made the field seem barren to her. She couldn't wait to escape its daily and cruel diminishment of her self-esteem and personal sense of worth.

Teacher Training in the Minds of Girls

Twenty years ago, I and others in the field suggested that systemic professional development for teachers in how boys and girls learn differently could lead to gains for girls in math/science. In 1997, this was theoretical and unproven, but by 2000 it was demonstrated in a two-year pilot study run by Dr. Patricia Henley, myself, and our colleagues in the School of Education at the University of Missouri-Kansas City. In this pilot, the efficacy of brain-based teacher training was tested via grades, test scores, and discipline referral data. Early in the pilot and continuing throughout, we found:

- grades and test scores went up for both girls and boys;
- discipline referrals to the principal went down;
- student satisfaction went up across the curriculum—in math, science, English, and social studies; and
- surpassing my own and Henley's hopes for the pilot, the teachers not only embraced the new success, but also personally and communally developed new innovations.

You can read about the six school districts that participated in the pilot in *Boys and Girls Learn Differently!* You can also read about other schools and school districts that have seen similar gains over the last two decades in our subsequent books and articles and on www.gurianinstitute.com.

Grounded in the success of the Missouri pilot, my GI team has operated out of the belief that every college or university school of education should teach a one semester course on the male/female brain to its future teachers. Most schools of education do not do so because of the "minefield" we discussed earlier in the chapter, but it can be done. I devised such a course in 1994 at Gonzaga University, and it was well received. A similar course can be taught anywhere. In this course, the professor can show brain scans to begin explorations of nature, nurture, and culture. As the course evolves, the many issues facing girls in STEM professions are revealed and solved, issues like these:

- *Lack of complex math comprehension early in life.* The Google executive who posited that birth-to-five training for parents and preschool/kindergarten teachers in STEM teaching might help girls was right. Early childhood training in STEM needs to be improved. Right now, teachers of math in pre-K and elementary grades often misread girls' signals, thinking girls are learning math well when they're not fully comprehending the lesson. Female math-frustration ensues and can accumulate into and through secondary school.
- *Fear of math* early in life and continuing through childhood. Math fear, especially on test day, is a very real thing, and it can lead to many years of accumulated and debilitating anxiety. As teachers and others receive training in how Social Emotional Learning (SEL) can enhance test scores, grades, student discipline, and self-esteem, girls' learning environments become more girl-friendly. Teachers like Mr. Peters alter the way they explain, support, and teach girls.
- Accumulating math anxiety compounds with *stereotype threat* in which the anxious girl feels less smart than the math-smart boy and decides math is a "boy" thing not a "girl" thing. New research has shown that girls do not consider themselves as "brilliant" as boys—their inability to succeed in math is one reason. As we train teachers and others in male/female learning difference (gender-differentiated instruction) we decrease stereotype threat.
- While respectable grade performance (often because of extra credit and extra homework) in middle and high school math classes can keep bad grades at bay, for those girls who are not naturally "math-smart," these extra-credit-grade-elevations correlate to 1) an *avoidance of higher-level math* classes, and 2) a

continuation of downward spirals in STEM learning such that, by the time these girls are through high school, they are often utterly disinterested in tech or math-related fields.

- Unfortunately, as higher levels of math are avoided by these girls in high school and college, it becomes nearly impossible for these girls to fulfill their potential early goals of entering computer coding and other tech specialties. These fields require not just some coursework in their specialty, but also a *love of higher math learning* which girls who have been struggling in math or science from the early years onward generally do not have.

- While our colleges are, happily, pushing for more females in higher math and tech classes, and while this culture-push is working in some cases, by the time many of these young women enter commensurate workforces, the corporations themselves notice many of the women engineers choosing to *step away from long-term self-development in the mechanical field.* Often these women move to an administrative, PR, or HR job at the engineering firm, or they quit to have children. These choices and decisions among women are complex, and we will explore them in this chapter and in Chapter 9, but the bottom line is this:

  1. Because of all these experiences and choices along the way, more men end up higher in the corporate or firm ladder throughout the corporate world and especially in tech fields, leaving women to earn lower aggregate wages and experience less leadership positioning in these fields.

  2. Overall, the negative consequences for women of STEM-learning issues earlier in life are partially responsible for fewer jobs at the top and fewer higher-paying jobs in high-tech and engineering.

If you are a science geek and want to look at original studies that support many of the items on my list, please look at:

Jillian E. Lauer and Stella F. Lourenco of Emory University (2016), *"Spatial Processing in Infancy Predicts Both Spatial and Mathematical Aptitude in Childhood."*

Daniel W. Belsky, et.al. (2016), *"The Genetics of Success: How*

Single-Nucleotide Polymorphisms Associated with Educational Attainment Relate to Life-Course Development."
Diane Halpern, et.al. (2007), *"The Science of Sex Differences in Science and Mathematics."*

You will find these and many more in the Notes and References at the end of this book. I strongly recommend showing these studies to your daughters and discussing them with both your girls and boys. They can help you develop citizen science in your home and in your children. And these studies can lead to systemic change in school buildings, as well. Teachers are hungry to learn more about the learning brains of girls and boys.

Try This

Explore the Single-Sex Educational Option for Math and Science

In the third study I listed, by Diane Halpern, et.al., you'll see the case made for culture-wide study of male/female brain difference in the math/science context. The study utilizes research from scientists who have collectively studied millions of brains and children. Overall, they support the position of this book and this chapter with a big "but." The "but" is inculcated in the study mainly by Diane Halpern, who argues the "minefield" or DGP position that while brain differences clearly exist, to teach to them will lead to gender stereotypes. Most specifically, she created a section in the study to argue that *single-sex classrooms and schools* are a bad thing.

I love this study, but the part of it in which she argues against single-sex schooling is not well-supported. In contrast, our Gurian Institute field research in more than two thousand schools has shown that:

1. Single-sex classrooms can improve girls' STEM confidence; and
2. Single-sex schools can powerfully enhance female self-esteem.

In *Successful Single-Sex Classrooms*, you will find research corroborating this kind of success in single-sex schools from around the country. I have listed other references for you in the Notes and References, in case you are contemplating this innovation in your community.

Unfortunately, in the public press, single-sex and co-ed schools are pitted against one another, e.g. "Are single-gender schools better than co-ed schools, or vice versa?" Neither is necessarily better or worse. Both can be quite helpful. Generally, the usefulness to students of co-education, single-sex classrooms, and innovative methods like Montessori or Waldorf depend on:

1. whether the teachers/staff are *trained* in male/female learning difference in general, and;
2. whether the teachers/staff use *science-based* strategies for STEM learning.

If staff and faculty at any school are not trained in how to teach to girls specifically, both co-ed and single-sex options can be inadequate to certain children and students.

If your community is pondering single-sex classrooms or single-gender schools, you might find that these single-gender schools/classrooms often show quicker success results than co-ed schools. In one of our Gurian Institute Model Schools, Farrell Girls Preparatory Academy in Tampa, Florida, it took only one year for the school to move to an "A" school (one of the highest performing schools in the district).

One reason for this fast success is the requirement in single-gender schools of training on male/female learning difference. As Director of Student Services, Carla Sparks, told me, "Because the brain-based professional development becomes an integral part of the pedagogy and professional learning community, the teachers more quickly absorb learning, discipline, and social-emotional development strategies that work for the student population; in Farrell's case, girls."

Without that training, either co-ed or single-gender schools can make systemic mistakes in learning and discipline, and, thus, lose both male and female learners. Quite often, co-ed schools are much slower than single-gender schools to provide this training and science-based systemic analysis, which results in old methods of teaching working less well than you might want them to.

An area of gain for girls in single-sex environments involves their individual gains in diverse leadership ability and self-confidence. Many shy and introverted girls shine better in single-gender classrooms, especially in math/science classrooms at the middle school age when there might be (in a co-ed classroom) two or three very assertive and math/science-smart boys (and girls) who dominate. In the girl-only classroom, more girls will generally talk, answer questions, and take more of the lead.

Single-sex classrooms and single-gender education are not a panacea, but the structure of single-gender classes/schools can be so beneficial to so many students, I believe it should be studied as a part of longitudinal research in all fifty states. As academic institutions study the innovation, our anecdotal Gurian Institute research will be corroborated. Already, single-gender and single-sex options are becoming a part of public schooling, and I hope this trend continues.

Naysayers often argue against single-sex education with, "If we separate boys and girls, we will increase gender stereotypes (similar to racially-segregated schools increasing racism), and this will crush girls' success." This ideological argument has been proven false, but it still dominates our media. In reality, single-gender schools are no more likely to create dangerous gender stereotypes than co-ed. Meanwhile, it is also important to note the false parallel between "racial segregation" and "single-gender schools."

The brain research in Part I, like that of David C. Page at MIT, makes this point. "If we compare a female and a male," Page noted, "genetic differences are 15 times greater than the genetic differences for two males or two females." In other words, two females of different races are far more similar genetically than a male and female of the same race. Comparing race and sex/gender is an error. When people who dislike single-gender education throw "segregation" into the argument, they are using a straw man argument that is not supportable by science.

If you are contemplating single-gender options, you gain a great deal by compelling people who attack your innovation to prove actual harm in single-gender classes or schools. To prepare yourself to ask this crucial question, go to the Notes and References where I have included more analysis. Naysayers will accuse single-sex and single-gender schooling of creating "dangerous gender stereotypes," but accusations of gender stereotyping without either longitudinal study or proof of harm are non-scientific at their core.

STEM Techniques for Birth-to-Five Girls

Single-sex and single-gender options are just one set of options your community can use to close gender STEM/STEAM and math/science gaps. Let me provide others now that our Gurian Institute research has proven effective.

To affect brain development early, remember to try *girls only day in the block corner.* Only girls (not boys) are allowed in a certain corner of the room for block building. Boys can have their own corner, but for this hour or day, they don't come into the girls' corner. This is a separate sex technique that can show big dividends, and here's why.

If you go to preschool to observe children for a period of seven days, you'll likely see a biological trend toward certain actions that favor males in spatial/physical play, e.g. the girls will end up watching as the boys build towers with blocks, then knock them down and laugh, then do it all over again. While this is natural play for boys, it may diminish girls' development of spatial intelligence. Because girls shy away from kines-thetic block play when aggressive boys dominate, they don't build up the spatial-mechanical centers we would like them to have. Girls only day in the block corner allows girls to try spatial building and mechanizing without interruption. This activity may stimulate synapses and func-tioning in spatial and mechanical centers of the brain.

Increased *gross motor play* can also help with spatial intelligence development. If you watch young children of both sexes for seven days in their play, work, and interactions, you'll see a greater tendency among the girls to occupy their time with "fine motor activity" (playing with dolls, drawing carefully, doing weaving and bead work, crafting their penmanship) and a greater tendency among the boys toward gross motor play (whole body play like roughhousing, running, hitting, kicking a ball, etc.). As you notice this pattern, you'll also see more impulsiveness in the boys, less in the girls; more aggression in the boys, less in the girls; more spatial intelligence development in roughhousing for boys, and more varied sensorial acquisition in the girls.

Like gender-specific block play, differences in gross and fine motor activity are natural. The male brain, driven in part by active spatial centers and a more active cerebellum (the "doing" center of the brain just above the brain stem), is formed with more testosterone at its baseline, and so would naturally tend toward more gross motor activity. Even at 30 or 50 or 70, males will (if health allows) tend to fidget more than females, stand up and move more, sit still less (unless their visual-graphic brains in the right hemisphere are substantially occupied by TV or some similar visual entertainment). But even when watching TV, you will notice males fidgeting on the couch, throwing arms in the air, etc. more than females. The brain differences are robust throughout life.

Knowing this cognitive difference, we can enhance female development of spatial intelligence by prodding them into more gross motor play as early as possible. By getting them to move around more, we help them become an object moving through space, which can stimulate more of their spatial intelligence development, and it is healthy for their bodies too!

With my own daughters, I became the "gross motor" parent in Gail's and my bi-strategic constellation, which is often typical of spatial-play fathers. I threw my children up and down, ran after them, made them run after me, played soccer with them, played football with them, rode bikes, and generally focused on development of spatial-kinesthetic intelligence. Now in their twenties, both Gabrielle and Davita are adept and unintimidated by spatial tasks (both are accomplished rock climbers). Davita works at a climbing gym and is now contemplating a graduate degree in physical therapy. The science worked with these girls.

Can our daughters survive and thrive as women without developing gross motor skills as little girls? Of course, they can. But will they end up successful in STEM fields if we don't focus on gross motors in the birth-to-5 age group? I don't believe so. While there will always be an exception to this statement (a girl whose brain is so genetically wired for spatial intelligence that she will become a mechanical engineer no matter what), we would do our girls a disservice if we believed a passive life will lead to the STEM gains we want for them.

Techniques for K – 12 STEM Learning

In making sure our little girls get a lot of uninterrupted spatial play and gross motor activity, we are affecting the birth-to-five pipeline of brain development, especially in connections that can get made in the right hemisphere and between the parietal lobe and memory, action, math, and critical thinking centers of the brain. We are likely also helping a little girl's brain construct and connect synapses in specific gray matter areas that may be used later for math and science acquisition (STEM/STEAM).

The reference to "gray matter areas" is crucial to future performance in actions and systems related to science, technology, engineering, art, and mathematics. These five areas occur in both white matter and gray matter in the brain, with specific emphasis on specialization in gray matter areas. This means that when a brain is doing physics, as was Alicia's in her physics class and Einstein throughout his career, it processes much of those tasks in a certain gray matter area. As I noted earlier, when Einstein's brain was cut open after his death, researchers found a thicket of cells in gray matter areas in the left inferior parietal area. It was clear that Einstein's math/science and spatial genius was somewhat localized there, in that part of the brain.

This did not mean that Einstein used no white matter activity to spread his thinking throughout his brain, but it did give all of us a clue to what is happening in brains that are working on math, physics, and science problems and innovations. To become effective in these fields, a brain needs to develop the gray matter areas that pertain to that specific brain functioning. Male brains, as we noted, already use up to 7 times more gray matter (localized) brain activity than do female brains; female brains use up to 10 times more white matter (diffused) brain activity.

In the biological sciences (biological research, nursing, medical school), where women are now as active or more active than men, a somewhat more equal combination of gray and white matter activity works well. However, in areas like mechanical engineering and coding, more localized gray matter activity is most likely needed. Since the male brain starts out using more gray matter activity, it has a leg up in areas that specifically require thick-building of cells in a localized brain area, generally one that involves abstract-concrete visual-spatial activity (physics, engineering) and/or quantitative reasoning (advanced mathematics).

If we have decided as a family, school, or corporate funder of programming that we want to enhance female STEM performance in workplaces during adulthood, a primary brain-based goal in K – 12, both in school and at home, should be enhancement of gray matter development, especially in the thickets (localized areas) that ground technology, engineering, and mathematics. Here are gray matter and spatial enhancers you can use in your homes and schools:

1. *Set a reasonable goal and protect the acquisition of that goal.* Teach your child to set the goal on paper, in her computer, or her smartphone. Have her write it down. Daniel Amen, in *Memory Rescue*, suggests having your daughter share her intention with a supportive friend or parent, and sending a regular progress report to that person. This is great advice for our daughters who can, through both the setting and sharing of the goal, use their social-emotional bonds with their friends as brain enhancers for focusing their brains on certain tasks.

2. *Have her use verbal skills (reading, writing, speaking) to connect specific areas of the brain to the task.* Because the female brain already devotes so much of its structure and activity to words, we can use this to our advantage. Use small groups (or parental one-on-one) to have your daughter talk about the task, write the task or numerical sequence down on paper (or type it into a computer), and/or take written notes in margins of books. As the word centers in the brain activate, they can stimulate other white matter activity, which can stimulate the gray matter areas needed for the STEM task.

3. *Have her draw the task on a whiteboard or storyboard.* The more space your girls use, the greater the likelihood of stimulating spatial centers in their brains—these are some of the centers that will help the math or science task to be fully realized. The more visual you help your girls to be, the more likely they will stimulate and build gray matter areas for the A (art) part of STEAM, which can help build gray matter activity for each of the other areas, S, T, E, and M.

4. *Along the same lines, use visual cues and drawing/graphics to punctuate mathematics work.* As much as a math sequence allows for drawn characters (even stick figures), suggest that your daughter draw and doodle pictures around the task

and sequence. If this drawing or graphic activity becomes distracting, then it is counterproductive. But in general, visual cues on computers, small cards, or pieces of paper can help stimulate visuospatial brain activity.

5. *Let her use squeeze balls in her non-writing hand and, as needed, let her toss balls in the air while she is working on a study task.* These spatial-kinesthetic activities can stimulate spatial centers of the brain, especially gray matter areas on the right side, areas we want that female brain to stimulate for math/science tasking. Gradually, over a period of years, the spatial tasks may even build more blood flow and cell development there.

6. *Have her constantly building things.* Help her experiment kinesthetically (by touching and physically creating objects) with a specific focus on building-mechanics (by building things with Legos or other physical objects). Give her a chemistry set and have her play with that for an hour a day. This kind of work activates the spatial and mechanical centers of the brain, which should make math/science learning more complete throughout the lifespan.

7. *Help her create a visual/verbal map for each of her difficult STEM tasks.* Most math problems involve sequencing (step 1, step 2, etc.) and science tasks are grounded in formulae. Math/science is, thus, a highly organized sequencing task-set that requires focus on each step in the sequence. Mapping out some of the sequence ahead of time can help the female brain feel less intimidated by the sequence. Words can be used in the mapping, e.g. "After I do _____, I need to remember to do _____."

8. *Help her learn the importance of failure in invention and STEM learning.* Math/science are failure-laden task sets. Perfectionism is okay as a part of the skill set of the learner near the *end* of the sequence, but not in the initial stages. To help girls realize this, ask them to study inventors' lives. As they do, they'll discover that these people kept doing something over and over again by taking risks, failing a lot, but persevering through the failures because each failure was "perfect" as a learning opportunity.

9. *Help her cut out distractions, especially phones and screens.* While doing the math/science task, help her to turn her

phone off so she avoids using words/images for anything other than the math or science task in front of her. Cutting out the distractions helps allow the "math" or "science" brain to flourish for two reasons: it cuts out use of words for other things, and it coerces the brain into working as much as possible in the gray matter areas needed to do best in the math/science task.

10. *Make STEM learning communal and, thus, fun.* Girls are communal people so it can be crucial that girls work with others to solve problems. I worked recently with a girls' school (grades 7 – 12). One of the reasons they asked me to consult for them was to improve STEM learning for the girls. I asked them to create a mentoring program in which older girls "big sistered" younger girls. Once the new mentoring program went into place, younger girls' STEM learning was enhanced by older girls' one-on-one teaching, and along the way, all the girls received social-emotional learning, bonding, and maturation.

We CAN Change the STEM Script for Girls

As I mentioned a moment ago, the S (science) part of STEM is trending female now with women comprising a majority of higher education students in medical and biology-related fields. However, issues in the technology, engineering, and math fields have been somewhat intransigent. While many colleges and universities are increasing the number of first-year students in college STEM-related classes, a new *Wall Street Journal* report quoted federal data, noting that only 20% of graduates in computer science and engineering are female. As you think about the analysis I've provided in this chapter, I hope you'll explore it with others, and look carefully at some educational and pedagogical issues that must, I believe, change if we are to see TEM improvement. We must do more in pre-K through 12th grade for TEM skill and interest building if we are to see more women in the fields in their twenties.

In our Gurian Institute school-based trainings, we provide analysis and tactics related to spatial learning, female/male brain difference, and STEM classwork. Once teachers receive training in the female brain, they tend to change things around as their own very insightful intuition links new innovations to science. As they shift their teaching methods, they often innovate in the following ways:

1. They no longer emphasize disappointment when girls (or boys) don't understand something abstract and only demonstrated once. Instead, they ask the girls something like, "Are you saying that my example was too abstract?" Upon hearing (or sensing) a "yes," they provide kinesthetic and concrete ways of building examples that fit the sensorial and experiential world surrounding the girl's life. This can become something like: "Talk in your group about what examples would work best for you. Give those examples. Look in your own daily life for a way to do that kind of numerical calculation." The group discusses this and comes up with concrete examples.

2. They make sure the girl repeats back to them the example, explanation, and concept until the teacher is sure the girl has understood it while also preparing multiple examples for all the minds in the classroom (some minds will immediately intuit the first example, while others will need a couple more examples to reach parity of comprehension).

3. They call on each girl in class to solve problems as much as possible, rather than allowing a few dominant math-science smart kids to receive most of the class attention.

4. They provide each student, as needed, with a math-smart mentor (like the older brother Alicia had, or the vertical mentoring program at the girls' school) who can work one-on-one with the girl in a brain-friendly way.

5. They lobby in the school and home life for diminishment of excessive multi-tasking, like extra homework. Higher levels of math and science are both equation and project-driven, requiring a lot of intricate and independent gray matter focus and less social multi-tasking. The more our girls' brains do long-term problem-solving projects and the less they do multi-tasking "busy work" in their various classes, the more their brains may be tuned toward larger projects in math and science.

This will mean asking teachers throughout the building to cut out most or all homework that is unnecessary for higher level learning. It also means teaching girls to quiet their multi-tasking social brains in pursuit of gray matter development in spatial and math-oriented centers.

New Testing for Spatial Intelligence Development

Meanwhile, if we are serious about closing the STEM gap, we will need to lobby the NEA and other educational organizations, including evaluators and testing organizations, *to test for spatial intelligence early on.* Though spatial intelligence is crucial to a child's future, we test for reading but not for spatial intelligence. We must change this. We must gather spatial data from birth to five and through elementary school, then let this data help us create new curricula that work with girls.

Using Choice Theory to Measure Female Success

I spoke recently at a tech company. An executive came up to me after my keynote and asked to speak privately. We moved to a private area where we could have coffee together and she said, "I can't say this in public, of course, so I didn't ask this question at the training. But here goes . . . What if, given the brain differences, we can never get 50/50 female/male in mechanical engineering and high tech? What if, given the differences in testosterone and aggression, we can never get 50/50 female/male in the C-Suite or upper leadership?"

"That is a minefield!" I joked, then agreed with her, saying what I mentioned earlier in this book. "If the brain science is accurate, and I believe it is, we will likely never get 50/50 in those areas, just like I don't believe we will ever get 50% male kindergarten or elementary teachers. And I don't think we will have 50% stay-at-home dads."

Nodding, she asked, "Okay, so . . . are we sure that's a bad thing? I mean, I have both sons and daughters and I want the best for my daughters, of course. But is all our push for 50/50 a little bit misguided? Aren't there casualties as a result—boys who don't get the help they need because we tell ourselves they have everything? Or girls who get forced into things they really don't want to do?"

Then she told me her own personal story.

"I'm not unhappy with where I am, but as a mom and a woman, I have to say, I don't want my daughters to feel the pressure I felt. When I was coming up in engineering, I was not going to be held back by any guy! I competed tooth and nail. I became one of those female bosses some guys, and some women too, called 'bitches,' but I didn't care. I'm proud to be who I am.

"But I didn't see options for myself back then. This was the life I chose, and I had gifts in what you call 'the spatial brain' and I pursued them. Also, I've always been competitive and aggressive. I think I'm what you call a 'bridge brain female', so it was okay for me to think, 'This is it, right here. This is what I must do.'

"Now though, I see things a little differently. One of my daughters might go into engineering, but she's not as competitive as I am. My other daughter's brain is much more like her dad's . . . he's a journalist . . . more verbal, more intellectual, not very spatial. She hated math, for instance, even with me helping her and trying to make sure she got the best tutors.

"The point is, I don't think either of my daughters really wants to live the life I'm living, and until today, I've thought that was a shame, a bad thing, a failure on my part. But in your keynote today, when you showed us the brain scans, I felt a wave of relief. I thought, 'What's wrong with my daughters being who *they* are?' So that's the context for what I'm saying. If we let go of the 50/50 idea, we see things differently."

This executive was anecdotally pointing toward "choice theory" as she assessed her daughters' lives. In Chapter 9, I will pursue this theory with you more deeply. While I am clearly vigilant about trying to help an educational system look at the female/male brain so that it can finally push through to maximum STEM success for girls in the future, I also believe we must set goals for STEM that are what girls and women really want. Nature, nurture, and culture are multi-causal in gender issues. When Harvard fired Larry Summers, it linked one of our country's leading universities with the very myopic culture-focused approach to girls and STEM. This link means that the nature part of the gender gap is woefully understudied. In fact, most researchers run scared from it. This helps no one, least of all girls and women.

Chapter 8

Protecting and Nurturing the Digital Girl:
Screen Time, Technology, and Social Media

> "Technology in girls' lives is both wonderful and troubling. The wonderful part is, girls' love their Pads, computers, and phones and these kids are brilliant at using them. But the troubling part is that same love. It takes over their lives. We have to take control of it very quickly because it can attack a girls' mental and physical health. This area of 'digital health' is one of the most important health areas of the new century."
> —Katey McPherson, Executive Director, the Gurian Institute.

I MET KATEY, 44, IN DENVER in 2013 when she was an assistant principal in a middle school in Phoenix, Arizona. She had come to our Gurian Summer Institute to become certified as a trainer. As we talked together, I learned that she had four daughters.

Having two daughters of my own, I grinned, "You must be very busy!"

Her smile back to me said, "You don't know the half of it."

Over the next four years, Katey became a powerful ally in our Institute's work and became Executive Director in 2016.

A dynamo of energy at five feet tall, she carries her wisdom with her wherever she goes. She has a winning smile, but behind the smile is acumen and intuition borne of two decades in the schools, more than a decade raising her daughters, and nearly a lifetime of digital avocation. She has studied digital technology, health, and citizenship, and co-authored the book, *Why Teens Fail*.

"This is about survival for me," she told me as we got to know one another. "I had to study this stuff to make sure I could work with students and raise my girls right."

Katey appears often on television as an expert on apps, predator websites, and school-digital interfaces among students and parents. She has helped me to focus this chapter, and I want to thank her in advance for sharing her knowledge of the digital world. In this chapter, I will take the position that while digital life is and can be a wonderful thing, especially as it helps girls master the world of technology (the world of the future), the natural girl can be somewhat erased by the digital girl if we aren't careful, and thus, technology can be a neurotoxin.

Try This

Set Healthy Digital Habits Right Away

The American Association of Pediatrics is a good resource for understanding best practices in technology use for children *in general*. Because our children spend an average of seven hours a day on entertainment media like televisions, computers, tablets, and phones, family members (first, second, and third) must become citizen scientists regarding a child's media time. As you may already know, screen time can turn into attention problems and other cognitive and academic issues; depression, anxiety, even suicide; problems with sleep and eating; obesity and physiological health issues. Because most devices now allow access to the Internet, moral and character development of our children are at stake.

In general, we need to:
- Limit screen time as developmentally appropriate— little or no screen time for children 18 months and under, and limited screen time on school nights after that (more on these limits in a moment).
- If our kids use screens a great deal in school already, have them spend most of their home screen time with educational media, not entertainment.
- Focus childhood on non-electronic formats (books, novels, nonfiction biographies and memoirs, newspapers, magazines, board games, chess, checkers, card games).

- When children (especially younger ones) watch media, we ought to deploy a family member (from any of the three families) to watch with the child as much as possible.
- Teach media literacy from the earliest ages so that children understand the connections between what they see and real life.
- Until the child is relatively mature, disallow screens in bedrooms (no televisions, computers, tablets, or video games in the bedroom).
- If older children use smart phones and other media in bedrooms, they should be moved to the living room by one hour before sleep time for overnight recharging.
- No TVs on during dinner time and no cellphones either!
- No more than one or two hours per day for entertainment media (TV, video games, etc.) except, perhaps, on a weekend day.
- Never sacrifice one-on-one mentoring for screen time. For example, every adult in a child's life can potentially teach the child a hobby. The hobby is preferable to screen time.
- Rarely sacrifice outside play time for media time. Outside play is more important.
- Rarely sacrifice reading time for media time. Reading is much more important for brain development than screen time, especially for the youngest brains.
- Rarely sacrifice imaginative free play with physical toys for media and screen time. Kinesthetic play is more valuable for brain development than screen play.
- Rarely sacrifice time in relational play and conversation with other human beings or care of animals (such as pets) for screen time.

Ensuring Your Daughter's Digital Health

Digital health is the interface of your daughter's natural template for brain and physical development with her habits of screen and digital technology use. Digital health will not feel exactly the same to one sister as another because use of technology does not have exactly the same effect on every child, but if you ensure digital health in seven stages—the stages of major brain development episodes—you can develop a plan of best practices for the digital health of each of your daughters.

Seeing Digital Health in Seven Stages

The female brain matures in seven developmental stages. In these stages, individual gene expression occurs in diverse environments including technological. While characteristics in each of the stages might exist simultaneously, each set of essential characteristics *peak* at different times, so they constitute a neuro-physiologically sequenced journey to mature adulthood. Because no two girls are exactly alike, this schedule of stages must be adjusted by you for best use.

The stages are listed here with bottom-line suggestions that I will explore further in a moment:

> **Stage 1: Pre-birth to 2 years old**. Little or no screen time. If screens are used, just use them for skyping with grandparents or, perhaps, a short TV program (not a movie). Shows in the vein of *Sesame Street* are sometimes used with this age group, but watch out—the images can often move too quickly for digital health in the 1-year-old's brain.
>
> **Stage 2: 3 – 5**. A bit of educational programming can work for this age group, but no use of phones yet. A short, animated movie can be okay, as long as the images don't move very quickly. No violence is recommended.
>
> **Stage 3: 6 – 9**. Increased use of educational programming, on-screen games, and animated movies. If live action films are used, content should be monitored, especially for sex and violence. No phones should be given to kids yet.
>
> **Stage 4: 10 – 13**. Still no phones until around 13 or 14 (reasons why to follow in a moment). If the school is using tablets and computers for a lot of lessons/classes and sending

kids online for homework, additional screen time should be kept to a minimum. Watch out for long drives in the car with screens on—audio (radio/music) and conversation are generally better, especially for a brain that already gets too much screen time.

Stage 5: 14 – 17. Cell phones are okay now, but privacy settings are for parents to set. Trust the child, but be vigilant. Keep screen time to four hours a day if possible. Everything else that is healthy should come before home screen time, e.g. chores, relationships, nature time.

Stage 6: 18 – 21 and Stage 7: 22 – 25 and beyond. By the time your daughter is 18, you will have very little control over screen time, but your mentoring is still essential, including presentation to your daughter of new research as it comes out. If you think your daughter is screen-addicted, it is generally essential that you help her get help before she fully enters adulthood.

Courageous Conversation

When Should We Give Her a Smartphone?

After a lecture, a mom, Andrea, said, "Danielle is always looking at her phone. How do I get her to stop?"

"How old is she?" I asked.

"Eleven," Andrea responded quickly, and my answer came just as fast.

"Take the phone away from her. Don't give it back until she is 13 or 14."

Andrea's face showed both surprise and suspicion—surprise that my response was so immediate, and suspicion that I didn't understand her plight. "I don't think I can do that," she said.

"Why not?" I asked. "It's your phone, right, not your daughter's?"

"It is," she agreed. "It is, yes, but . . ." she paused, thinking about it, almost physically fidgeting her body to try to wear the idea around. "Well, it is," she repeated, feeling better about it.

"It is."

"It is," I encouraged. "Her attention to it is actually harming her brain development. There is no solution except to take it away until her brain is ready for it."

When Andrea walked away, I believe she felt resolved to take the phone away, but I don't know. For tweens, once the phone is given, it is tumultuous to take it away. Yet I have heard other parents say, "I took it away and thought life would become terrible but, you know, after a few days my daughter ended up thanking me. She said, 'Mom, I have a life now. I'm not addicted to that phone.'"

This is the outcome we hope for.

The Trinity of Digital Health

When you are trying to decide what is best regarding digital childhood and healthy screen use, there is a trinity of health categories to study: *cognitive, physical,* and *social-emotional.* If your own daughter is having difficulty in any of these three areas (falling behind in school work/grades, becoming obese or not getting enough exercise, relational difficulties with adults and/or peers), the cell phone and screens might be a culprit. She may be spending so much time on the phone and other screen-media and thus becoming:

- too sedentary (a recent study showed that 19-year-old girls today are sitting as much as people in their 60s);
- distracted from academic performance and cognitive development; and/or
- engaging in too much immature relational activity to remain socially healthy.

As Katey and I recently discussed this trinity, she said, "Regarding the third health concern, sometimes moms and dads I work with honestly don't know how much "relational health" fits with their kids' devices. So many moms just this week at a training asked me, 'If I don't give her SnapChat to her, is she missing out on something relationally important? Even worse, will she be so out of sync with peers she'll get socially harassed?' In the group I was working with, some moms were in tears with worry about this.

"We ended up talking about 'end goals?' I asked them, 'What is your end-goal in giving devices and Internet access to your daughter, or your son?' As we talked, it was clear that everyone's end goal was good health, and after we discussed the question about SnapChat at length, the group of moms did realize that fear of a girl being out of sync is not enough relational ammunition for giving devices to kids before their brains are ready. A friend of mine posted this mom-friendly blog for families that have already allowed a lot of devices. (http://amycarney.com/blog/7-things-your-daughter-should-not-post-on-instagram/). Amy Carney is a wonderful citizen scientist of this kind of thing.

"The bottom line, I believe, is this: relational health is rarely compromised by good decisions that parents make on behalf of kids. Knowing what decisions to make at the various stages of a child's life is a great boon to the process of doing what is best for our family."

Stage 1 – 2: Birth through Five

As much as possible, we must keep young children away from overuse of screens. Little or no screen time is appropriate for children under 18 months, and for toddlers and pre-K children, an hour a day is plenty. The brain is growing in this age group through kinesthetic and sensorial input and activity. When screens get involved, some of this brain growth does not occur.

In the last few years, parents are increasingly handing their toddlers their phones as distraction devices in airports or during road trips, in the grocery store or while the parent is working. When we do this, we may not realize child-gaze on the smart phone can endanger natural neural processing. In that airport, it would be far better to interact with and interpret the environment around the child, lift her up and down, toss a ball to her, or just walk and talk. Bill and Melinda Gates did not give their children cell phones until they were 14 years old. This family modeling is powerful and very useful.

Between Stages 1 and 2, it is especially crucial to be vigilant about how much any child care provider is setting kids in front of screens, and it is essential to avoid the popular idea that if you start a girl using a screen device early in life, she will somehow gain an advantage later. There is no scientific proof for this, nor does it fit with findings in brain science. The brain early in life doesn't need *any* screen to grow up capable of later cognitive tasks. Our human brain development evolved for more than a million years in nature, with all five senses activated in environmental contact. Even if there's something active happening on-screen, such as a visually acted story, the screen itself is passive in comparison to kinesthetic activity, so it is generally less adequate for brain development than natural life is. In Stages 1 and 2 especially, from birth to around five years old, the less screens the better.

Better than screens is putting some music on and letting a girl dance. Build a fence in the backyard or find a park and just let her toddle around, fall, cry, get comfort from you, get up, and fall all over again. Her brain learns naturally from these activities, as it does when seeing a cat and chasing it, laughing at the cackling of a squirrel, cuddling with Mom or Dad, getting thrown up in the air by Dad or Mom, being read to by Grandma or Grandpa, and then rushing into the kitchen because the smell of cinnamon suddenly puts the brain into a joyful trance of sensorial excitement.

Recently I brought up all these protections and activities at a conference lecture and some concerned parents came up to me afterwards. A mom said, "If we don't start our girls on these screen technologies early in life, they won't function well enough in the world of technology later—they'll be behind other kids. I read an article about how coding can help with sequencing which can help brain development. What you said tonight doesn't fit with the science."

Sequencing is indeed an essential cognitive function that girls may need help with, but they can learn sequencing through hundreds of other cognitive tasks. They don't need a phone or an iPad for it at 4 years old.

"Study your daughters carefully," I replied. "Ask yourselves, 'Is learning sequencing skills with an electronic technology so important that I'd risk difficulties with my daughter's maturation in other areas?' It was a question Gail and I asked ourselves constantly as parents," I admitted. "It is a never-ending question, a constant weighing of options."

"But I won't fit in," our daughters told Gail and me more than once as we curtailed their screen time. "I won't 'belong' if I don't know all the shows and don't have a cell phone like my friends do!"

Evil parents, we said, "Children can get along just fine without screens all the time. We never had cell phones, so you don't need one until 13."

Our kids grumbled, but now that they are grown and contemplating having families, they have thanked us for protecting their digital health.

Stage 3: 6 – 9 years old

As your daughter grows into and through the kindergarten years, she will tend toward more screens. By elementary school, she will likely watch movies and TV, get on your computer or iPad, look at your phone, and perhaps use screens for some classwork in school. Because screen time can be toxic to her brain, it must be limited. Especially if she is using laptops or tablets in school, it is important to make sure most screen time at home is educational rather than entertainment. Educational programming is the least passive and most cognitively stimulating, while entertainment programming is the most passive and least helpful to brain development.

In terms of hours, four hours of screen time a day for a 7-year-old is generally too much—probability of maturation errors in cognitive, physical, or social-emotional health rise in this circumstance. Most likely, two hours will have little negative impact on health. As with all of this information in all the stages of maturation, you must tailor these generalities to fit your child.

An argument against this kind of vigilance is, "By nine, my daughter is a tween living in communities or families that are very screen-focused. Mom and Dad have screens with them all the time, older siblings might be playing video games every night, and peers at school have cell phones by now. It's impossible to limit screen time the way you suggest."

It is not impossible, but it does require family contracts and strong citizen science. Nine-year-olds are able to discuss science and the human brain. As tech companies donate laptops or tablets to elementary school children (and in some cases, kindergartners), the daily use of screens is growing in hours. As all or most learning moves to screens, the child will do even less real-world functioning, which is potentially dangerous to cognitive, physical, or social-emotional development. Thus, the vigilance at home may need to be taken up a notch. Danger lies in four hours of screens at school, then another two at home.

But is it dangerous for every child? Every girl? Probably not. So how can a parent know for whom it could be dangerous? As with many potential neurotoxins, genetic testing might help resolve this question, but there is not (as far as I know) any way presently to test for screen-time danger.

However, there is a back-door test you can use—testing for obesity genes, which can correlate directly with screen-time issues in growing children. As we noted earlier, you can test for the three obesity genes: DRD2 (an eating behavior gene), MC4R (an appetite gene), and FTO (a body fat gene). You can contact your physician or other professional to ask if they are able to order genetic tests like those we've referred to in earlier chapters that will help you understand your daughter's genome.

If you discover that your daughter has the genetic template for higher body fat and weight gain, you will have a scientific—though non-direct—way of making your case for highly limited screen time and, in contrast, at least 2 – 3 hours of physical activity per day, including walking, sports, and chores. This "back-door" genetic test for unhealthy screen time is one with which you can currently use to prove that screen time will be potentially neurotoxic for *your* child. Within the next decade, I hope, geneticists will be able to discover other "front door" genetic tests so that every family can determine the pluses and minuses of screen time for their individual child.

Did You Know?

One School Allows No Screens

If you become one of those "vigilant" parents who is looking for every possible angle by which to protect your child, you can get help from innovators who are walking the path with you. In Los Altos, California, in the tech-dominated Silicon Valley, a Waldorf School uses no electronic technologies for learning. Pens, paper, knitting needles, animal parts, dirt, and other tools and elements of nature fill its classrooms—no screens. Parents of the kids in this school work at eBay, Google, Apple, Yahoo, and Hewlett-Packard. In an article in *The New York Times*, Alan Eagle, 50, who works for Google, explained why he sends his children to this "no screen time" school.

"Technology has its time and place," he says. "If I worked at Miramax and made good, artsy, rated R movies, I wouldn't want my kids to see them until they were 17. Remember: at

Google and all these places, we make technology as brain-dead easy to use as possible. There's no reason why kids can't figure it out when they get older."

One of the teachers at the school, Cathy Waheed, a former computer engineer, teaches fractions "by having the children cut up food — apples, quesadillas, cake — into quarters, halves and sixteenths. 'For three weeks, we ate our way through fractions. When I made enough fractional pieces of cake to feed everyone, do you think I had their attention?'"

She did.

And without any screens.

Stage 4: 11 – 14 years old

By eleven years old, your daughter is likely in pre-puberty or puberty, with new hormone flow even if she does not yet menstruate. Beyond hormone flow and huge leaps in synapses and structural expansion, each brain is developing its own unique neural footprint for dopamine release. Dopamine is our brain's reward chemical. The centers of the brain that handle it, such as the *nucleus accumbens* and *caudate nucleus,* are now in a massive process of transformation.

This process needs our assistance in order to build neural pathways upward to the cerebral cortex in ways that will be most socially functional in the long-term. This early adolescent needs the dopamine rush to happen from real life, not mainly through screens because the screens don't fit as well with natural reward chemistry and gene expression. You will be able to study your child's digital health by looking again at cognitive, physical, and social-emotional markers. Is she doing well in school, growing physically without obesity or other disorders, and making "real life" friends and connections in the family system?

One of the miracles of the Stage 4 brain is its "pruning" activity. Pruning is the human brain's way of getting rid of cells that are not being used, to make room for the greater influx of cells and brain activity that adolescence anticipates and needs for full maturation. For instance, if your daughter is taking music, karate, or voice lessons, her brain will likely retain the cells used for those activities. If she stops, her brain will get rid of a lot of the cells associated with these tasks.

Similarly, if she spends a lot of time in front of screens and curtails time in real-life situations, her brain will retain the "virtual activity" cells and lose the real-life cells—to the potential detriment of her maturation.

In all this, sex and gender are important because the male and female brain develop their hormonology, cellular activity, dopamine flow, and pruning tempo somewhat differently, including a quicker tempo of maturation for girls than boys, and for the female brain than the male.

Girls' speedier maturation occurs in these areas:

1. Speedier myelination of cells that coat the brain, thus, speedier development of more white matter activity in the female brain, making neural pathway development between the limbic emotional centers and frontal lobe thinking centers a faster-growing natural process in the brains of the natural girl than the natural boy.
2. More rapid and earlier pruning of unneeded and higher-risk brain cells and brain activity. The female brain starts its pruning back in Stage 3, and it peaks in Stage 4. The male brain may not begin its heavy pruning until Stage 4, and it may not peak until Stage 5.
3. Quicker development and completion of brain centers used for emotive processing, such as the *anterior cingulate cortex* which, as we mentioned earlier, is involved in rumination. Complex social-emotional skills develop more quickly in the female brain than in the male and are naturally designed to do so, giving the female brain a head start, which makes our attention to her screen time in early adolescence so very important.
4. Quicker development by 2 to 4 years of connectivity between various limbic areas and the pre-frontal cortex. The natural boy and natural girl are not on the same page in maturation of executive decision-making. Female brains move quicker to get some of their decision-making centers of the brain activated.
5. Girls also utilize a great deal of white matter multi-tasking and oxytocin-based bonding, making it important to help them focus on specific areas of growth and protect themselves in relationships. If at 12, a girl has unfettered access to the Internet, she may seem to be maturing quite well, but in fact may make very confused and dangerous executive decisions, bonding with predators or engaging in constant drama online.

Given how quickly the female brain matures during Stage 4, and knowing what is at stake, it is crucial to deepen your assessment of your daughter's use of screens through the lens of the trinity we discussed.

- *Physical.* Is she developing physically in the normal range? Is she moving around in the home and other environments at least 2 – 3 hours a day? If you have any doubts at all about what would be a suitable amount of exercise for your daughter, ask your pediatrician for science-based standards that fit *her.* In general, for a ten-year-old girl, more than two hours a day would be ideal. Remember, her ancestors generally walked to school or into fields and other places at least two hours a day, if not more.
- *Cognitive.* Is she developing her critical thinking skills and other cognitive abilities at the normal pace? Can she organize, think, feel, problem-solve, get good grades, and perform well enough on tests. By 9 years old, you may see some talent sets beginning to clarify. She may be great at math or reading or both. If she needs extra help in a certain area, like math, a math program via the Internet might be helpful. This is a way of using technology as an asset, focusing screen time on educational products, then limiting screen time for other entertainment.
- *Social-emotional.* Does she have friends? If she is very shy, does she have a friend or two? Does she interact well with parents and elders? Is she involved in interactive environments like Girl Scouts that help her grow social-emotional pathways in the brain? On the other hand, perhaps she's not spending enough time with Mom, Dad, other "parents," or other kids. If this is the case, she is likely spending too much time in front of screens. Study her for a few weeks. Talk in your family about her social-emotional development. If needed, cut back her screen time.

Overall, an early adolescent might gain more from chess or board games as a good substitute for part of the screen time. Board games with family members are also, generally, better for the brain. Sales of these "hobby games" have gone up in the last few years as families seek alternatives to excessive screen time and digital life. Research in the neuroscience of chess has shown benefits in potential increase in IQ and math skills, attention span and memory, ability to concentrate, verbal skills development, strategic and critical thinking, development of patience, work ethic, and sportsmanship. Meanwhile, there is no neuroscience research to show that these benefits will come from spending excessive time in front of screens.

Is a Kindle Considered a "Screen?"

People often wonder how e-readers fit into a girl's developmental map.

"My daughter loves to read and likes the Kindle better than holding a book," a dad recently told me. "I don't want to get in the way of her love of reading, but is the e-reader considered 'screen time?' If so, is it dangerous? Claire spends three or four hours a day on the weekends looking into that Kindle."

If a child is spending two hours with an e-reader and an additional four hours in front of other screens, then the whole "screen time" as an aggregate must be dealt with. But outside of that kind of excessive screen use, the e-reader is one of the least dangerous screens for the brain because it's merely a glass lens through which to see the original book.

However, if the e-reader is used at bedtime, it can become detrimental. The blue light in the e-reader, tablet, or computer tricks the melatonin in a child's (and adult's) brain to think it's time to wake up. You want just the opposite near bedtime. You want the melatonin to put the girl to sleep because her maturation and health depend greatly on getting the right amount of sleep.

Remember, just because the Kindle leaves the bedroom an hour before bed, books do not have to go. A real book can get read, or other projects completed with pen and paper.

And like all issues of digital health, while keeping screens away from a child's bedtime is good for all kids, for girls with anxiety or depression issues, it can be a life-saver. Her brain may especially need more real-world functioning and interaction.

Stage 5: 14 – 17 years old

All the developmental steps your daughter's brain, hormones, and socio-biology are going through in Stage 4 continue into Stage 5. Stage 5 also involves an almost climactic increase in American children's screen time. As of 2016, the typical American consumed 43 gigabytes of data per day which is an increase of 350 percent in the last three decades. For adolescents without digital tethers, information can become mostly visual via computers, tablets, television, YouTube, movies, videogames, and visual stimuli on websites.

This is both good and bad for a dopamine-obsessed adolescent brain. What stimulates reward will feel beloved; what is harder to do, may go by the wayside. The more time a Stage 5 brain stares into a screen, the more likely that brain will become screen addicted. As the brain prunes, explodes dopamine centers, and builds pathways between emotional impulse and critical thinking centers, it needs help from us in all the areas we have already discussed—assessment of the trinity, and scaling back screen time to an hour or two a day at home if nearly every hour at school is spent in front of a screen.

The Natural Girl vs the Digital Girl: Be Aware of the Maturity Gap in the iGeneration

What is at stake is maturity itself because the digital girl tends to be less mature than the natural girl. Nature matures children because it is a world of life and death. Spending an afternoon with a dying grandmother will naturally mature a Stage 4 or 5 girl. That same afternoon spent online is less maturing because it generally will not challenge her to realize that she must make ultimate decisions about how to live.

These decisions, and the work ethic and relational maturity that come from them, has been called "adulting" by millennials and Gen X/Y/Z. Jean M. Twenge, a psychologist at San Diego State University, has studied this phenomenon, publishing in 2017, *iGen: Why Today's Super-Connected Kids are Growing up Less Rebellious, More Tolerant, Less Happy—and Completely Unprepared for Adulthood,* a book that I highly recommend.

The iGeneration, Twenge found, are behind previous generations in reading, writing, critical thinking, understanding of government/current affairs, academic skills, and many other markers of maturity during adolescence. She concludes, "The iGenerations sit at the forefront of the worst mental health crisis in decades, with rates of teen depression and suicide skyrocketing since 2011."

The gift that digital life was supposed to bring our adolescents—more happiness—it has not brought at all. About today's adolescents, Twenge notes that "the more time they spend online, the worse they feel."

Excessive screen time and use of technology is invading brain development as a potential neurotoxin for any child, especially our adolescents. It confuses the adolescent brain's dopamine-release system. As many of the iGeneration avoid adulting for as long as possible—well into their twenties—they are grappling with what began in early- to mid-adolescence as digital life overwhelmed natural life. They try in their twenties to accommodate their own brain development anomalies, hoping they can slow down independence-seeking, marriage, child-bearing, and thus help their brains catch up to maturity at some point. But unaware of the loss of natural life to digital life, they and their parents often think their depression and anxiety—their fear of life itself—grows from something relational, some inadequacy in the family. It well might, especially if there has been trauma or addictive disease to grapple with during childhood, but often a child's life has not been traumatic—that young adult's mental health crisis grows from combinations of environmental neurotoxins we described earlier and digital neurotoxicity.

These young people can get by, mainly subsidized by parents and bolstered by medications, well into their twenties. Sometimes, that subsidy is necessary as jobs these young people might want are not plentiful. Meanwhile, the basic iGen entitlement of Stage 5 adolescence extends far into adulthood, and time expands and contracts not on the rhythms of maturity, but on the rhythms of digital life.

It is in Stage 5, if not before, that we must all come together to stem this tide. If we do not, we will compromise adulthood. Once adulthood is compromised, what we consider mature success will become engulfed in fear-based ideas like "gender microaggressions" (which we will look at in more detail in Chapter 9) and obsessions with celebrities and entertainment rather than good policy and a life of service.

Digital Citizenship

Ultimately, digital life must come second to natural life or we will poison two or three generations of children without even realizing we are doing it. While encouraging our daughters to engage in a healthy digital life, we can also ensure maturity by insisting on *digital citizenship*. Discussions at home and in the community on what a good digital citizen is will have begun earlier in middle school, but now it becomes like health insurance for a middle adolescent.

There are numerous powerful "digital citizenship" curricula offered online, and I have listed some of them for you in the Notes and Resources.

Dealing with Cyberbullying

Hannah and Chloe were constantly at one another's throats in social media. Each of them wrote just enough to get a response, and the other girl couldn't resist writing a new response which brought on another response. And on and on it went into terrible drama, hurt feelings, and gossip thrown out into other Facebook and Instagram accounts, as well as Twitter feeds.

When I met with these 15-year-olds, I learned that Hannah and Chloe thought consciously, "This is a good thing to do. I'm sticking up for myself. I am speaking my truth. I have a voice." They blamed one another for bad behavior, escalation, "inappropriate stuff," and "meanness." It took some time to get them to track their own heightened and constant anxiety—the upload of cortisol (the stress hormone) in their blood and brains. In a heightened and stressed state, they become more and more anxious, and more and more angry. They had a voice and stuck up for themselves, yes. But at the cost of self and soul.

The neuropsychiatrist, Daniel Amen, calls their internal emotive consciousness ANTs (anxious, negative thoughts). Social media is amplifying our brain's capacity for these ANTs—what we called "negativity bias" when we looked at depression and anxiety earlier. Once ANTs take over the brain, Amen says, girls can't disengage from the stimulus, and the brain just keeps creating more ANTs. This vicious cycle often becomes cyberbullying. Often, the victim becomes the bully and the bully the victim, then the roles reverse again. Cyberbullying and victimization have been linked to numerous suicide attempts and completions nationwide.

Disengagement is a key to ending any bullying activity, but especially crucial to dealing with cyberbullying. I worked with Hannah and Chloe on disengagement by showing them that cyber-reactivity extends the time of the bullying activity, which swells up the limbic areas of the brain (*hippocampus, cingulate gyrus, amygdala*) with stressful hormonal and neurochemical activity, even if the slight or argument is minor. We traced together how Hannah could not get out of her head the feeling that her friend, Chloe, had been "condescending." Chloe corrected something Hannah did during a soccer game, but made the correction, Hannah told her mother, "in a condescending way, like I didn't mean anything, like I was stupid." The mother was empathic and figured Chloe and Hannah would patch things up.

But social media sent the families in a different direction. Chloe began to cyberbully Hannah, while accusing Hannah of bullying her. Revealing and inappropriate pictures were sent out to most of the high school. In the end, Hannah had to leave the school because of the tribalism that erupted in the school between these friends and their own crews. Both girls said and did things they regretted and Chloe's family could not prove that Hannah had sent the sexualized photos, but the damage was done.

This is our new reality. This can happen to any girl. It can happen to your daughter. More than one in five girls in the U.S. will experience cyberbullying, according to the Centers for Disease Control and Prevention. Cyberbullying is insidiously dangerous because our children can't escape it—day or night, they may be bullied—and because the bullying that used to be kept within a small group can now expand into the whole school community, or beyond.

Studies at the Girl Scout Research Institute show that girls are especially susceptible to cyberbullying because they spend more time than adolescent boys on certain social media platforms and because they define more of their self-worth than males, on average, on how many people like them.

While each school and community puts in place its own education programs to help stop cyberbullying (there are many good ones available), each of us as parents can help our kids to disengage before the enmities begin. Disengaging will help girls learn to not take things personally (a crucial maturation lesson) and help girls experientially stop themselves from excessive rumination stimulated by social media push-pull and anger-anxiety responses.

Disengagement will likely require bi-strategic and multi-strategic parenting and mentoring—everyone's assets have to be brought to bear. It will also require helping girls to get offline, even if that means giving them a month off their devices. And it will likely require counseling and mental health options, especially if it has gotten to the point of depression, anxiety, or self-cutting. Cyberbullying can lead to suicide attempts. If you have a sense that your daughter is being cyberbullied, I hope you will seek help from the school counseling staff or private professionals right away.

Girls Constantly Expressing Themselves Is Not Necessarily Healthy

Cyberbullying is a form of self-expression. The bully (and, as we noted, the victim) become so expressive as to become verbally and digitally violent. Especially in today's very verbal and expressive society—in which children are told to "have a voice and speak up for yourself no matter what" and our political leaders attack one another without filters or civility—it should come as no surprise that our children are growing up believing that self-expression is the key to personal emotional health.

Having a voice is a good thing in theory, but self-expression is not a panacea. In fact, it can be counter-productive to healthy brain development.

Ohio State University psychologist, Brad Bushman, has been studying the various ways that we "vent and express our feelings," including online in social media. In his lab at OSU he especially wanted to test the common cultural idea that verbally expressing our feelings to another, including online, leads to greater self-esteem and mental health. To test this idea, he created a series of studies and controls that tested whether thinking about feelings (rumination) and then using words for feelings (verbal expression) would: 1) lower the subjects' stress levels, 2) assist them in forming and keeping good bonds and relationships, and 3) help them act more successfully in groups.

The common cultural theory was borne out, to some extent, by Bushman's experiments, published in *Personality and Social Psychology*. But in a majority of cases, Bushman found, "the students in the rumination group were angrier and most aggressive while those in the control group, who did nothing to vent their feelings, were the least angry or aggressive."

The common cultural assumption is, in many cases, including online cyber-relationships, wrong. While it's certainly a good thing to "have your voice" and "stand up for yourself," expressing feelings can also raise stress levels dangerously.

Bushman's studies have been replicated by neuropsychiatrist Daniel Amen who tracks rumination and feeling-expression in brain scans. Amen told me, "The more rumination about feelings in the brain we experience, the more risk of those anxious thoughts, which just continues the stress cycle, potentially increasing emotional distress and the likelihood of anxiety and depression. Women have up to four times more activity in the rumination part of the brain (*the cingulate gyrus*) than men so there is a lot of gender involved in all of this. Without realizing it, women tend to value, sometimes too much, the constant processing and expressing of feelings."

Amen concluded, "No one wants to tell their child not to express herself, but healthy expression is really what we want—not just constant expression."

Social media and online activity for ventilation of feelings is not, from a health standpoint, essential. Fewer males get involved in cyberbullying activities and their negative aftermath, in part, because they don't process and ventilate as much online. Our girls will absolutely gain by curtailing their time online.

Sexuality Online

If not in Stage 4, then certainly in Stage 5, we should assume that our daughters are exploring sexuality in some way online. Perhaps by visiting a porn site alone or with a boyfriend or partner; perhaps by stumbling on sexual content via YouTube; perhaps by pretending to be someone older than themselves in order to get a date online. In myriad ways, social media is set up for early sexual maturation. To help you set strong family values in this area, here are some suggestions:

- Don't overreact to normal visual-sexual curiosity and normal sexual fantasies, masturbation, etc. There is a wonderful book on normal sexuality called *Slippery When Wet* by reproductive physiologist Joanna Ellington. Dr. Ellington has a powerful "mom-friendly" perspective—both as a scientist and a mother—on what is normal for adolescents.
- Keep strict tabs on the websites your daughter visits, both via phone and computer/tablet, if necessary. If possible, keep parental controls on all visual devices (including television, Netflix, Hulu, etc.), but assume that your daughter may find a way around those, so keep checking everything to see where she went if you are at all worried about her visual porn use.
- Learn about apps! Katey advises:

If it is on their device, it should be on yours. You can use mechanisms like Family Share Approval from your carrier to approve app downloads and purchases, as well as give each child their own Apple ID and password so you can monitor their every move. Without these mechanisms, there is no way to truly know what kids are doing online and within apps and messaging services.

Simple apps like OurPact, Circle with Disney, and Screen Time *allow you to monitor and filter content and restrict by the hour which child can access what. Websites like safesmartsocial.com and commonsensemedia. org allow you to keep up with the latest and greatest apps. You can also easily turn off your kids' online access and router to your home remotely—for instance, from your date night at a restaurant.*

Talk weekly with your children about their social media platforms. *Have a "tech talk Tuesday dinner" where everyone shares something brave, kind, crazy, disrespectful, or even sexually risky from their news feeds. This allows you and your family to discuss your family's values and guiding principles. When the use of a platform or technology does not align with your family's guiding principles, changes can be made.*

Remember, underdeveloped brains are double agents. They can pretend to be okay when they are really in distress, so above all else, be vigilant.

- When and if you approach your daughter about apps or websites, avoid shaming her. Try to understand why she went to the site, what she wanted to learn. If consequences are needed, give your daughter at least a second chance. Two chances to change her behavior helps her to self-regulate so she can develop her own boundaries and emotional intelligence on this issue.

- If nothing works, look carefully at the possibility of a sex addiction and get help from professionals immediately. If your daughter seems inordinately attracted to sexual behavior online, you may not have known it, but she may have been sexually abused and your tracking of her apps and online activity can be a gift to you—a clue to a courageous conversation in which you discover and treat the source of her trauma. In these cases, get professional help immediately.

Teaching the Habits of Mindfulness

Fr. Bill Watson of the Sacred Story Institute, in collaboration with high school girls, has created a program, *True Heart*, to help build *mindfulness* in high school students. Even if you aren't Catholic, you might still be fascinated by its regimen. Among many other assets, the program is a way into your child's (and your own) study of scientific research on the importance of mindfulness in adolescent development. The program helps girls get offline for various times per day. Students work instead on mindfulness and prayer, as well as developmental journaling and self-reflection. The program, at its core, is about helping girls mature in healthy ways.

Especially given how stimulated our girls' brains are by digital life today, making sure they are mindful—practicing elements of meditation, prayer, quiet time—can help them be happy in ways technology cannot. Pastor Tim Wright (timwrightministries.org) has a powerful rite of passage program for girls that teaches mindfulness. The practice of yoga or sitting meditation can also help girls to quiet their minds.

Ironically, the middle teen years are the very years when the growing mind yearns for the practice of quietness and mindfulness, but with fewer adolescents spending time in worship in this generation than ever before, essential maturation through practice has diminished. Even if you never go to a place of worship, I hope you will help your daughter be mindful. Especially as she enters Stages 6 and 7 (18 years old and beyond), she will need to know her own soul if she is to both survive and thrive through life's inevitable peaks and valleys.

The Real World

By the time your daughter is 18, you may have very little leverage anymore to help her with technology or maturation. You may no longer be able to ensure that she spends most of her developmental time in the real world. Hopefully, your daughter seems like a young woman to you now—relatively mature, resilient, strong, capable of independence, and able to plan her freedom gradually, and consciously.

In her adulthood, technologies may afford her the real world itself as she uses them to explore and be. Hopefully, by the time your daughter enters Stage 6, she will feel like you do about digital life—that it is useful, but should not overwhelm.

In traveling the country to speak on this topic, I have learned that tens of millions of us feel like we have experienced a "sin" not of commission but omission regarding our children's digital life. We realize we may have "omitted" our authority as parents and adults to control toxins, including technological.

On August 24, 2017, Melinda Gates shared her own anxieties about this omission in a Washington Post article headlined: "Melinda Gates:

I spend my career in technology. I wasn't prepared for its effect on my kids." In the article, she writes, "I spent my career at Microsoft trying to imagine what technology could do, and still I wasn't prepared for smart phones and social media. Like many parents with children my kids' age, I didn't understand how they would transform the way my kids grew up—and the way I wanted to parent. I'm still trying to catch up."

If you have children at home, this article should feel very supportive to you. Gates notes the power of Instagram and Snapchat and admits to worrying over the use of technologies among children. She extolls the virtues of technologies for potentially increasing a child's ability to empathize with others far away, and she admits that many young people today know they are addicted to their devices, and wish they weren't. She points to an article in *The Atlantic*, "Have Smartphones Destroyed a Generation?" and notes the connection between these technologies and the increase of emotional distress in children and adults.

She suggests that parents watch the documentary *Screenagers* with their children and show it in their communities. She recommends parents utilize the resources of Common Sense Media and the American Academy of Pediatrics' "Family Media Plan" to help them control technology in their home. Like Katey, she recommends device-free family time around the dinner table, and courageous conversations about media itself. Like Katey has done with her children, Gates recommends the Netflix series, *13 Reasons Why*, which explores teen suicide (parents should view this first in order to decide whether their children are old enough to view its potentially distressing content).

The Gates family is a premier family from which to take advice on use of technology—and it is inspiring, I think, to see these two parents grappling with the issues of omission and confusion all parents of digital children grapple with. I hope we can all join them in taking our digital authority back. Like Katey and the Gates family, we can celebrate the healthy educational and globalizing influences of digital technologies while remaining vigilant to never supplant real life with digital life. This key principle, if well followed, marks our taking back the decision about who and what to allow into our home. We alone bear the responsibility of deciding who and what will become a member of our family

Chapter 9

Girls of the Future:
Building a New Gender Equity Paradigm and Healing the War with Men

> "In order to come fully to the encounter with whatever gives ultimate meaning, in order to really wrestle with the angel, one must be a free agent, not defined by another, or by cultural imperatives."
> —Marilyn Sewell, *Cries of the Spirit*

IN JUNE OF 2017, the movie *Wonder Woman* came out. In it, Diana is a warrior woman who is also a lover and empath, a strong woman who is also ready to exercise her natural vulnerability, a proud woman who is also humble; a woman whose physical beauty is not overwhelming of mind but a part of it, such that the physical, the emotional, the intellectual, and the spiritual are balanced in her. Diana gains herself and her place in the world through both emotional self-reflection and intense and passionate action, a servant of truths greater than herself. She works well with men, a female leader who does not have to lead by proving men inherently defective (though she clearly knows herself as equally competent with men and, because she is daughter of Gods and Goddesses, more powerful than men). As she battles an evil man and his minions, she does not confuse his evil for manhood or maleness. Rather, she integrates the masculine into the feminine (and vice versa) and partners with males in an intuitive embrace of gender equity.

Until this film came out, I had difficulty finding an action movie that fit the concept of the "whole woman" I believe parents of girls today hope to embolden and support. There were movies like the Lara Croft series in which a woman showed her prowess as a warrior, but to me, she did so either by curtailing her inward emotional life or by making men inferior. When *Wonder Woman* came out, I could talk to girls and boys in both co-ed and single-sex schools about "the whole woman" in ways they would understand and enjoy.

Behind the fun of the movie itself, I hoped children and adults would use the movie to talk about what the future for girls is and will be. Women are becoming increasingly holistic and experiencing a world of many options and much power, yet the battle for gender equity continues. My approach to that battle is generally somewhat different than the popular approach of our time, and *Wonder Woman* helped me explain what I have called "a science-based approach to gender equity."

The assets of, and battle for, that kind of gender equity is the subject of this chapter.

Ensuring Gender Equity

Much of the material in this chapter grows from working in communities to help define what kind of political and personal action the future girl, the future woman, is moving into as she builds a new world. Parenting has become political, especially in America. There is a tacit journey every family of girls makes today, a journey that can, if we study it and utilize its assets, nurture whole women. In that journey, we are all poised—women and men—to re-invent what we mean by *gender equity*. Our daughters, I believe, are desperate for us to do so.

Because so much girls' advocacy is now done through social media, I am not only going to provide you with analysis in this chapter but hope, too, that you will take a moment to go online to see blogs you can share with your friends and colleagues via social media. Both look at gender equity issues from a science-based lens: one is about mansplaining and gender microaggressions, and the other about Google's firing of Andrew Damore in 2017. You can find these blogs at:

- http://www.gurianinstitute.com/blog--newsletter/archives/06-2017.
- http://www.gurianinstitute.com/blog--newsletter/archives/08-2017.

I hope you will find the blogs and my analysis in this chapter to be useful "screenshots" of the public debate every parent must (I believe) join if we are to fully protect our daughters today. I further hope these screenshots will inspire you to blog and write your own opinions, or at least support organizations that support the kind of science-based advocacy that can best protect the future for our daughters and our women.

2018 is not 1968.

New ideas are needed if we are to fully advance girls and women in the new millennium.

Protecting Our Daughters from Four New Gender Myths

If you decide to turn your citizen science into political action, you may run into the same four gender myths I have run into over the last thirty years. Because I have explored and responded to these myths in previous works such as *The Wonder of Girls, Boys and Girls Learn Differently, Saving Our Sons,* and *Leadership and the Sexes,* and because I have already responded to some of the myths in the earlier chapters of this book, I won't repeat that material here. Rather, I will take my analysis forward.

Some of the prominent myths are:

Myth 1: Women and girls must stop depending on males if they are to become truly gender equal because women's equality requires near or complete autonomy from males.

Myth 2: Gains in women's power and gender equity are best measured by quantitative financial gains.

Myth 3: White male privilege and the systemic sexism it creates are the primary reason for both female and male distress today, including rampant micro-aggressions that harm women.

Myth 4: Gender science, including the science of gender trait difference, is a dangerous form of gender stereotyping because it perpetrates patriarchal and restrictive gender roles.

In this book thus far, I hope I have made a case for countering Myth 4 especially, providing science-based evidence to help you do so in your community. In this chapter, I will help you counter myths 1 and 2. This chapter will also provide some response to Myth 3, as did Chapter 5. For even more analysis of that myth, please see the two blogs I mentioned earlier, and *Saving Our Sons* (2017).

In total, these four new gender myths harm our daughters by:

- making males the enemy when most men are allies of women and children;
- diminishing the development of resilience and success among our women;

- negating and devaluing the choices that our women and girls are making; and
- pretending that science is not useful in the gender equity debate when there is no discipline more useful to gender equity in the new millennium than the natural sciences.

Good Early Ideas Became Encrusted Myths

If you've read my early works, you'll know that I often utilized the work of Joseph Campbell, a follower of Carl Jung, and author of *The Hero with a Thousand Faces*. Having studied myth-making on all continents, he discovered both the positive and negative "power of myth." On the positive side, myths create iconography for whole civilizations to follow into substantial progress, even necessary revolution. On the negative side, arbiters of ideologically entrenched social orders—religious, political, or cultural—"press onto people mythological structures that no longer match their human experience." This happens, Campbell argued, when symbols and ideas are "reduced to the concrete goals of a particular political system of socialization."

This reduction is what has happened, I believe, with some of the early ideas we fought for in the latter 20th century.

These four early ideas got encrusted into the new gender myths:

Idea 1: Men oppress women, so women must become independent of men.

Idea 2: Men control the flow of money, so for women to become equal to men, each woman must make as much money as each man makes.

Idea 3: Women's inequality, like colonization and enslavement of indigenous and African races, was perpetrated by white men for the most part, so those men should now have little or no power (privilege). If they possess it, they are part of the problem.

Idea 4: We can't have equality if we don't have "gender sameness," thus any science that says women and men are different is a part of the system of oppression we must overthrow.

Some of these original ideas, powerful culture-changers in the 20th century, carried truth in them. Decades later, however, they have become ideas reduced to the four newly encrusted myths that, I believe, match the politics of the people who believe in the Dominant Gender Paradigm, but no longer match our collective experience. Constant adherence to them in academics, government, and the media (the Big Three) does the ultimate harm that blind adherence to any mythology has always done—it harms the future health and wellness of our children.

Much of America and the West no longer buys into the myths, even though many people in the Big Three still do. Feminist Sheryl Sandberg pointed out the contradiction in *Lean In* when she noted that the majority of American women no longer call themselves feminists. My family enjoyed this book, with Gabrielle saying, "Sandberg really gets it . . . women are constantly leaning back, leaning out. We need to lean in, be assertive, take hold of what we want."

Few things in life could be truer than that. But even while enjoying the book, Gabrielle joined me in wondering if Sandberg fully understood why so few women, especially young women, self-identify as feminists. When I ask the women in my family why they avoid "feminist," they say, "I'm not a victim, and the most important thing to me is not to call myself a victim of men or the patriarchy. I need men, and I don't want to be part of an ideology that accuses men of nearly anything bad."

Gail said, "Our problems are deep and important, but the feminist myths don't work for me anymore."

Countering Myth 1: Ending the War with Men

Camille Paglia, author of *Sexual Personae*, and a favorite philosopher of Davita's, gives voice to Gail's and my daughters' reasons for leaning into work and love, but "leaning out" of feminism.

"A peevish, grudging rancor against men," she wrote in *Time* in December of 2013, "has been one of the most unpalatable and unjust features of second and third wave feminism. Men's faults, failings and foibles have been seized on and magnified into gruesome bills of indictment—including by ideologues at our leading universities."

She continues, "When an educated culture routinely denigrates masculinity and manhood, women will be perpetually stuck with boys. And without strong men as models to either embrace or resist, women will never attain a centered and profound sense of themselves as women."

The once revolutionary idea that women must go it alone, without men, was already hyperbolic in the 20th century and has become even more harmful now as women struggle to make gains, raise families, and discover self-actualization without men. While my daughters were growing up, we talked a lot about this.

In her teens, Gabrielle said, "I mean, yes, a woman has to become independent, but it's kind of lame to make men always the destroyers and women always the creators. That's just a kind of gender stereotype."

Davita, younger then, concurred in concrete terms of her own. "Everyone has to take responsibility for herself. Blaming men because I'm shy isn't really going to help me."

As our daughters went to college, Davita especially found herself an outlier who pointed out the four myths and was attacked in her college classes as she argued her point of view.

Noretta Koertge, a philosopher of science at Indiana University, has studied the prevalence in academic settings of the four myths via the "gender microaggressions" movement. Many people in many academic fields related to gender, she notes, get away with providing ideological opinions that exaggerate their claims, making the gender field one in which there is often little rigorous science. In the area of gender microaggressions, for instance, this kind of thing happens daily. Nearly every "micro-aggressor" happens to be male, and there is no proof offered that a woman is hurt by a mansplain or call-out by a man for acting in some way that a man doesn't like. Maybe the man is wrong, but where is the harm? And how is there more harm in a man doing this with a woman than a woman with a man?

Maturity, my daughters always learned, comes from calling out the man back—that is a resilient response. But in the academic world, Koertge argues, proof of harm is not required and resilience is not protected. What is protected is female fragility, which is assumed constantly. When someone argues against this kind of thing, they are attacked for being aggressors (or abusive) because they apply logic that is disliked by the ideologues. The reason this happens successfully, Koertge points out, is that "All manner of logic itself is patriarchal anyway—logic is, thus, suspect . . . Even to force the study of logic on female students is to aggressively support the patriarchy that devalues women."

In many colleges, academic rigor is under siege by students opposed to non-DGP ideas about sex and gender. At a university I spoke at recently, I was accused of "abusing" the students by talking about "binary ideas of gender" (i.e. the male and female brain). The use of the word "abuse," though incorrect, was not questioned by others in the classroom because "microaggressions" had already been adjudicated in academic student opinion as "abusive," "patriarchal," and "dangerous." Students lobbied for safe rooms in which to avoid hearing the words of white males.

This new mythology has taken hold of academics despite the early feminist tenet that 1) women and men should be treated equally, without special treatment for either; and 2) that male protectiveness of fragile females should finally be shelved in favor of female independence and resilience. The academic environments that first bore feminism into our consciousness have fallen into the very trap they once promised to avoid. They are treating girls and women as highly fragile creatures who cannot be independent without blaming males for nearly anything. This approach fails our daughters who do not develop resilience, and often, quite frankly, do not find the love they need and want.

Courageous Conversation

Exploring the Gender Politics Around You

In your community, your book group, your social media, I hope you will take on these sorts of gender-political topics as you can.

One women's group in Wisconsin wrote me about their discussion following the 2016 election.

We are all women between 25 and 50. Some of us had read The Wonder of Girls *when our daughters were young. Then we started talking about all this again after reading one of your blogs on single-sex education and then hearing you give an evening keynote on raising girls at our school. You came here right after the 2016 election, and we have a lot to say about gender issues, I can tell you!*

One thing we noticed in Secretary Clinton's campaign was the way she exaggerated the whole 77 cents on the dollar thing. We all know it's true that men make more money than women, so our issue with her doing that wasn't that she was lying—we know this is a difficult issue, especially because women take so much time off to raise kids. Our issue was with the way she lost the election, in our opinion, because of her obsession with pitting women as victims and never talking about the needs of boys or men.

I should tell you, all of us who got together to send this email to you, we all have daughters. We should be the kind of women who say Clinton was right to just talk about women's needs and how girls are behind boys. But many of us have sons, too, and we're married to or divorced from men. We know men and boys do not have it easy.

What I'm saying is, we think Hillary's feminism backfired. She only talked about women's issues and left boys and men out completely and Trump won the election by talking about men, unemployment, and those themes. While none of the women in my group like Trump himself, we don't think Trump won the election, we think Hillary lost it by using the old feminist-victim-of-men approach. We can't prove it, but that is what we think.

P.S. By the way, I am not one of those people who thinks we should have voted for Hillary because she was a woman—I voted for her because I thought she was better qualified than Trump, but she was stuck in the past, in my opinion.

This book group took on deep topics of sex and gender with a keen eye for the political landscapes around us. I wrote Mary back, thanking her for sharing her group's courageous conversation.

Interestingly, to her point about voting for Hillary because she was a woman: while everyone in my family voted for Clinton, I was the only person who did so, in part, because she was a woman! Gail, Gabrielle, and Davita all said they would not vote for a candidate based on their sex or gender. I felt that Hillary's election would fulfill my long-held aim to finally see a woman lead our country. As I believe my colleagues and I proved in the research for *Leadership and the Sexes* (2008), women and men lead differently. I was excited to see the science reflected through a female lens in the White House. Clearly, our country will have to wait a bit longer to test this theory out in the White House, but we do certainly have a lot to discuss in our courageous conversations!

Countering Myth 2:
Revising What We Mean by "Power."

Power is a multi-faceted concept, but "equal power for women" has lately become a mainly or solely *quantitative* idea. Many power wielders in the Big Three believe that gender equality cannot exist until 1) each woman makes the same amount of money each man makes, and 2) there are the same number of women at the top of corporations as men. While "power" and "money" are useful standards of equity, this impossible-to-reach myth negates women's qualitative choices. Without our realizing it, women are making choices and have the freedom to make them in ways that many males do not. This, too, is a part of gender equity to celebrate.

Money and Power

Males as a group make more money than females (i.e. President Obama and Hillary Clinton pointed out in 2016 that "women in America make 77 cents for every dollar men make") and specific men (alpha males) have more money or higher-paying CEO positions than specific women. Given this reality, why would women like Mary and those in her group feel that Hillary Clinton overplayed the statistic?

Two reasons stand out, I believe.

First, because the statistic does not pertain to equal pay for equal work. As numerous studies have shown (I have listed some for you in the Notes and Resources), equal pay for equal work is well-adjudicated now. Rarely do women and men not get paid the same amount of money for the same time spent doing the same work. When men do get paid more, it is generally because they spend more hours at work, in the commute, in cross-country travel, etc.

The 77 cents on the dollar statistic is, then, about female/male *aggregate income*. Because women often take so much more time off work to raise children; because they make choices for work/life balance that many males do not or cannot make; and because many of the professions women choose are not as well-paid as many of the professions (and hierarchy climbs) that males choose, aggregate male income is 23 cents on the dollar higher than aggregate female income.

Second, many women understand the power of *choice*. They seek the freedom to *choose* their profession and *choose* the amount of time they will spend in it, including the amount of time and energy they will spend climbing a hierarchy. Most women know that men on average work more hours away from home than women. Men tend to want to climb hierarchies toward higher pay more than women, especially once women have children. Additionally, men have always tended to do the most dangerous—and therefore more lucrative—jobs, like working on skyscrapers.

Given women's choices, men will likely always earn more, on average, than individual women if aggregate male earning and aggregate female earning are kept separate in the gender debate. But because most American workers (both female and male) marry/partner to pool their assets and raise children, financial assets are only artificially separated in a gender debate. In most cases, men/women are earning the income, not women vs. men. This is not reflected in the 77 cents on the dollar statistic.

Given all these realities, if measurement of success for women remains solely in the province of money earned by every individual woman, women will likely remain the "victims" of men, masculine systems, and the patriarchy. Men will be blamed for continuing to earn a greater amount of aggregate money in comparison to women. The women's rights movement will not be applauded for its progress in allowing tens of millions of women to see money, choice, and partnership in tandem. We will continue to systemically neglect women's reality—and continue to attack males and "male systems" as inherently dominant and unfair.

Better would be to see the myth for what it is. When men get more pay for equal work, this is unfair to women, and we will take it to court. But for the majority of women, "freedom to choose" (qualitative power) should now be seen as equal in cultural importance to personal pay or hierarchical (quantitative) power. Once we add qualitative power to the social debate, we take a major step forward. This addition moves us beyond the 1960s gender-equality paradigm of pure quantitative measurement toward a new gender-equity paradigm that includes choice theory.

Not to move in this direction is to negate what most women want. As we noted earlier, a comprehensive study based on Pew Research published in 2011 found that nearly two-thirds of American women hoped they would be able to *choose* to stay home when they have children or only work away from home part-time. Just over one-third wanted to work full-time outside the home while raising their children, and most of them hoped that their husbands/partners would also work to earn income.

Given this reality and given the natural instinct in most men to try to facilitate this choice and freedom for women, the sole use of the myth of quantification felt repugnant to Mary and her group. Her women's group saw through the mythology of pure quantitative power and thought qualitatively too. They partnered with males or other partners who shared financial assets so that they could work 25 or fewer hours away from home while spending the rest of their time with their children, family, and community. In this model, women value their ability to live and care for others at a deep, primal level that is not counted in DGP gender-equality conversations.

Most males, I believe, understand the logic of the women's group. Men know that girls and women have a lot of power. We respect women's choice in large part because our moms were very powerful and guided our lives until we became independent, bonded with powerful women in love and marriage, and then raised empowered daughters. We are aware of women in impoverished communities that do not have power, and we fight to help them. Meanwhile, in those same communities, we see that men do not have power either. We fight to help them too. In college, in graduate school, in law school, in medical school, in the workplace, in divorce court, in the neighborhood, in the PTA, in the counseling office, in the hospital, even in the church or synagogue, we see that women's power is growing and, in some ways, surpassing male power.

Did You Know?

In Many Ways, Female Power Surpasses "Male Power and Privilege"

In 2015, the World Health Organization published the Global Burden of Disease Study led by the Institute for Health Metrics and Evaluation. After evaluating data from all countries and continents, the study authors revealed: "In most parts of the world, health outcomes among boys and men continue to be substantially worse than among girls and women. Yet this gender-based disparity in health has received little national, regional or global acknowledgement or attention from health policy-makers or health-care providers."

The study's authors discuss their awareness of the popular myth that males, including white males, have more power than females, including white females. But they also note that female power in health surpasses male power despite the concept that females are victims of more mental and physical disease in patriarchal cultures.

The study authors conclude that, "Including both women and men in efforts to reduce gender inequalities in health as part of the post-2015 sustainable development agenda would improve everyone's health and well-being."

Health is just one area where female power surpasses male. Education, personal safety, longevity, and employment are others. Girls surpass boys in pre-K, K – 12, college, and graduate education. Girls are also less likely to be victims of violence, less likely to die young, and less likely to be homeless or without financial resources than males.

The latter point was made in a new study, *Wayward Sons*, by Drs. Autor and Wasserman at MIT. Elaine C. Kamarck and Jonathan Cowan, who commissioned the Autor/Wasserman study for the think tank, Third Way, confirmed just how much better the employment/choice picture is getting for females when compared to males.

"The growing disparity between men and women is easy to overlook given the fact that at the very top of our society, power and money is still overwhelmingly held by men. And yet, when we move to the realm of more ordinary people we see a tectonic shift. Over the last three decades, the labor market trajectory of males in the U.S. has turned downward along four dimensions: skills acquisition; employment rates; occupational stature; and real wage levels . . . These emerging gender gaps suggest reason for concern.

"First, because education has become an increasingly important determinant of lifetime income over the last three decades—and, more concretely, because earnings and employment prospects for less-educated U.S. workers have

> sharply deteriorated—the stagnation of male educational attainment bodes ill for the well-being of recent cohorts of U.S. males . . . (who) are likely to face diminished employment and earnings opportunities and other attendant maladies, including poorer health, higher probability of incarceration, and generally lower life satisfaction. Of equal concern are the implications that diminished male labor market opportunities hold for the well-being of others—children and potential mates in particular."

While a lot of good things have happened in the last five decades, especially in the fight against gender-role restrictions, tens of millions of under-nurtured boys and men can erase many of our gains for women and girls, as well as place all of us in potentially grave danger. Given that women are more likely to receive government assistance than men, to most men and women—as to Mary and her group—the DGP insistence that quantitative power is more important than qualitative power becomes a kind of white lie, and we avoid too much affiliation with it.

Yet both women and men support women and girls. As men observe many of our daughters, wives, and mothers also avoiding the DGP now—not calling themselves feminists—we see that the DGP does not necessarily fit the grassroots of American life. In your own citizen science, you can study this around you. You can talk about the various ways of studying success as women—power, money, and choice. Hopefully, you will have conversations that intersect with the past, but which also keep their footing in the present.

In the present, race and socio-economic status are complex factors in female choice-making—white women, in general, have more choices and freedom than many women in other races. At the same time, even in different racial groups, girls and women of color are doing better in many ways than boys and men of color. Though certain alpha males with white male privilege still run certain systems and certain males tacitly or directly denigrate females, their actions don't rob all or most women of their power today. If they did, women would not be succeeding in the ways they are succeeding, and males would not be falling behind today in the multiple ways they are struggling across the racial and socio-economic spectrum.

A Case Study in Choice Theory: STEM Jobs

We hinted at a case study in choice theory in Chapter 7. Let's fully explore it here.

More males than females (about an 80/20 ratio) work in spatial-mechanical jobs that pay a lot, e.g. mechanical engineer. As we saw in earlier chapters, while some women are and can be brilliant in the spatial fields, there are distinct elements of the male and female brain difference that attract more males than females to mechanical engineering. Even when young women are guided to these fields through helpful college and graduate school scholarships and mentoring, fewer women choose to stay in the highly isolative, non-relational, non-verbal science fields as compared to men.

Isaac Cohen, of *Forbes Magazine*, provided in-depth investigative reporting on this male/female difference in 2014. As he researched the story and presented his findings, he took on—and received not a little controversy for it—Myths 2 and 4 on our list.

Cohen wrote, "Non-physical (brain) or behavioral differences between the sexes have become the *mokita* of our era; they are the 'truth we all know but agree not to talk about.' Certain types of findings are routinely ignored, slighted, or repressed (in the media). Social science that points to discrimination against women is shouted from the rooftops, but research that casts doubt on such sources or identifies other causes is hastily shoved under the rug."

In his deep dive into this subject, Cohen discovered that even at universities like Harvard and MIT that have committed massive resources to empowering women in certain STEM fields, women comprised the minority of enrollees, "including computer science (19%), circuits and electronics (9%), and elements of structures, a physics course with a side of linear programming (5%). Women who do take these courses get the same grades as men and they actually have higher completion rates than their male counterparts. But on average, even in the privacy of their own homes (via online coursework) and without the pressures and publicity of the classroom, they don't seem as eager to develop these skills."

Cohen noticed the choice theory women were employing as they prioritized work/family balance. "Female professors reported that they enjoyed childcare much more than male professors," Cohen wrote. "The gender gap in enjoyment of childrearing was not associated with gender role attitudes or leave-taking. Rather, it seemed to reflect genuine differences in how professionally committed men and women felt about the day-to-day experience of taking care of kids."

At John Hopkins University, professors Camilla Benbow and David Lubinski confirmed that gender differences in choice and preference skew percentages of males and females in hierarchy-climbing because women tend to be less acutely focused on climbing to the highest leadership positions than men, even in areas where they are highly gifted. Benbow and Lubinski's results grow from following thousands of gifted teen girls and boys over a twenty-year period, well into their careers. Both the boys and girls (then men and women) thought of themselves as "successful in their chosen professions," liked their career (including homemaker careers), enjoyed "continuing to develop my intellectual interests," "continuing to develop my skills and talents," "having leisure time to enjoy avocational interests," and "having time to socialize," among others. But as the children became adults, the males "placed greater importance than women on 'being successful in my line of work,' 'inventing or creating something that will have an impact,' and 'having lots of money.'" The women, however, tended to stress "having strong friendships," "living close to parents and relatives," and "having children."

Benbow and Lubinski also found that, "The sexes were similar in self-esteem and other self-concept indicators. Most importantly, men and women, on average, entered different fields and professions, and they varied in how they chose to allocate their time."

After completing his research, Cohen challenged the DGP this way: "Some people may find these results discomfiting. Resistors are tempted to set up a straw man: 'Are you saying you want women to be 1950s housewives again?' But that's not what these data imply. It helps to remember, as Steven Pinker has written, that 'equity feminism is a moral doctrine about equal treatment that makes no commitments regarding open empirical issues in psychology or biology.' This sort of common sense feminism, which stresses equality of choice over equality of outcome, tends to get lost in the breast-beating over diversity."

Interesting proof of disparate preference and choice theory comes to us from Scandinavian countries such as Denmark and Sweden. In these cultures, governments have developed quotas to ensure equal leadership positioning for women in high government positions. But their free market sector, which is more reflective of our American free market system, still shows only 10 percent females in the C-Suite of corporations. Women have the freedom to say: "I don't want to kill my quality of life to climb to the top for those jobs," and they are exercising that freedom.

Try This

Use "Centric" more than "Dominated"

One of the ways that choice theory is negated in our public discourse—and women's choices are devalued—is the DGP insistence on naming all or most professions that do not have 50% female ascension "male dominated." Because the DGP adherents believe in the myth of quantification as the sole marker of equality, and because women-to-men ratios are not 50/50, they argue that there is systemic gender inequality —privileged men dominating oppressed women. While this scenario is no doubt an accurate one in some cases, it is mythology to see it as accurate in most. Once we employ choice theory and gender trait difference theory, we see things differently. We see DGP concepts as accusative and, in most cases today, inaccurate.

This new vision requires new language. You can institute this new language, where appropriate, in any area of gender-equity research—your home, office, and neighborhood—by substituting the word "centric" for "dominated." When males are being dominating and females are being oppressed, we must call them out. "Male-dominant" is absolutely appropriate for Sharia Law in parts of Afghanistan. But mechanical engineering is not a dominance/oppression system. These professions are "male-centric."

Pre-K through sixth-grade educational environments, equally so, are "female-centric." These teaching professions are chosen by women. Women are not oppressed in making the choice, and males have not dominated them into these choices.

Football will always be male-centric, as is much of the financial services industry, especially at the alpha levels. Social services and human services are generally, today, female-centric, with most therapists and social workers female.

With each profession, you can study the numbers and data to see which ones you believe are still patriarchal or male-dominated and which ones are female and male-*centric*. I personally tested out the "centric" language in my corporate trainers. Some corporate leaders and managers liked it and felt relieved of political pressure by the language. Others felt more politically motivated to help women if "male-dominated" got used everywhere. "Why let up," one senior manager in financial services told me. "Why give an inch? Males dominate women wherever they are, and all women has is to call them on it."

But not every woman in male-centric fields agreed. A 27-year-old female firefighter told me this story.

"Let's face it, I work in a very male field and I work with almost all competitive guys. Even though I'm competitive too, I'm different than them. I've learned that they are going to try to beat me at everything, so I compete just enough that I have their respect and I compete to the level I want to get to. I don't need to compete all the time to be happy like a lot of them do. I respect, though, that most of them do, and they respect me for who I am. I had to prove myself, but once I proved myself, there wasn't much drama with them anymore. We understand each other.

Until you used the term 'centric' today, I would have said firefighting is male dominated, but I like 'male-centric' better actually. These guys aren't trying to dominate me, they are trying to compete with me, and you know what, I can't say that's a bad thing. A competitive guy is just who I want by my side when I move into the forest to fight a brutal fire."

Seven Best Practices for Ensuring Gender Equity

By sharing the information of this chapter (and, indeed, this whole book), I am hoping to convince you and inspire our culture to apply the gender war to situations that need it, but transcend that war in most situations. Thirty years working in your communities has shown me that while some situations of female distress may correlate to something the Dominant Gender Paradigm focuses on (e.g. gender stereotypes, stereotype threat, or sexism) most distress among our girls is not *caused* by those elements.

Causation is most important—we have to target that—and to target it, Myth 4 has to move aside. I hope this book has proven how robust female/male difference is, and how powerful a community can become when it embraces that science. Best practices empower girls and women at deep levels. Many of these practices and skills are what the business world especially is hoping girls will have by the time they become women in the workforce. To me, these are skills that can ensure gender equity for women.

> **Teach girls how to be effective at self-promotion, accepting a compliment, and taking credit for their ideas and their work**. Men often mansplain and take credit for ideas that a woman had. While continuing to point out this competitive behavior to men, women are also best served by parents and communities that raise them to speak louder and more forcefully. Self-promotion is key to women's empowerment, especially because women will need to compete for resources continually—and that is not a bad thing.

> **From the moment that you think a girl has developed inner strength, teach girls not to take things personally.** In infancy and the early years of a girl's life we instinctively protect her from tears and emotional pain. But as she grows, we must refocus on helping her long-term self-esteem by teaching her to stop crying or whining when whining serves only to weaken her resolve. Inner strength is somewhat preserved by processing feelings, but it can also disappear when only the feelings themselves become paramount. Problem-solving skills and taking very little personally are crucial too.

> **Prepare girls for the possibility of violence and aggression by engaging them in sports, martial arts, or other self-protective systems.** The more that girls are involved in physical play, aggression nurturance, and activities like martial arts, the more likely they will survive and thrive beyond potential violence in later life. Play It Safe is an organization that teaches child safety and self-protection in Arizona and California. Laurie Latham, a former police officer and Play It

Safe executive, told me, "The girls and boys that go through our training program are much more likely to be able to stand up to violence and abuse. Empowerment is as much a matter of action as feeling. We teach kids to be safe by being powerful."

Use science rather than popular opinion to help girls through their journey of personal development. This includes the sciences of environmental toxicology and healthy nutrition; gene testing when appropriate; hormonal analysis as needed; gender/brain science throughout the lifespan; sleep, exercise, and sports sciences especially during adolescence, and all the citizen science we've looked at in this book. Once we commit to using science, we cut out a lot of the noise from the blogosphere and focus on the key areas of a daughter's development.

Turn away from victim culture. When girls and women are victims of bullying, sexual assault, abuse, or sexism, we must help them confront this pain and the people who caused it. But victim culture is something else, as we've noted; victim culture perpetuates the idea of female weakness. That idea is detrimental to the long-term efficacy of girls and women in the world.

Help girls find their passion and their purpose. Girls can often feel isolated and even a bit lost, especially if they are very shy and/or just don't make friends very well. These girls especially may need constant, courageous conversations with us about passion and purpose. "What are you doing with your life?" "Why are you here on this earth?" "What are your most profound values?" "What skills do you need to develop right now?" "Isn't it time to get off social media and get into something important?" Guiding girls toward passion and purpose provides them with a permanent way to raise their own self-esteem—through action of purpose and a sense of passionate engagement in the world—*and* it helps each community thrive. An engaged, passionate, purposeful girl is good for her community!

While continuing to make sure women are given equal pay for equal work in male-centric fields, insist also that our culture pays more for female-centric work. Child care providers, who are mainly women, are paid very little. This devalues their profound work. Similarly, pre-K through 6 school teachers are mainly women and are paid far less than a mechanical or industrial engineer. The true gender pay gap appears in the lack of valuation our culture gives to female-centric professions. This pay gap won't be solved by attacking males, masculinity, male privilege, and sexism since the gap mainly grows from capitalist competition in the corporate world, which is not a negative or bad thing—we are a thriving culture because of competition. Solutions, generally, will not come from male-centric professions, most of which thrive in the competitive marketplace and assign valuation from that marketplace. Because many female-centric jobs and wages are paid via government and nonprofits, the way to attack the pay gap is through foundation and government help. Foundations will need to increase their giving to female-centric non-profits, and legislators will need to pass laws that pay female-centric professions more. We are the only people who, with our votes and voice, can convince them to do that.

Developing Gender Symbiosis

I hope this book has provided you with ideas, strategies, and theory that will help you deepen the gender-equity dialogue in your community. I hope you have gained tools of empowerment and resilience and I hope you have enough evidence and logic at your disposal to counter the four myths when they darken the social dialogue about sex and gender in your part of the world.

That darkening, I insist, does girls no good.

While gender stereotypes exist and perhaps always will, these optics and images don't compare in negative consequence to the loss of the father or the addicted mother or the increase in autism, joblessness, suicide, cyberbullying, and other mental health issues among children in our era. While some bad men do terrible things to women and girls, and while some of these men escape punishment, most men are good people who want to work with empowered daughters and resilient women.

Beyond using the term "centric" in your conversations, I hope you will also look at using the term *gender symbiosis*. It can serve as a counterpoint to our present culture-gender war.

Symbiosis is the natural pattern of mutual dependency among organisms (sometimes called biological mutualism). It allows for the needs of both and all genders to be met so that the needs of the other genders will be understood. While symbiosis can, at its extreme, denote a parasitic relationship (like a barber fish attaching to a shark to live off the detritus on the shark's skin) or hyper-dependency (an infant and mother), it most often connotes a close relationship between two or more people in which each person is dependent on the other for survival and thriving—not only of self but, most especially, of offspring.

From the viewpoint of gender symbiosis and mutual dependency (interdependence), we will see advantages in gender trait difference.

Here is a tool I use in corporations and communities to compare female/male prioritization of the four primary parental functions asserted in the fields of anthropology and ethology. The four functions are:

> **Protect** (protect children at all costs, and make their lives as safe as possible for as long as possible)
> **Provide** (food, shelter, clothing, social advancement, and ultimately, development of children's ability to independently provide for themselves)
> **Nurture** (attachment, bonding, love, and mentoring via bi-strategic and multi-strategic empathy)
> **Grow** (personal self-actualization, often accomplished then sacrificed for others in need).

Here is how females and males tend to prioritize these four functions, especially once they have children together:

Females	Males
Protect	*Protect*
Nurture	*Provide*
Provide	*Nurture*
Grow	*Grow*

When women (and men) take time off to raise kids, these change further. Since most of the people who take this time off are women, the priorities generally shift this way:

Females	Males
Protect	*Protect*
Nurture	*Provide*

211

Grow	*Nurture*
Provide	*Grow*

From a statistical viewpoint, including exceptions, the rule for females and males once children come is for males to put off personal growth and females to engage in more personal growth. Furthermore, because males are doing the majority of the employment/wage earning, females are doing more of the hands-on nurturing of children.

At the same time, it is interesting to note that even in families in which both parents work, males still tend to spend more time "providing" (working longer hours farther away from home) and females still tend to spend more time nurturing. Some research shows that even in lesbian/gay couples, the more masculinized of the two tends to more specifically fit the "male" model, and the more feminized the "female."

When I use this grid in my work, I receive a lot of "aha" nods of the head, but also some naysayers. They call this gender stereotyping, and they feel that I am pushing a traditional notion of gender roles onto the culture. Always, I point them to the science. These grids are not built from people's opinion, but from research, such as the 2011 study I shared earlier (and more in the Notes and Resources) that reveal gender trait difference in statistical analyses of female/male partnership and parenting.

Living in the New Reality

Once this reality is understood—even including the facts that 1) any particular relationship can reverse some aspect of the female/male prioritizations, and 2) sexual orientation may not be heteronormative—both women and men may find passion to build symbiotic relationships. Rather than gender trait difference being seen as a weakness, it is seen as a strength.

For this reality to become a subject of family life, we will need to focus on the primary areas of prioritization as we carry on courageous conversations with our children to help them understand that no matter the configuration they create, when they marry and raise children, symbiosis will be of paramount importance. The kinds of partnerships that expose different but symbiotic priorities do so because they are primarily biological. All our sociology comes second to our biological drive to raise healthy children together and in concert with multiple caregivers and assets in our three families.

The natural bottom line the DGP avoids is that we are not independent of one another—we are interdependent. Where he has a weakness, she needs to be strong, and vice versa. Where she needs assets, he needs to provide them, and vice versa. The future for girls depends on this kind of interdependence as much as it does on female or male independence.

Bi-strategic prioritization does not always look like a traditional family of dad working and mom staying at home—millions of families don't look that way at all—but the symbiotic relationship between the partners is always crucial to the family's stability and survival.

Thus, gender symbiosis and gender equity, especially once both the patriarchy and the DGP are deconstructed, become one of the most courageous conversations girls and women can have—not just among themselves, but among the boys and men who love them and will sacrifice nearly anything so that these girls and women can have success and empowerment.

Epilogue

"We must get to the place where truth never frightens."
—Catherine of Sienna

ONE OF MY EARLY HEROES was the biologist E.O. Wilson. From his research in Africa and back home in the hallways of Harvard's Museum of Comparative Zoology, he has been generating ideas about human nature for decades, including books like *Sociobiology* and theories such as "Consilience." His latest book, *The Meaning of Human Existence*, published near his 85th birthday, continues his ethological exploration in a political-academic context.

"During the civil rights movement and rise of resentment against the Vietnam War," he recalls in his latest book, "the country's intellectuals and its professors shifted far left. As part of this we adopted a belief that everything is due to culture and history, and nothing is due to the way the brain is wired."

In his memoir, he goes on to talk about bucking this trend by remaining adamant about the role of genetics. In so doing, he became a man among a minority of academics who studied human nature itself, and received attacks as a racist, sexist, and "old-fashioned" thinker. He was, of course, none of these, but "if you could have a genetic basis for your behavior," he recalls, "then somebody could say there could be a genetic basis for differences from one race to the other, and that is what frightened the academics."

I first discovered his work in the 1980s as I was reading the ethologist Konrad Lorenz to begin building my own gender theory. Studying Lorenz, Wilson, and the work of neurobiologist Ruben Gur at the University of Pennsylvania, I began to posit the idea of gender symbiosis.

While genetics and other research in the neural sciences has evolved over the decades—transcending the "politically correct" view Wilson lamented in the sciences—this transcendence has not happened enough in the field of sex, sexual politics, and gender. In gender studies, especially funded by the Big Three, to suggest that nature plays as large a part as culture in gender equity still results in being called sexist, old-fashioned, and patriarchal. Even knowing this, E.O. Wilson writes wisely, "There's nothing more satisfying than that slaughter of an old theory, provided you can replace it."

We can now replace the DGP just like early feminist theory replaced traditionalist and patriarchal theory before it. But neither feminism nor the DGP needs slaughtering. Their best principles are still of profound value to our civilization. Gender symbiosis, nature-based theory, and feminist theory can all run parallel courses. Traditionalist theory still exists in some parts of American life, especially in some religious communities, running parallel to feminist theory, and there is room in both theories to repurpose their mythos with natural sciences.

Our girls can help us become the revolutionaries they need us to be, as Gabrielle and Davita have helped me to be a better man. They have taught me that "Woman" is both obvious and amorphous. They have shown me that if, in caring for girls, we pretend that all of us are just "people," our feet will be stuck in the quicksand of "nothing" and "anything," lost between polarities, unstable, error-prone. At some point, each of us must step out of the muck of ideology to understand the differences between a "man" and a "woman."

It is in that context, they have taught me, that "gender identity" will always evolve socially, while sex and sex-on-the-brain will always be female and male. Both happen on parallel courses. To pretend they don't is to neglect human nature; to forget or neglect human nature is to create dangerous social systems of abuse or neglect and not even realize it.

God doesn't choose sides between women and men, nor should culture. One way is not better—both ways are necessary and beautiful. One half of emotional intelligence is female and the other half is male. That is a good thing, something we should love and cherish, not attack or denigrate.

If you will choose this complex way of living—this ultimately loving way of raising your daughters—I believe you will be utilizing all the new cultural and technological assets available to us, while still respecting "old" assets as well.

But living out this path may not be easy, including accessing the kind of testing I hope you'll discover. The changes to diet, exercise, and sleep; the recasting of math/science classes; adaptations in digital life and use of technology; understanding workplace issues differently; revising concepts of sexism and microaggressions—all this adds up to a path that you may well need a lot of support to walk. Our culture's present obsession with "microaggressions" will take a massive human effort to fully understand and put into helpful context.

I hope you'll join our Gurian Institute community and find the support you need. If you click the Membership button on www.michaelgurian.com you'll see how we are building a community of passionate and science-based educators, parents, and professionals like you. Please join us.

"Stepping into the fray of life," the feminist Rita Dove wrote in 2000, "does not mean dissipation of one's creative powers . . . the reward is a connection on a visceral level with the world as it reshapes its destiny for a new century's countdown." This visceral and creative power is *you*. It is *us*. Parents of girls are in this fray every day, and much of the fray is so biological and so visceral we need hard and difficult sciences to help us do our job well. I am in the fray and I can say, looking back at 30 years of advocating for girls and women, my advocacy has changed somewhat because of the fray.

Thirty years in the fray has taught me that ideology, when it is first rising within us, feels like a new, exploding light. For a time, that light shines on everything and makes sense of everything, including every ideological projection of self and culture. Feminism exploded like light, and because of it, our culture regenerated and improved. I still believe in feminism, just as I believed in many of its principles when I voted for Hillary Clinton. The problem we must face communally is not feminism, in my opinion, but the DGP.

To me, it is not the need for gender equity that blinds us, but the ideological principals of the DGP. They blind us, create gender war, and foment a culture that is now suffering the consequences of blind affiliation to superficial attacks and theories. While DGP adherents—a minority in our country, but a very loud and well-placed one—can find new recruits by pushing their ideology, they mainly help bind our culture to their ideological purities, not to progress, because progress comes when people stop breaking children's lives into pieces, and finally understand what diversity is, and what each child needs.

In her novel, *The Waves*, early feminist Virginia Woolf writes, "Another stage has been reached. Stage upon stage. And why should there be an end of stages? And where do they lead?"

I hope you can use this book to help you develop a new stage of feminism, if you are a feminist, and a new stage of cultural progress whoever you are, one that is activated not by people in an ideologically-pure environment, but by you and your friends and cohorts who will use your citizen science, even when it's messy, to change the world for girls.

The End

Acknowledgments

The Minds of Girls represents the culmination of three decades of research, practice, and advocacy in applied gender science. I stand on the shoulders of many others working in the field. You know who you are, too many to name, but each one of you played a huge part of my vision and theory. Our devotion to interdependence of disciplines will ultimately change the lives of our children.

My deep thanks also to my Gurian Institute co-authors and co-researchers: Katey McPherson, Kathy Stevens (of blessed memory), Dakota Hoyt, Patricia Henley, Adie Goldberg, Peggy Daniels, Stacie Behring, Arlette Ballew, Kelley King, and Barbara Annis. You have strengthened my ability to think strategically and practically about the needs of girls and boys, and women and men, from the trenches and "on the ground."

For all the other people who have aided us in the Gurian Institute's wisdom-of-practice research over the last twenty years, I also wish to express my deepest appreciation. We could not conduct our research without your help. To all the parents, teachers, citizens, leaders, and fans who have written letters (back when we did that!) and e-mails, I express my humble gratitude.

Among the many gifts your correspondence has offered me, one that influenced this book and my others, is your ongoing challenge that I provide a resource for every possible reader that not only dives deep into what children need to thrive, but also takes on the acute challenges of advocating for girls and boys in our present political climate. I hope this book fulfills some of that challenge.

My thanks also extend to colleagues in publishing, including editors Jon Gosch, Gail Reid-Gurian, and Russ Davis.

To my clients: thank you for allowing me to serve you. You have helped me become increasingly more effective with girls, boys, women, men, and everyone across the gender spectrum.

To Gail and our daughters, Gabrielle and Davita, I extend the kind of gratitude that can barely be expressed in words. As women, you have insisted I work diligently for females and males both, and throughout this insistence, you have kept me focused on diverse sides of various gender equations.

Everyone I have thanked here has taught me that there is a great deal at stake in our work. The aggregate result we hope to achieve with the diverse people we serve is a whole culture's discovery of essential science-based and common-sense strategies for every child.

My thanks to all of you for helping me to do this for three decades—I can't do what I do without you.

Notes and Resources

Preface

From the poem "Where Does the Temple Begin, Where Does It End?" by Mary Oliver.

The research in this book integrates these sources:

- Results from my meta-analysis of 1,542 studies on female development.
- Statistical benchmarks and analysis from think-tanks and governmental agencies such as the Department of Justice, the National Institute of Mental Health, the Pell Institute, the OECD, the WHO, and the United Nations.
- Action and wisdom-of-practice research from the Gurian Institute team. We have trained more than 60,000 professionals and reached more than one million parents. In meetings with stakeholders in hundreds of communities, and in our data and analysis from social services and educational clients, we have thousands of responses to surveys and questionnaires, some of which appear in this book. These emails, correspondence, and research come from ordinary people like you who are working with girls and boys around the world.
- Interviews and interactions with members of the legislative and executive branches, government officials, and corporate leaders from Fortune 500 companies who are concerned about the iGeneration, girls' lives, women's resilience, and women's workplace issues.
- Case studies and clinical research from my own counseling clients, with details changed for confidentiality.

In these Notes and References, various forms are used for reference notation based on the source from which I have taken the reference.

As my daughters were growing up, we talked about the DGP a great deal; I gradually understood the DGP as espousing these ideas:

1. Nature is a small part of a girl's life. Nurture and culture are much more powerful.
2. Most girls' distresses grow from female victimization by males, masculinity, the patriarchy, and male-forced gender roles. This victimization creates gender role pressure and female suffering via male violence and oppression (toxic masculinity).
3. The feeling among girls of victimization from masculinity and male privilege is so systemic that no girl or woman can escape its distress, especially in the shadow of gender stereotypes and norms that constantly keep females oppressed.
4. Given male defect and female victimization, maleness (masculinity)

must be removed from schools, businesses, colleges, children, and families to protect girls and women from constant male microaggressions and to help empower girls and women.

One of the ways that the DGP adherents push their attack politics is to claim that sex and race are the same thing, i.e. claiming that girls-only STEM classrooms, for instance, are like racial segregation. I was discussing this with my colleague, Leonard Sax, recently (who is also a target for these folks) and he told me that Supreme Court Justice Ruth Bader Ginsburg pointed out in 1996 in the majority ruling in U.S. v. Virginia that sex and race are not the same. Yet the DGP keeps pushing the idea. If we don't fight this kind of overreach, we will not be able to fully help our daughters use all the innovations they may need.

Chapter 1

Steven Pinker. *The Blank Slate.* New York: Penguin, 2003.

David Page is quoted from "Every Cell Has a Sex: X and Y and the Future of Health Care," in *Women's Health Research at Yale*, August 2016, by Rick Harrison.

"Beyond He or She," *Time,* March 2017.

See www.michaelgurian.com/research and see studies referenced in later chapters of this book regarding male/female differences.

Friederici AD, Pannekamp A, Partsch CJ, et al. "Sex hormone testosterone affects language organization in the infant brain." *Neuroreport.* 2008;19(3).

Gruygrok, Amber, et.al., "A Meta-Analysis of Sex Differences in Human Brain Structure," *Neuroscience and Bio-Behavioral Reviews,* 2014.

Bodenmann, Guy, et.al., "Effects of Stress on the Social Support Provided by Men and Women in Intimate Relationships," *Psychological Science,* 2015.

For more detail on female/male brain differences, see the May 2005 *Scientific American* issue on "His Brain, Her Brain."

Horizon, on the BBC in 2015, "What Sex Is Your Brain?"

Conant, Eve, "In Their Words: How Children Are Affected by Gender Issues," *National Geographic,* January 2017.

Savin-Williams, Ritch C., "Who's Gay? Does it Matter?" *Current Directions in Psychological Science,* Vol 15., 2006.

Madsen, Sue Lani, "State's New Gender-Restroom Rule," *The Spokesman Review,* January 16, 2016, quoting Williams' University of UCLA School of Law study, "0.3 percent of population are transgender."

See original study at: Gates, G.J., "How Many People Are Lesbian, Gay, Bisexual, and Transgender?" Retrieved from http://williamsinstitute.law.ucla.edu/qp-content/Gates.

Olson, Kristina R., et al. "Gender Cognition in Transgender Children," *Psychological Science,* 2015, Vol. 26 467-474.

The whole March/April 2016 issue of *Psychotherapy Networker* is devoted to "The Mystery of Gender."

Gates, G.J., "How Many People Are Lesbian, Gay, Bisexual, and Transgender?" Retrieved from http://williamsinstitute.law.ucla.edu/ qpcontent/Gates.

The November/December 2005 issue of *Family Therapy Magazine*, "Gay and Lesbian Relationships," is a comprehensive resource on issues and science regarding LGBTQ populations.

Schmid, Randolph E., "Study of Gays, Brothers Finds Prenatal Effect," *Associated Press*, June 27, 2006.

"The Mystery of Gender," *Newsweek*, May 21, 2007.

1994 Harvard Medical Letter on the genetics and biology of homosexuality and transgender.

Norris, Alyssa L., et al. "Homosexuality as a Discrete Class," *Psychological Science*, 2015, Vol. 26, 1843-1853.

Baily, J.M., et al. "Genetic and Environmental Influences on Sexual Orientation and its Correlates in an Australian Twin Sample," *Journal of Personality and Social Psychology*, 2000, Vol. 78.

Fergusson, D.M., et al. "Sexual Orientation and Mental Health in a Birth Cohort of Young Adults," *Psychological Medicine*, 2005, Vol. 35.

Peters, M., et al. "The Effects of Sex, Sexual Orientation, and Digit ratio (2D:4D) on Mental Rotation Performance," *Archives of Sexual Behavior*, 2007, Vol. 36.

Sanders, A.R., et al. "Genome-wide Scan Demonstrates Significant Linkage for Male Sexual Orientation," *Psychological Medicine*, 2015, Vol. 45.

Peltz, Jennifer, "New York Moves to Stop LGBT 'Conversion Therapy,'" *Associated Press*, February 6, 2016.

Russo, Francine, "Is There Something Unique about the Transgender Brain?" *Scientific American Mind*, January 1, 2016.

Kranz, G, et.al., "White matter microstructure in transsexuals and controls investigated by diffusion tensor imaging," *Journal of Neuroscience*, 2014.

Wu, Katherine J., "Between the (Gender) Lines: The Science of Transgender Identity," *Harvard University Science in the News*, October 25, 2016.

Some resources you can find online are:

   Transgender Revolution Guide from National Geographic.
   The 2015 "Schools in Transition" guide.
   The "Welcoming Schools Starter Kit."

Carlozzi, Al, "Counseling Transgender Persons and Their Families," *Counseling Today*, August 2017.

Walsh, Mark, "Transgender Advocates Buoyed by Student's Court Victory," *Education Week*, June 7, 2017.

Baldor, Lolita C., "Military Chiefs Seek Delay in Transgender Enlistment," *San Diego Union-Tribune*, June 25, 2017.

Wilson, Stephen, "IOC Relaxes Transgender Guidelines for Athletes," *Associated Press*, January 25, 2016.

McKibben, Sarah, "Creating a Welcoming Environment for Transgender Students," *Education Update Newsletter,*

Blad, Evie, "How Many Transgender Children Are There?" *Education Week,* March 8, *2017.*

Stephen Wilson, "IOC Relaxes Transgender Guidelines for Athletes," *Associated Press*, January 25, 2016.

Meyers, Laurie, "LGBTQ Issues Across the Life Span," *Counseling Today,* April 2017.

Olson, Kristina R., et al. "Gender Cognition in Transgender Children," *Psychological Science,* 2015, Vol. 26. (The references/end notes in this study are a gold mine for anyone researching a science-based perspective on LGBTQ.

"Citizen Science" has grown in popularity with the advance of the Internet, Google, etc. While it is generally an anecdotal science, I believe it is the wave of the future for parenting and child developmental issues. Given how easy it is now to get access to primary science studies, and given the power of parents to observe and study their own children, citizen science seems a revolutionary way to discover best practices for child development. At the same time, citizen science can go awry, as it has in the anti-vaccination movement. We must be rigorous and vigilant.

Flaccus, Gillian, "Citizen Scientists Map Impact of El Nino," *Associated Press,* January 25, 2016.

Wang, Shirley S., "Why Medial Researchers Experiment on Themselves," *The Wall Street Journal,* January 26, 2016.

Degler, Carl. *In Search of Human Nature.* Oxford: Oxford University Press, 1992.

Johnson, Wendy, et.al, "Sex Differences in Variability in General Intelligence," *Psychological Science,* Vol. 3, August 2008.

Tyson, Neil deGrasse. *Astrophysics for People in a Hurry.* New York: Horton, 2017.

Bogan, Louise. *A Poet's Alphabet.* New York: McGraw-Hill, 1970.

Chapter 2

Halpern, D.F., et.al., "The Science of Sex Differences in Science and Mathematics," *Psychological Science in the Public Interest.* Vol. 8., August 2007.

Brizendine, Louann. *The Female Brain.* New York: Three Rivers Press, 2007.

Brizendine, Louann. *The Male Brain.* New York: Harmony, 2011.

Gur, Ruben, and Raquel Gur, "Complementarity of Sex Differences in Brain and Behavior," *Journal of Neuroscience Research,* November 2016.

Haier, Richard, "Intelligence in Men And Women Is A Gray And White Matter." *ScienceDaily*, January 22, 2005.

Spear, L. P. "Neurobehavioral changes in adolescence." *Current Directions in Psychological Science.* Vol. 9, 2011.

Spitzer, J. A. "Gender differences in some host defense mechanisms."

Lupus Vol. 8, 1999.

Spitzer, J. A., and P. Zhang. "Gender differences in neutrophil function and cytokine induced neutrophil chemoattractant generation in endotoxic rats." *Inflammation*. Vol 20. 1996.

Spitzer, J. A., and P. Zhang. "Protein tyrosine kinase activity and the influence of gender in phagocytosis and tumor necrosis factor secretion in alveolar macrophages and lung-recruited neutrophils." *Shock* Vol. 6, 1996.

Taylor, R. W., et.al., "Gender differences in body fat content are present well before puberty." *International Journal of Obesity and Related Metabolic Disorders*. Vol. 21, 1996.

Taylor, S. E., et.al., "Biobehavioral responses to stress in females: tend-and-befriend, not fight-or-flight." *Psychological Review* Vol.107, 2000.

Susman, E. J., et.al., "Hormones, emotional dispositions, and aggressive attributes in young adolescents." *Child Development*. Vol. 58, 1987.

Smith, S. S., et.al., "Oestrogen effects in olivo-cerebellar and hippocampal circuits," *Novartis Foundation Symposium*, Vol. 230, 2000.

Nickerson, D. A., et.al., "DNA sequence diversity in a 9.7-kb region of the human lipoprotein lipase gene," *Nature Genetics*, Vol. 3, 1989.

Nicolette, J., "Searching for women's health: a resident's perspective." *Journal of Women's Health & Gender-Based Medicine*. Vol 9. 2000.

Nishizawa, S.C., et.al., "Differences between males and females in rates of serotonin synthesis in human brain," *Proceedings of the National Academy of Sciences of the United States of America*, 1997.

McEwen, B. S. "Clinical Review 108: The molecular and neuroanatomical basis for estrogen effects in the central nervous system." *Journal of Clinical Endocrinology and Metabolism*. Vol 84, 1998.

Becker, J. B. "Gender differences in dopaminergic function in striatum and nucleus accumbens." *Pharmacology, Biochemistry, and Behavior*, Vol. 64, 1999.

McEwen, B. S. and S. E. Alves. "Estrogen actions in the central nervous system." *Endocrine Reviews*, Vol. 20, 1999.

McFadden, D. "A masculinizing effect on the auditory systems of human females having male co-twins." *Proceedings of the National Academy of Sciences of the United States of America*, Vol. 90, 1993.

Bachevalier, J. and C. Hagger. "Sex differences in the development of learning abilities in primates." *Psychoneuroendocrinology*. Vol. 16, 1991.

Hurst, L. D., and H. Ellegren. "Sex biases in the mutation rate." *Trends in Genetics*, Vol. 14, 1998.

Hyde, J. S. and M. C. Linn. "Gender differences in verbal ability: a meta-analysis." *Psychological Bulletin*. Vol. 104, 1988.

As you can see from these Notes, sex differences in the brain (what we now popularly call "gender differences") appear at all ages, including in earliest childhood and latest life-stages.

For early childhood to late adolescent differences, see especially:

Yu, Vickie., et al. "Age-Related Sex Differences in Language Lateralization: A Magnetoencephalography Study in Children," *Developmental*

Psychology, 2014, Vol.50.

Ingalhalikar, Madhura, et al. "Sex Differences in the Structural Connectome of the Human Brain," *Proceedings of the National Academy of Sciences,* 2014, Vol 111.

Killgore, William, et al. "Sex-Specific Developmental Changes in Amygdala Responses to Affective Faces," *NeuroReport,* 2001, Vol. 12.

Gummadavelli, Abhijeet, et al. "Spatiotemporal and Frequency Signatures of Word Recognition in the Developing Brain," *Brain Research,* 2013, Vol. 1498.

Sacher, Julia, et al. "Sexual Dimorphism in the Human Brain," *Magnetic Resonance Imaging,* 2013, Vol 31.

Dizik, Alina, "The Secret Subtext of Menus," *The Wall Street Journal,* March 25, 2015.

Winslow, Ron, "Genes May Explain Why Cancer Varies by Gender," *The Wall Street Journal,* May 17, 2016.

Shors, Tracey J. and Miesegaes, George, "Testosterone in Utero and at Birth Dictates How Stressful Experience Will Affect Learning in Adulthood," *Proceedings of the National Academy of Sciences 99,* no. 21, October 15, 2002.

Shors, Tracey J., "Stress and Sex Effects on Associative Learning: For Better or for Worse," *Neuroscientist 4,* no. 5, September 1998.

Wade, Nicolas, "Peeking into Pandora's Box," *The Wall Street Journal,* May 14-15, 2016. Wade explores themes in the new book by Siddhartha Mukherjee, *The Gene,* (Scribner, 2016). He makes a point that is perhaps common sense, but also can get lost as we try to understand what is "sex" and what is "gender" from a biological viewpoint.

While we can discuss "gender" as happening on a spectrum as male/female brains do happen on a spectrum, these brains are still male and female. So, while gender can feel fluid, when we come right down to living our lives and doing our daily tasks of surviving and thriving, sex (neurobiology) is far more powerful in us than some of the present debate allows for. Everyone who has had children has peeked into this truth; parents see the genes in their own family lab. Few, if any, parents of boys and girls cannot tell within five years of the child's birth that there are gender-different brains in those gendered bodies. Even the parents of a transgender child are seeing male/female brains—and so are their children who are trying to "become" the brain they already are by altering the body.

In a 2008 study published in the *Journal of Personality and Social Psychology,* a group of international researchers compared data on gender and personality across 55 nations and confirmed that, throughout the world, women tend to be more empathically nurturing, risk averse, and emotionally expressive in words, while men are usually more competitive, risk taking, and emotionally flat in comparison (men feel fewer feelings and express fewer of those feelings in words).

These differences were obvious in all cultures, but highest in frequency between men and women in the more prosperous, egalitarian, and educated societies such as our American culture and Europe. According to the authors,

"Higher levels of human development—including long and healthy life, equal access to knowledge and education, and economic wealth—were the main nation-level predictors of sex difference variation across cultures."

The idea, then, that male/female differences disappear in an economic democracy is incorrect. The more males and females have the freedom to "be who they are," the more they evidence gender differences. While their gender roles become more parallel, their gender differences—which affect their ability to learn well, grow well, survive, and thrive—are robust and must be taken into account by all social theories or we will lose huge portions of both males and females to distress.

Halpern, D. F. *Sex Differences in Cognitive Abilities*, 3rd ed. Mahwah, NJ: Lawrence Erlbaum Associates, 2000.

Hampson, E., "Sex differences in human brain and cognition: the influence of sex steroids in early and adult life." In: *Behavioral Endocrinology*, 2nd ed. J. B. Becker, S. M. Breedlove, D. Crews, and M. McCarthy, eds. Cambridge, MA: MIT Press/Bradford Books, 2000.

Hampson, E. "Variations in sex-related cognitive abilities across the menstrual cycle." *Brain and Cognition*. Vol. 14, 1990.

Hampson, E. "Estrogen-related variations in human spatial and articulatory-motor skills. *Psychoneuroendocrinology*, Vol. 15, 1990.

Hampson, E. and D. Kimura. "Reciprocal effects of hormonal fluctuations on human motor and perceptual-spatial skills." *Behavioral Neuroscience*, Vol. 102, 1988.

Gaillard, R. C. and E. Spinedi. "Sex- and stress-steroids interactions and the immune system: evidence for a neuroendocrine-immunological sexual dimorphism." *Domestic Animal Endocrinology* Vol. 15, 1998.

Gallagher, A. M., et.al., "Gender differences in advanced mathematical problem solving." *Journal of Experimental Child Psychology*, Vol. 75, 2000.

Ehrhardt, A. A. and S. W. Baker. "Fetal androgens, human central nervous system differentiation, and behavior sex differences, pp. 3351. In: *Sex Differences in Behavior*. R. C. Friedman, R. R. Richart, and R. L. Vande Weile, eds. New York: Wiley & Wilson. 1974.

Ingalhalikar, Madhura, et.al., including Ruben and Raquel Gur and Ragini Verma. "Sex Differences in the Structural Connectome of the Human Brain," *Proceedings of the National Academy of Sciences,* January 2014. The following is the Abstract for the study.

"Sex differences in human behavior show adaptive complementarity: Males have better motor and spatial abilities, whereas females have superior memory and social cognition skills. Studies also show sex differences in human brains but do not explain this complementarity.

"In this work, we modeled the structural connectome using diffusion tensor imaging in a sample of 949 youths (aged 8–22 y, 428 males and 521 females) and discovered unique sex differences in brain connectivity during the course of development. Connection-wise statistical analysis, as well as analysis of regional and global network measures, presented a comprehensive description of network characteristics.

- In all supratentorial regions, males had greater within-hemispheric connectivity, as well as enhanced modularity and transitivity, whereas between-hemispheric connectivity and cross-module participation predominated in females. However, this effect was reversed in the cerebellar connections.
- Analysis of these changes developmentally demonstrated differences in trajectory between males and females mainly in adolescence and in adulthood.
- Overall, the results suggest that male brains are structured to facilitate connectivity between perception and coordinated action, whereas female brains are designed to facilitate communication between analytical and intuitive processing modes."

As you are reading through these studies and the other thousand or so studies I have collected in the lists noted earlier, I hope you'll see three things especially:

1. That we've known about these sex differences for thousands of years and began proving them fifty years ago;
2. That the studies include people from all races and ethnicities in the U.S. and throughout the world; and
3. That the studies include all age groups, beginning at birth and extending throughout the lifespan.

These are important points, I believe, because they can bolster nature-based thinking in communities and organizations.

Epting, L. K., and W. H. Overman. "Sex-sensitive tasks in men and women: a search for performance fluctuations across the menstrual cycle." *Behavioral Neuroscience*, Vol. 112, 1998.

Breedlove, S. M., "Sexual differentiation of the human nervous system." *Annual Review of Psychology*, Vol. 45, 1994.

Broman, K. W., et.al., "Comprehensive human genetic maps: individual and sex-specific variation in recombination." *American Journal of Human Genetics*. Vol. 63, 1998.

Brizendinem Louann. *The Female Brain.*

Gurian, Michael. *Nurture the Nature.* San Francisco: Jossey-Bass/John Wiley, 2007.

Gurian, Michael with Barbara Annis. *Leadership and the Sexes.* San Francisco: Jossey-Bass/John Wiley, 2008.

Pashler, H., et.al., "Does multitasking impair studying? Depends on timing." *Applied Cognitive Psychology*, Vol. 27, 2013

Pereira, C. S., et.al., "Music and emotions in the brain: Familiarity matters." *PLOS ONE*, Vol 6, 2013.

Mehl, Matthias R. et al., including James W. Pennebaker, "Are Women Really More Talkative Than Men?" *Science,* Vol. 317, p. 82, July 2007.

OECD – PISA data can be accessed via *www.oecd.org/Pisa* and by exploring the oecd.org site. Particularly instructive is to go back over the last few decades and watch the evolution of the scores.

NAEP data can be accessed through https://nces.ed.gov/

nationsreportcard. As you go through the years and grades (go back twenty years, if possible), you'll also see an evolution of test scores by gender.

Amen, Daniel. 2013. *Unleash the Power of the Female Brain*. Bantam. New York.

Please see the studies noted above, including Halpern, Gur, Benbow, et.al., "The Truth About Sex Differences in Mathematics and Science," and:

Gur, Ruben C., et.al., "An fMRI Study of Sex Differences in Regional Activation to a Verbal and Spatial Task," *Brain and Language*. Vol. 74, 2000.

Cherry L. and Lewis, M. "Mothers and two-year-olds: a study of sex-differentiated aspects of verbal interaction." *Developmental Psychology*. Vol. 12, 1976.

Weinberg, M.K., et.al., "Gender differences in emotional expressivity and self-regulation during early infancy." *Developmental Psychology*, Vol. 35, 1999.

Simon Baron Cohen's *The Essential Difference* (updated, 2004) is a very powerful read on male/female brain differences.

Hertel, Paula, et.al., "Looking on the Dark Side of Rumination: A Cognitive Bias Modification Study," *Clinical Psychological Science*, April 16, 2014.

Orth, Ulrich and Robins, Richard, W., "The Development of Self-Esteem," *Current Directions in Psychological Science*, Vol. 13, 2014.

Kircanski, Katharina., et.al., "Rumination and Worry in Daily Life: Examining the Naturalistic Validity of Theoretical Constructs," *Psychological Science*, 2015.

Judith Shulevitz, "The Science of Suffering, *New Republic*, November 2014.

Middlebrooks, Catherine D., et.al. "Selectively Distracted: Divided Attention and Memory for Important Information," *Psychological Science*, 2017.

Cohen, M. S., et.al., "Value-based modulation of memory encoding involves strategic engagement of fronto-temporal semantic processing regions." *Cognitive, Affective, & Behavioral Neuroscience*, Vol 14. 2014.

Craik, F. I. M., et.al., "The effects of divided attention on encoding and retrieval processes in human memory." *Journal of Experimental Psychology*: Vol. 125, 1996.

Richard Haier, "Intelligence in Men and Women Is a Gray and White Matter." *ScienceDaily*, January 22, 2005.

Amen, Daniel G., et.al., "Gender-Based Cerebral Perfusion Differences in 46,034 Functional Neuroimaging Scans." *Journal of Alzheimer's Disease*, 2017.

Chapter 3

Theresa M. Wizemann and Mary-Lou Pardue, Editors, *Exploring the Biological Contributions to Human Health: Does Sex Matter?* National Academy of Sciences, Committee on Understanding the Biology of Sex and Gender Differences, Board on Health Sciences Policy. Washington, D.C. National

Academies Press, 2001

Michael Gurian. 2017. *Saving Our Sons.* Gurian Institute Press. Spokane, WA.

See the Walsh Research Institute in Illinois. *Nutrient Power* by William J. Walsh, the founder of the institute, is fascinating and very useful.

Amy Dockser Marcus, "Scientists Fix Gene Defect in Human Embryos," *Wall Street Journal.*

Jane E. Brody, "A Mysterious Rise in Type 1 Diabetes," *The New York Times,* April 21, 2015. The title of this article implies that it is only about diabetes, but in fact the article goes into helpful depth on new genetics-based research on the effects of stress on juveniles and adults, i.e. how stress affects epigenetics.

Melissa Healy, "Study Links Autism, Anti-Depressants in Pregnancy," *The Los Angeles Times,* December 15, 2015.

Luc Goossens, et al. "The Genetics of Loneliness: Linking Evolutionary Theory to Genome-Wide Genetics, Epigenetics, and Social Science," *Perspectives on Psychological Science,* 2015, Vol. 10(2) 213-226.

Staff Report. "Women with Bulimia 'Wired' Differently," *Medpage Today,* July 18, 2017.

Gustavson, Daniel., et.al., "Genetic and Environmental Associations Between Procrastination and Internalizing/ Externalizing Psychopathology," *Psychological Science,* 2017.

Simon Makin, "What Really Causes Autism," *Scientific American Mind,* November/December 2015.

Robert Lee Hotz, "China Genetically Modifies Monkeys to Aid Autism Study," *Wall Street Journal,* January 26, 2016.

Anna Mikulak, "Across the Spectrum," *Association for Psychological Science Journal, the Observer.* May/June 2017. This article features new thinking on the genetics of autism.

Laurie Meyers, "Reconsidering ADD," *Counseling Today,* August 2016.

Alan Schwarz. 2016. *The Ritalin Generation.* Scribner. New York.

Nigg, Joel T., et.al., "Variation in an Iron Metabolism Gene Moderates the Association Between Blood Lead Levels and Attention-Deficit/ Hyperactivity Disorder in Children," *Psychological Science,* 2015.

Daniel Amen, *Healing ADD,* New York: Berkley, 2013. I highly recommend Dr. Amen's approach to ADD which not only uses brain scans to aid in diagnosis and treatment, but also divides ADD into various types so that parents and professionals can fully understand the exact kind(s) of ADD/ADHD a child has. Like genome testing, the use of brain scans to aid in correct treatment can be very helpful.

Medications given for ADD/ADHD (like any brain disorder or condition) can affect the human body and brain in ways unforeseen or misunderstood until much later and so are not necessarily "benign." Even though they are needed by many of our children, they can also, ironically, cause issues with lack of motivation as well as other side effects. See:

Robinson, Terry and Kolb, Bryan, "Structural Plasticity Associated with

Exposure to Drugs of Abuse," *Neuropharmacology*, 2004, Vol. 47.

Carlezon, William, et al. "Understanding the Neurobiological Consequences of Early Exposure to Psychotropic Drugs, *Neuropharmacology*, 2004, Vol. 47.

Gramage, Esther, et al. "Periadolescent Amphetamine Treatment Causes Transient Cognitive Disruptions and Long-Term Changes in Hippocampal LTP," 2013, *Addiction Biology*, Vol 18.

Robinson, Terry and Kolb, Bryan, "Persistent Structural Modifications in Nucleus Accumbens and Prefrontal Cortex Neurons Produced by Previous Experiences with Amphetamine," 1997, *Journal of Neuroscience*, Vol. 17.

Pardey, Margery, et al, "Long-term Effects of Chronic Oral Ritalin Administration on Cognitive and Neural Development in Adolescent Wistar Kyoto Rats," 2012, *Brain Sciences*, Vol. 2.

Alpha Genomix is one of the companies that uses a DNA test to determine how medications are metabolized by each person's genes and physiology. The company produces a comprehensive list of a wide array of medications and their efficacy. Medications are listed as 1) able to be prescribed according to standard regimens, 2) adjusting dosages or increased vigilance while on the medication 3) potentially reduced efficacy or increased toxicity.

23 and Me is another company that provides genetic testing. With its results in hand, you can use the Genetics Genie software, with professional assistance, to interpret results. I have personally used 23 and Me for genetics study and found the company reputable and professional.

Let me make clear, however, that I am not "selling" any of these companies. They are companies I know of, ones that my and some of my colleagues' clients and patients have utilized.

I recommend that you get the help of psychiatrists and/or other qualified medical professionals to help you learn which tests are best and how to interpret the results. The tests need some very qualified eyes to read them for use by the family and the individual child or adult whose genes have been studied.

A very intriguing science-based approach to treatment of autism and other conditions is GAPS (Gut and Psychology Syndrome) natural treatments. A practitioner is Dr. Natasha Campbell-McBride (www.doctor-natasha.com).

For more on obesity genetics, see: http://www.ncbi.nlm.nih.gov/pubmed/21717811.

Daniel Akst, "Delay That's in Our DNA," *The Wall Street Journal*, April 12, 2014.

Ayorech, Ziada, et.al., "Genetic Influence on Intergenerational Educational Attainment," *Psychological Science*, February 2017.

Mehr, Samuel A., et.al., "Genomic Imprinting Is Implicated in the Psychology of Music," *Psychological Science*, August 2017.

Ayorech, Ziada., et.al., "Genetic Differences Linked with Social Mobility, *APS Journal*, August 11, 2017.

Alison Gopnik, "How to Get Old Brains to Think Like Young Ones," *Wall Street Journal,* July 8/9, 2017.

Amy Dockser Marcus, "The Hard, New Family Talk: Our Genes," *The Wall Street Journal,* September 28, 2015.

Anna Gorman, "Doctors Encourage Shoppers to Skip 'Bad Food'," *Tribne News Service,* January 5, 2016.

Cynthia M. Bulik, et. al. "Significant Locus and Metabolic Genetic Correlations Revealed in Genome-Wide Association Study of Anorexia Nervosa.*" American Journal of Psychiatry*, 2017.

Yiend, Jenny, et.al., "Negative Self-Beliefs in Eating Disorders: A Cognitive-Bias-Modification Study," *Clinical Psychological Science*, April 9, 2009.

Keel, Pamela K., et.al. "Influences of Ovarian Hormones on Dysregulated Eating," *Clinical Psychological Science,* March 16, 2014.

Klump, Kelly L., "Differential Effects of Estrogen and Progesterone on Genetic and Environmental Risk for Emotional Eating in Women," *Clinical Psychological Science,* 2016.

Sumner, A. E., et.al., "Sex differences in African-Americans regarding sensitivity to insulin's glucoregulatory and antilipolytic actions," *Diabetes Care.* Vol. 22, 2000.

Nicklas, B. J., et.al., "Daily energy expenditure is related to plasma leptin concentrations in older African-American women but not men," *Diabetes,* Vol. 46, 1997.

Chapter 4

Ulrich Orth and Richard W. Robins, "The Development of Self-Esteem," *Psychological Science.* Vol. 23, 2014.

Alexander Todorov. 2017. *Face Value.* Princeton University Press. Princeton, NJ.

The June 2017 issue of *Current Directions in Psychological Science* includes a gold mine of studies on face perception, facial cues, individual differences in picking up social cues, and many of the other topics covered in this section.

Scott Sleek, "The Science of Sameness: The Neural Mechanics of Conformity," *Association for Psychological Science Journal,* Vol. 29, December 2016.

Malcolm Ritter, "Paving the Way for Motherhood," *Associated Press,* December 27, 2016.

Susan Pinker, "Lessons from Chimp Mothers Last a Lifetime," *Wall Street Journal,* December 10-11, 2016.

Treva Lind, "Bridging Generations," *Spokesman-Review,* June 5, 2017.

Richard O. Prum. 2016. *The Evolution of Beauty.* Doubleday. New York.

Bonnie Rochman. 2017. *The Gene Machine.* Farrar, Strous & Giroux. New York.

Adrian Woolfson, "A Genetic Pandora's Box, *Wall Street Journal,* March

11-12, 2017.

Katarina Salmela-Aro, "Study: As Many as 20% of Top High-School Girls May Burn Out." *Science Daily,* May 14, 2017.

The American Counseling Association, in August of 2012, reported a new Substance Abuse and Mental Health Services Administration (SAMHSA) report that revealed the percentage of girls experiencing a major depressive episode triples between the ages of 12 and 15, growing from 5.1% to 15.2% respectively. "SAMHSA also indicates that an annual average of 1.4 million adolescent girls between the ages 12 to 17 experienced a major depressive episode in the past year. One positive sign emanating from the report was that adolescent girls are increasingly seeking treatment for their depression."

Eli Francovich, "Forum Tackles Youth Suicide," *Spokesman-Review,* June 11, 2017.

Ron Steingard, "Mood Disorders and Teenage Girls," *Child Mind Institute Newsletter,* July 20, 2016.

Rachel Ehmke, "What is Body Dysmorphic Disorder?" *Child Mind Institute Newsletter,* June 27, 2017.

Sara Burrows, "Depression is a Disease of Civilization," *Return to Now,* February 24, 2016, featuring *The Depression Cure* by Stephen Ilardi.

Andrea Petersen, "Training the Brain to Cope with Depression," *Wall Street Journal,* January 19, 2016.

Fortunately, there are programs to help girls in nearly every city and state. The "Girls Leadership program" provided through the United Nations can be used worldwide. Rachel Simmons, the author of "Odd Girl Out," offers summer leadership camps for girls. In Arizona, www.notMYkid.org shows workshops led by graduating seniors and older teens for younger girls. Girls Rule is a national program focusing on helping girls.

Bethany Bray, "Living with Anxiety," *Counseling Today,* June 2017.

The September/October 2015 issue of *Family Therapy* is titled "Therapy, Medication, and the MFT." It is packed with useful articles on brain disorders and medication.

Resources on suicide include:

- Maggie Fox, "Suicides in Teen Girls Hits 40 Year High," *NBC Health News,* August 3, 2017.
- Lindsay Holmes, "Suicide Rates for Teen Boys and Girls Are Climbing," *Huffington Post,* February 2017.
- Keri O'Driscoll, "Teen Suicide," *Grown and Flown.* August 8, 2017.
- Gregg Zoroya, "The Tragic Tide of Suicide: 4 an Hour," *USA Today,* October 10, 2014.
- Mark Emmons, "Williams' Death Opens Discussion on Often-Private Issue of Suicide," *McClatchy-Tribune,* August 14, 2014.
- Betsy McKay, "Suicides Climb After Years of Declines," *The Wall Street Journal,* April 22, 2016.

Dr. Max McGee, retiring superintendent of the Palo Alto School District, is a great resource in the suicide prevention area. In Phoenix, Arizona, where the Gurian Institute has co-sponsored Suicide Prevention services, these weblinks are useful. They can be used and/or replicated by any district.

www.communitybridgesaz.org

www.teenlifeline.org

www.crisisnetwork.org

www.thepathwayprogram.com.

Also see the websites for the Suicide Resource Prevention Center. They have a ready-to-use toolkit for schools and communities at www.heardalliance.org/help-toolkit.

For more insight on rumination, worry, anxiety, and depression among girls, see:

Kircanski, Katharian, et.al., "Rumination and Worry in Daily Life: Examining the Naturalistic Validity of Theoretical Constructs," *Psychological Science,* 2015.

Brown, T. A., et.al. "Current and lifetime comorbidity of the DSM-IV anxiety and mood disorders in a large clinical sample." *Journal of Abnormal Psychology*, Vol. 110, 2001.

Bylsma, L. M., Taylor-Clift, A., & Rottenberg, J. (2011). "Emotional reactivity to daily events in major and minor depression." *Journal of Abnormal Psychology*, 120.

Carels, R. A., Coit, C., Young, K., & Berger, B. (2007). "Exercise makes you feel good, but does feeling good make you exercise? An examination of obese dieters." *Journal of Sport & Exercise Psychology*, Vol. 29.

Cooney, R. E., Joormann, J., Eugène, F., Dennis, E. L., & Gotlib, I. H. (2010). "Neural correlates of rumination in depression." *Cognitive, Affective & Behavioral Neuroscience,* Vol. 10.

Thomsen, D. K. (2006). "The association between rumination and negative affect: A review." *Cognition & Emotion*, Vol. 20.

Treynor, W., Gonzalez, R., & Nolen-Hoeksema, S. (2003). "Rumination reconsidered: A psychometric analysis." *Cognitive Therapy and Research*, Vol. 27.

Watkins, E., & Moulds, M. (2005). "Distinct modes of ruminative self-focus: Impact of abstract versus concrete rumination on problem solving in depression." *Emotion*, Vol. 5.

Watkins, E., Moulds, M., & Mackintosh, B. (2005). "Comparisons between rumination and worry in a nonclinical population." *Behaviour Research and Therapy*, Vol. 43.

Yook, K., Kim, K.-H., Suh, S. Y., & Lee, K. S. (2010). "Intolerance of uncertainty, worry, and rumination in major depressive disorder and generalized anxiety disorder." *Journal of Anxiety Disorders*, Vol. 24.

McLaughlin, K. A., Borkovec, T. D., & Sibrava, N. J. (2007). "The effects of worry and rumination on affect states and cognitive activity." *Behavior Therapy*, Vol. 38.

Meyer, T. J., Miller, M. L., Metzger, R. L., & Borkovec, T. D. (1990). "Development and validation of the Penn State Worry Questionnaire." *Behavior Research and Therapy*, Vol. 28.

Moberly, N. J., & Watkins, E. R. (2008). "Ruminative self-focus and negative affect: An experience sampling study." *Journal of Abnormal Psychology*, Vol. 117.

Moberly, N. J., & Watkins, E. R. (2010). "Negative affect and ruminative self-focus during everyday goal pursuit." *Cognition & Emotion*, Vol. 24.

Leonard Sax, "Why Do Girls Tend to Have More Anxiety Than Boys?" *New York Times*, April 21, 2016.

Verhallen, Roeland J., et.al., "The Oxytocin Receptor Gene (OXTR) and Face Recognition," *Current Directions in Psychological Science*, Vol. 28(1), 2016.

Guastella, Adam J. and Andrew H. Kemp, "The Role of Oxytocin in Human Affect: A Novel Hypothesis," *Current Directions in Psychological Science*, August 9, 2011.

Taylor, Shelley E., et.al., "Are Plasma Oxytocin in Women and Plasma Vasopressin in Men Biomarkers of Distressed Pair-Bond Relationships?" *Current Directions in Psychological Science*, December 17, 2009.

Fang, Angela., et.al., "Attachment Style Moderates the Effects of Oxytocin on Social Behaviors and Cognitions During Social Rejection," *Clinical Psychological Science*, April 2014.

Bartz, Jennifer A., "Oxytocin and the Pharmacological Dissection of Affiliation," *Current Directions in Psychological Science*, 2016, Vol. 25.

Elahe Izadi, "How Men and Women Process Emotions Differently," *Washington Post*, January 23, 2015, referring to research in the *Journal of Neuroscience*.

A wonderful example of male/female difference was provided to me by Rob Kodama, a Gurian Master Trainer who is Director of Admissions and Marketing, as well as Head Soccer Coach, for Crespi Carmelite High School in Encino, California. He told me:

"The first thing I think about when it comes to sports and gender difference is communication styles when it comes to how boys and girls receive instructions. The volume levels I have to use with boys always tends to be louder than with girls. I have to be more careful how I speak to the group of girls because they read the body language and tones much better than boys. There will be times I am working with the high school boys and go straight to a second session with all girls and forget to change my tones and they will interpret it as me yelling at them."

Cohen, Noga, "Linking Executive Control and Emotional Response: A Training Procedure to Reduce Rumination," *Clinical Psychological Science*, 2014.

Eisenbruch, Adar B., et.al., Lady in Red: Hormonal Predictors of Women's Clothing Choices, *Psychological Science*, 2015.

Alloy, Lauren B., et.al., "Pubertal Development, Emotion Regulatory Styles, and the Emergence of Sex Differences in Internalizing Disorders and Symptoms in Adolescence," *Clinical Psychological Science*, 2016.

Krems, Jaimie Arona, et.al., "Is She Angry? (Sexually Desirable) Women 'See' Anger on Female Faces," *Psychological Science*, 2015.

Roberts, Craig, et.al., "Partner Choice, Relationship Satisfaction, and

Oral Contraception: The Congruency Hypothesis," *Psychological Science,* 2014.

Mendle, Jane, "Beyond Pubertal Timing: New Directions for Studying Individual Differences in Development," *Current Directions in Psychological Science,* Vol. 23, 2014.

Daniel Goleman, *Emotional Intelligence.*

Sumiya, Ahmad, et al. "Emotional Intelligence and Gender Differences," 2009, *Suhrad Journal of Agriculture,* Vol. 25, No. 1.

Amen, Daniel. *Sex on the Brain.*

Baron-Cohen, Simon. *The Essential Difference.*

Taylor, Shelley E. *The Tending Instinct.*

The July 2008 *Anesthesia & Analgesia Journal* is devoted to the topic of sex, gender, and pain response. Fifteen clinical studies comprise the volume and make powerful reading for anyone interested in how men and women respond to pain differently. Volume 107: 1.

Also, see the work of Jay Giedd, M.D., at the National Institute of Mental Health (nimh.gov). He and his lab team have posted some of their brain scans on their site, some of which show differences in the male and female brain. According to the NIMH website, "The lab studies sexual dimorphism in the developing brain (especially important in child psychiatry where nearly all disorders have different ages of onsets, prevalence and symptomatology between boys and girls)."

For more on male/female brain difference in emotional processing, please see the resources listed in the Notes for earlier chapters; my previous books on this topic; and the work of neuroscientists Louann Brizendine, Leonard Sax, and Daniel Amen.

Sumathi Reddy, "The Problems of Treating Several Chronic Conditions," *The Wall Street Journal,* August 11, 2015.

Daniel Goleman, *Emotional Intelligence.*

Kivlighan, Katie, et al. "Gender Differences in Testosterone and Cortisol Response to Competition," *Psychoneuroendocrinology,* 2005, Vol. 30.

Cashdan, E., "Are Men More Competitive Than Women?" *British Journal of Social Psychology,* 1998, Vol. 34.

Geary, David and Flinn, M.V., "Sex Differences in Behavioral and Hormonal Response to Social Threat," *Psychological Review,* 2002, Vol. 109.

David Brooks, "Is Chemistry Destiny?" *The New York Times,* September 17, 2015.

Bushman, Brad, "Does Venting Anger Feed or Extinguish the Flame? Catharsis, Rumination, Distraction, Anger, and Aggressive Responding," *Personality and Social Psychology,* 2002, Vol. 28.

Lyubomirsky, S., and Nolen-Hoeksema, S. "Effects of Self-Focused Rumination on Negative Thinking and Interpersonal Problem Solving." *Journal of Personality and Social Psychology.* 1995, Vol. 69.

Feinberg, Matthew, et.al., "Gossip and Ostracism Promotes Cooperation in Groups," *Psychological Science,* Vol. 25(3), 2014.

Stroud's research is featured in Sue Shellenberger, "Advice on Helping

Teen Girls Thrive," *Wall Street Journal,* April 12, 2017.

Laura Thomas, "Rejecting the Mean Girls Framework," *Edutopia.org,* July 11, 2017.

Lisa Damour. *Untangled.*

Hertel, Paula, et.al., "Looking on the Dark Side of Rumination: A Cognitive Bias Modification Study," *Clinical Psychological Science,* April 16, 2014.

David C. Geary, "Evolution of Sex Differences in Trait- and Age-Specific Vulnerabilities," *Perspectives on Psychological Science,* Vol. 11(6), 2016.

Maria Donilova, "School Bullying Persists While Reports of Sex Crime Up," *Associated Press.* May 17, 2017.

Saylor & Leach, 2009, "Perceived Bullying and Social Support in Students Accessing Special Inclusion Programming," *Journal of Developmental and Physical Disabilities,* Feb. 2009, Vol. 21, Issue 1.

Laura Thomas, "Rejecting the Mean Girls Framework," *Edutopia.org,* July 11, 2017.

Resnick, M., et al., 1997, "Protecting young people from harm: Findings form the National Longitudinal Study of Adolescent Health." *Journal of the American Medical Association,* 278, 823-832.

Gingsburg, K., 2015 3rd edition, *Building Resilience in Children and Teens: Giving Your Child Roots and Wings,* pgs. 21-30, American Academy of Pediatrics.

Especially with more girls becoming more violent in our era, see also "Lighter Penalties for Those with 'Violent Genes,'" by Melvin Konner, *The Wall Street Journal,* July 23-24, 2016. Dr. Konner analyzes the role of the monoamine oxidase (MAO) gene, which helps process dopamine and the enzyme linked to violence, as well as the connection of both to ventral striatum processing in the brain. Bringing together new studies from Finland, the U.S., and Canada, he provides a helpful summary of the research connecting genetics and violence. He also notes a link between alcohol and substance abuse (and the genetics related to alcohol and drug use) and violence.

Meanwhile, bullying statistics vary depending on the source because what is defined as bullying differs between sources. Check out the Center for Disease Control, for instance, http://americanspcc.org/bullying/statistics-and-information/?gclid=Cj0KEQjwyum6BRDQ, and you can find further statistics at http://americanspcc.org/bullying/statistics-and-information/.

Any bullying or violence at all is too much, obviously, e.g. see: Kathleen Smith, "The Many Faces of Domestic Violence," *Psychotherapy Networker,* November 2014, pp 11-12. Simultaneously, we must become more realistic about what is bullying in school and what is not. By some present definitions of bullying, every child is bullied, and if you spend time on Google, you can even find reputable "studies" that claim exactly that. If that is the case, then every sibling has bullied his/her sibling repeatedly and been bullied repeatedly. To me, this approach to bullying trivializes the actual and dangerous bullying that goes on among our children and adults.

Frank Dilallo, a veteran educator and Gurian Institute Trainer, has written a series of very helpful resources on bullying. Some come under the category of *Bullying Redirect: New Strategies for Educators and Parents.* These books are written separately for secular parents and schools and Christian/Catholic parents and schools. You can access them online.

LGBTQ children often experience heightened bullying. Some resources for families of these children include:

- American Psychological Association—(202) 336-5500
- Association of Gay and Lesbian Psychiatrists—(215) 222-2800
- National Association of School Psychologists—(301) 657-0270
- National Youth Advocacy Coalition—(800) 541-6922
- Parents, Families, and Friends of Lesbians and Gays—(202) 467-8180.

Kitayama, Shinobu., et.al., "The Dopamine D4 Receptor Gene (DRD4) Interdependent Social Orientation Moderates Cultural Difference in Independent Versus Interdependent." *Psychological Science*, April 18, 2014.

Chapter 5

The endnotes for this chapter include not only the references within the chapter, but also more references by which you can explore this nature-based approach to suffering, privation, and issues our girls face. Neurotoxins attack not only our children's cells, but the cells of us, as parents (which then creates negative effects down through the generations). Many neurotoxins are physical/environmental (food, etc.) and many are behavioral, such as violence/trauma we experience(d) at neurotoxic levels.

Robert M. Sapolsky, "Sperm Can Carry Dad's Stress as Well as Genes," *Wall Street Journal,* September 6, 2014.

The September/October 2015 edition of *Family Therapy* is devoted to looking at issues regarding medication that I discuss in this chapter and this book. If you have a child on medication, you might especially find this article useful: "Children, Adolescents, and Psychiatric Drugs," by Dr. Jacqueline A. Sparks.

David Klein, "Label Salon Products to Disclose Health Risks," *San Francisco Chronicle,* August 21, 2017.

Melissa Healy, "Acetaminophen Use Linked to Behavioral Issues in Kids," *Los Angeles Times,* August 16, 2016.

Daniel Amen, "Brain Health Guide to Red Dye," Amen Clinics Newsletter, June 14, 2016.

Bazer, F.W., et.al., "Environmental Factors Affecting Pregnancy: Endocrine Disrupters, Nutrients, and Metabolic Pathways," *Molecular and Cellular Endocrinology,* Vol. 298(1-2).

Sumathi Reddy, "Treating Sensory Disorders in Children," *Wall Street Journal,* August 16, 2016.

Gary Taubes. (2015). *The Case Against Sugar.* Knopf. New York.

Robert Lee Hotz, "Study Finds Allergy Risk Starts in Infant's Gut," *Wall Street Journal.* October 11, 2016.

Michael Biesecker, "EPA Chief Met with Pesticide CEO Before Reversing Ban," *Associated Press,* June 28, 2017.

Sumathi Reddy, "For More Children, Puberty Signs Start at 8 Years Old," *Wall Street Journal,* June 21, 2016.

Thomas Gremillion and Gabrielle Gurian have produced a powerful action report on healthy eating, "Going Local: Initiatives to Reduce Antibiotics in the Food Supply," October 2017, at http://consumerfed.org/wp-content/uploads/2017/10/going-local-report.pdf.

Geller, A.M., et al. "Gender-Dependent Behavioral and Sensory Effects of a Commercial Mixture of Polychlorinated Biphenyls," *Toxicological Science,* 2001, Vol. 59.

Palanza, Paola, et al. "Effects of Developmental Exposure to Bisphenol A on Brain and Behavior in Mice," 2008, *Environmental Research,* Vol. 108.

The May and June 2015 *Scientific American* provides a number of very readable and powerful articles on the workings of genetics, gene expression, and effects of neurotoxins on genes. Diana Maron is quoted from this volume. Frank Biro is quoted from May 2015, "The Science of Health." We introduced this topic in Chapter 2 and Chapter 3, and those endnotes include more references for this section. Also see Leonard Sax, *Girls on the Edge.*

Grandjean, Phillippe, et al. "Neurobehavioral Effects of Developmental Toxicity," *Lancet Neurology,* Vol. 13, March 2014.

See also the online summary: "Endocrine-disrupting Chemicals Pose Threat to Male Reproductive Health" in *News Medical: Science and Health,* December 11, 2015.

Colborn, Theo, et al. "Developmental Effects of Endocrine-Disrupting Chemicals in Wildlife and Humans," *Environmental Health Perspectives,* 1993, Vol. 101.

Fisher, Jane, "Environmental Anti-androgens and Male Reproductive Health: Focus on Phthalates and Testicular Dysgenesis Syndrome," *Reproduction,* 2004, Vol. 127.

Golub, Mari, et al. "Endocrine Disruption in Adolescence," *Toxicological Sciences,* 2004, Vol.82.

Travison, Thomas, et al. "A Population-Level Decline in Serum Testosterone Levels in American Men," *Journal of Clinical Endocrinology and Metabolism,* 2007, Vol. 92.

Ozen, Samim and Darcan, Sukran, "Effects of Environmental Endocrine Disruptors on Pubertal Development," *Journal of Clinical Research in Pediatric Endocrinology,* 2011, Vol. 3.

Masuo, Yoshinori and Ishido, Masami, "Neurotoxicity of Endocrine Disruptors: Possible Involvement in Brain Development and Neurodegeneration," *Journal of Toxicology and Environmental Research,* 2008, Vol. 14.

Aksglaede, Lise et al. "The Sensitivity of the Child to Sex Steroids:

Possible Impact of Exogenous Estrogens," *Human Reproduction Update,* 2006, Vol. 12.

"Chemicals Present in Clear Plastics Can Impair Learning and Cause Disease," March 28, 2005, retrieved from *www.yale.edu/opa/ newsr/05-30-28-02.all.html.*

Hojo, R., et al. "Sexually Dimorphic Behavioral Responses to Prenatal Dioxin Exposure," *Environmental Health Perspectives,* 2002, Vol. 110.

Roy, Jonathan, et al. "Estrogen-like Endocrine Disrupting Chemicals Affecting Puberty in Humans—A Review," *Medical Science Review,* 2009, Vol. 15.

Makin, Simon, "What Really Causes Autism," *Scientific American Mind,* November/December 2015.

Thomas E. Brown, "ADHD: From Stereotype to Science," *Educational Leadership,* October 2015

Daniel Amen, *Healing ADD.*

Yoshinori, Masuo, et al. "Motor Hyperactivity Caused by a Deficit in Dopaminergic Neurons and the Effects of Endocrine Disruptors," *Regulatory Peptides,* 2004, Vol. 123.

Swan, Shanna H., et al. "Decrease in Anogenital Distance Among Male Infants with Prenatal Phthalate Exposure," *Environmental Health Perspectives,* 2005, Vol. 11.

Duty, S.M, et al. "Phthalate Exposure and Reproductive Hormones in Adult Men," *Human Reproduction,* 2005, Vol. 20.

Duty, S.M., et al. "Phthalate Exposure and Human Semen Parameters," *Epidemiology,* 2003, Vol. 14.

McEwen, Bruce, "Steroid Hormones and Brain Development: Some Guidelines for Understanding Actions of Pseudo-hormones and Other Toxic Agents," *Environmental Health Perspectives,* 1987, Vol. 74, 177-184. As far back as the 1980s, we knew endocrine disruptors could harm our children, but we did not act with scientific rigor. Now, we must.

MacLusky, Neil, et al. "The Environmental Estrogen Bisphenol A Inhibits Estradiol-Induced Hippocampal Synaptogenesis," *Environmental Health Perspectives,* 2005, Vol. 113.

Fisher, Claire I, et al. "Women's Preference for Attractive Makeup Tracks Changes in their Salivary Testosterone," *Psychological Science,* Vol. 26(12).

Michael Hawthorne, "Exposed: Studies Show Link Between Childhood Lead Levels and Violent Crime Years Later," *Chicago Tribune,* June 15, 2015.

Kris Maher, "City Urges Aid after Lead Found in Water," *The Wall Street Journal,* December 16, 2015.

Cameron McWhirter and Mike Vilensky, "Water Contamination Found in Vermont Wells," *The Wall Street Journal,* March 16, 2016. Flint, Michigan is not the only area of the country that must look carefully at the water our children drink. PFOA (perfluorooctanoic acid), which is used in various industrial products, joins chemicals in aluminum, lead, and other metals as potentially toxic to the brains of our children.

Ronal Serpas, "Understanding Violence as a 'Contagion,'" *The Wall Street*

Journal, April 6, 2015.

Thomas F. Denson, "Naturally Nasty," *Journal of the Association for Psychological Science,"* January 2014 – Vol 27, No 1.

Charlene M. Alexander, et al. "Adolescent Dating Violence: Application of a U.S. Primary Prevention Program in St. Lucia," *Journal of Counseling and Development,* October 2014, Vol. 92.

Dahlberg LL, Mercy JA. "History of Violence as a Public Health Issue." *AMA Virtual Mentor,* February 2009. Volume 11, No. 2: 167-172. Available on-line at http://virtualmentor.ama-assn.org/2009/02/mhst1-0902.html.

Khullar, Dhruv and Jena, Anupam B. "Homicide's Role in the Racial Life-Expectancy Gap," *The Wall Street Journal,* April 28, 2016.

Gapp, Katharina, et al. including Isabelle M. Mansuy, "Implication of sperm RNAs in transgenerational inheritance of the effects of early trauma in mice," *Nature Neuroscience,* March 2014, Vol. 17.

Lisa Gillespie, "Struggles Now—And Later," *Tribune News Service,* March 8, 2106.

Robert M. Sapolsky, "The Price of Poverty for a Developing Brain," *The Wall Street Journal,* April 12-13, 2016.

Roxanne Nelson, "Violence as an Infectious Disease," *Medscape Medical News,* April 29, 2013.

Manuel Jimenez, "Kindergartners with Traumatic Life Experiences Struggle More in School," *Healthday News,* January 15, 2016.

Brand, C.R., et al. "Personality and General Intelligence." In G.L. Van Heck, P. Bonaiuto, I.J. Deary & W. Nowack (eds.), *Personality Psychology in Europe* 4, 203-228. Tilburg University Press. 1993.

David C. Geary, "Evolution of Sex Differences in Trait- and Age-Specific Vulnerabilities," *Perspectives on Psychological Science,* Vol. 11(6), 2016.

Joanna Ellington, *Slippery When Wet.*

The studies in *Pediatrics* can be found in Leonard Sax's *Girls on the Edge.* That book has many other similar studies in it as well. It is a very important read for parents of daughters.

Also see: Daniel Amen, "Is There a Link Between Depression and Birth Control?" *Amen Clinics Newsletter,* December 5, 2016.

James Greenblatt, "Low Cholesterol and Its Psychological Effects," *Integrative Psychiatry,* August 17, 2017.

Jie-Yu Chuang, et al, "Adolescent Major Depressive Disorder: Neuroimaging Evidence of Sex Difference during an Affective Go/No-Go Task," *Frontiers in Psychiatry* (2017).

Daniel Amen, "Do You Have an Abusive Relationship with Sugar," Amen Clinics Newsletter, August 16, 2017.

Shanna Swan, "Parents Needn't Wait for Legislation to Shield Kids from Toxins in Products," *San Francisco Chronicle,* January 9, 2006.

In a tiny two paragraph story off the wires, the headline reads, "Artificial Ingredient Sliced." The story is about Pizza Hut ending the use of artificial ingredients over the next year in its U.S. restaurants. Pizza Hut executives have studied the science and agree that BHA and BHT must be cut from meat to protect customers, as must artificial preservatives from cheese.

This is the kind of responsible citizenship that should make front-page news, in my humble opinion. The epigenetics issues that preservatives, artificial ingredients, red dye, artificial sweeteners, and even simple things like aluminum can cause our children should be front page news whenever possible.

The information and research on LGBT mentioned in this chapter can be found in the notes for Chapter 1. Also see:

Sarah Knapton, "Being Homosexual is Partly Due to Gay Gene, Study Finds," *Daily Telegraph,* February 13, 2014.

Bailey, J. Michael, et.al., "Sexual Orientation, Controversy, and Science," *Psychological Science in the Public Interest,* Vol. 17, 2016.

Chapter 6

Karen Salmansohn is a female empowerment writer and speaker who can be reached at www.notsalmon.com.

Angela Duckworth and James J. Gross, "Self-Control and Grit: Related but Separable Determinants of Success." *Psychological Science.* Vol. 23. 2014.

Eric Adler, "Millennials Not Leaving the Nest," *Tribune News Service,* May 1, 2017.

Alison Gopnik, "Against Parenting," *Wall Street Journal.* July 9-10, 2016.

Jennifer Breheny Wallace, "Children Should Be Heard, But Only So Much," *Wall Street Journal,* July 22-23, 2017.

Rick Wormeli, "Motivating Young Adolescents," *Educational Leadership,* September 2014.

David S. Chester, "The Role of Positive Affect in Aggression," *Current Directions in Psychological Science,* Vol. 26, August 2017.

Ellis, Bruce J., et. al. "Beyond Risk and Protective Factors: An Adaptation-Based Approach to Resilience," *Psychological Science,* Vol 12: 2017.

To learn more about OPRMI genes, go to the American Psychiatric Association and search OPRMI genes, for example, *https://www.psychiatry. org/.../am_newrese..* See May 13, 2000 - NR654 Association of *OPRMI* +118A Allele, *Charles* A. *Cloutier,* Department of Psychiatry, Duke University.

Gillespie, Charles F., et al. "Risk and Resilience: Genetic and Environmental Influences on Development of Stress Response," *Depression Anxiety,* 2009, Vol. 26.

Kuzelova, H., et al. "The Serotonin transporter gene (5-HTT variant) and psychiatric disorders: review of current literature," *Neuro Endocrinology,* 2010, Vol. 31.

For more on 5-HTT and related genetic coding, see *Nurture the Nature.*

Garwood, Philip, "Neurobiological Mechanisms of Anhedonia," *Clinical Neuroscience,* 2008, September 10(3).

Daniel Goleman. *Emotional Intelligence.*

Hall, J. A. (1990). *Nonverbal sex differences: Accuracy of communication and expressive style.* Baltimore, MD: Johns Hopkins University Press.

Wisco, Blair E., et.al., "Self-Distancing from Trauma Memories Reduces Physiological but Not Subjective Emotional Reactivity Among Veterans with Posttraumatic Stress Disorder," *Psychological Science,* 2015.

Randy Dotinga, "Fatal Opioid ODs on the Rise Among U.S. Teens, "*Health Day News*, Aug. 16, 2017.

David M. Buss, "Sexual Conflict in Human Mating," *Psychological Science,* Vol 26, 2017.

Buss, D. M. (1996)." Sexual conflict: Evolutionary insights into feminism and the "battle of the sexes." In D. M. Buss & N. M. Malamuth (Eds.), *Sex, Power, Conflict: Evolutionary and Feminist Perspectives* (pp. 296–318). New York, NY: Oxford University Press.

Buss, D. M. (2016). *The Evolution of Desire: Strategies of Human Mating* (rev. and updated ed.). New York, NY: Basic Books.

Berkley, K. J. 1997a. "Female vulnerability to pain and the strength to deal with it." *Behavioral and Brain Sciences, 20.*

Berkley, K. J. 1997b. "Sex differences in pain." *Behavioral and Brain Sciences* 20:371–380.

Berkley, K. J. 2000. "Female pain versus male pain," in: *Sex, Gender, and Pain*, R. B. Fillingim, ed. Seattle: IASP Press.

Berkley, K. J., and A. Holdcroft. 1999. "Sex and gender differences in pain," in: *Textbook of Pain*, 4th ed., P. D. Wall and R. Melzack, eds. Edinburgh: Churchill Livingstone.

Hawley, Patricia H., "The Duality of Human Nature: Coercion and Pro-sociality in Youths' Hierarchy Ascension and Social Success," *Current Directions in Psychological Science,* Vol. 23(6).

Sue Shellenbarger, "Moms, Let Dads Be Dad," *The Wall Street Journal,* June 17, 2015.

Barbara Kay, "Want to help society? Let kids know their fathers," *National Post, June 16, 2016.*

http://news.nationalpost.com/full-comment/barbara-kay-want-to-help-society-let-kids-know-their-fathers

Megan Daley, "Five Things Pediatricians Want Dads to Know about Fathering," *The Los Angeles Times,* June 13, 2016, reporting multiple studies in *Science* and other journals corroborating the importance of fathers in building emotional intelligence, social success, and cognitive development in boys and girls.

Martin Daubney, "How Dad Deprivation May Be Eroding Society," *The Daily Telegraph,* June 22, 2016.

Laura Landro, "Why Learning to Be Resilient is Good for Your Health," *The Wall Street Journal,* February 16, 2016.

Judy Foreman, "The Discomfort Zone," *The Wall Street Journal,* February 1 – 2, 2014.

Paul Bloom, "The Empathy Trap," *Wall Street Journal,* December 3-4, 2016.

Lyn Mikel Brown, www.hardygirlshealthywomen.org.

Lisa Gutierrez, "Can't Sit Still While Reading This? Keep Fidgeting—Research Says It's Good for You," *Tribune News Service,* September 27, 2016.

Some recent books that teach resilience are: *The Song from Somewhere Else,* by A.F. Harrold, *Overboard! (Survivor Diaries)* by Terry Lynn Johnson, *The Paper Flower Tree,* by Jacqueline Ayer, all published in 2017

Nancy Szokan, "Want Healthy Kids? Let Them Play in the Mud," *Washington Post,* November 29, 2016.

Steven Poole, "The Serious Business of Play," *Wall Street Journal.* November 19-20, 2016.

Howard Fendrich, "Muguruza Beats Her Role Model," *Associated Press,* July 16, 2017.

John Carucci, "Wild Ride for Wilde in Broadway Debut of Orwell's 1984," *Associated Press,* June 25, 2017.

James Patterson is quoted in "Along Came a Writer," an essay in *Wall Street Journal,* June 16, 2017.

Ben Sasse. 2017. *The Vanishing American Adult.* St. Martin's Press. New York.

Mary Oliver is quoted from *American Primitive.*

Chapter 7

Dr. Sydney Baker is interviewed by Dr. Kara Fitzgerald at: www.drkarafitzgerald.com/2016/06/27/episode-15-art-medicine-soul-stirring-chat-sidney-baker-md/

Michael Gurian with Barbara Annis, *Leadership and the Sexes.*

The following are references not just from recent years but from the '60s, 70s, and 80s. We've known what we know about the science of girls/boys, women/men, and STEM for a long time, but we've been politically paralyzed in using the brain-based information.

Stones, I., M. Beckmann, and L. Stephens. 1982. "Sex-related differences in mathematical competencies of pre-calculus college students." *School Science and Mathematics* 82.

Stanley, J. C., and C. P. Benbow. 1982. "Huge sex ratios at upper end." *American Psychologist* 37.

Economics and Statistics Administration, Department of Commerce, "Women in STEM: A Gender Gap to Innovation," http://www.esa.doc.gov/Reports/women-stem-gender-gap-innovation, August 3, 2011.

The 2013 national poll on modern parenthood was conducted by the Pew Research Center. The study asked mothers and fathers to identify their "ideal" working arrangement. Fifty percent of mothers said they would prefer to work part-time and 11 percent said they would prefer not to work at all. Fathers answered differently: 75 percent preferred full-time work. *And the higher the socio-economic status of women, the more likely they were to reject full-time employment.* Among women with annual family incomes of $50,000 or higher, only 25 percent identified full-time work as their ideal.

Bian, Lin, et.al., "Gender Stereotypes about Intellectual Ability Emerge Early and Influence Children's Interests," *Science*. January 27, 2017.

Jessica Guynn, "Women in Computer to Decline Even More," *USA Today*, October 21, 2016.

Maria Danilova, "Little Girls Doubt That Women Can Be Brilliant, Study Shows," *Associated Press*, January 27, 2017.

Susan Barnett's "Complex Questions Rarely Have Easy Answers" is the introduction to "The Science of Sex Differences in Science and Mathematics," 2007 study. This introduction says it all: many factors in nature, nurture, and culture create a STEM gap.

Goetz, Thomas, et.al., "Do Girls Really Experience More Anxiety in Mathematics?" *Psychological Science*, Vol 24(10). 2013.

Philip B. Gnilka and Alexandra Novakovic, "Gender Differences in STEM Students' Perfectionism, Career Search Self-Efficacy, and Perception of Career Barriers," *Journal of Counseling and Development*, January 2017.

Melissa Korn, "Colleges Move to Close Gender Gap in Science," *Wall Street Journal*, September 26, 2017.

Ceci, Stephen J., "Women in Academic Science: A Changing Landscape," *Psychological Science in the Public Interest*, 2014.

To study American test scores and other STEM data disaggregated by sex, visit the American Enterprise Institute's website and search for Mark Perry. For instance, search for "Mark Perry and Bachelors' Degrees by Field and Gender."

To go deeply into this issue, check out two books from 2010: Stephen Ceci and Wendy Williams, *The Mathematics of Sex*, which makes the case for a much-expanded conversation about girls/women and STEM issues, including an inclusion of science-based information; and *The Science on Women and Science* published by the AEI Press and edited by Christina Hoff Sommers, a resident scholar at the American Enterprise Institute.

Michael Gurian with Patricia Henley, Terry Trueman, and Kathy Stevens, *Boys and Girls Learn Differently*.

J. E. Lauer, S. F. Lourenco. "Spatial Processing in Infancy Predicts Both Spatial and Mathematical Aptitude in Childhood." *Psychological Science*, 2016.

Pruden, Shannon M. and Levine, Susan C., "Parents' Spatial Language Mediates a Sex Difference in Preschoolers' Spatial Language Use," *Psychological Science*, Vol. 1 – 14, 2017.

Belsky, Daniel W., et.al., "The Genetics of Success: How Single-Nucleotide Polymorphisms Associated with Educational Attainment Relate to Life-Course Development," *Psychological Science*. Vol 27(7). 2016.

Garon-Carrier, Gabrielle, et.al., "Persistent Genetic and Family-Wide Environmental Contributions to Early Number Knowledge and Later Achievement in Mathematics," *Psychological Science*, Vol 1 – 12, October 2017.

Harrison J. Kell, et.al., including Camilla Benbow, "Creativity and Technical Innovation: Spatial Ability's Unique Role," *Psychological Science*, July

11, 2013.

Bailey, Drew H., et.al., "State and Trait Effects on Individual Differences in Children's Mathematical Development," *Psychological Science,* 2014.

Carlezon, William, "Biological Substrates of Reward and Aversion: A Nucleus Accumbens Activity Hypothesis," *Neuropharmacology*, 2009, Vol. 56.

Cornwell, Christopher, et al. "Non-cognitive Skills and the Gender Disparities in Test Scores and Teacher Assessments: Evidence from Primary School," May 1, 2012.

Thomas S. Dee, "How a Teacher's Gender Affects Boys and Girls," *Education Next*, 2006.

Proudfoot, Devon., et.al., "A Gender Bias in the Attribution of Creativity: Archival and Experimental Evidence for the Perceived Association Between Masculinity and Creative Thinking," *Psychological Science,* 2015.

Matal, Rui, et al., "Propensity for Risk Taking Across the Life Span and Around the Globe," *Psychological Science,* 2016.

Lubinski, D., & Benbow, C. P. (2006). "Study of Mathematically Precocious Youth After 35 Years: Uncovering Antecedents for the Development of Math-Science Expertise." *Perspectives on Psychological Science*, 1.

Lykken, D. T. (1968). "Statistical Significance in Psychological Research." *Psychological Bulletin*, 70, 151–159.

Meehl, P. E. (1990). "Appraising and Amending Theories: The Strategy of Lakatosian Defense and Two Principles That Warrant It." *Psychological Inquiry*, 1.

Morrison, D. F. (1967). *Multivariate statistical methods.* New York, NY: McGraw-Hill.

National Science Board. (2010). "Preparing the Next Generation of STEM Innovators: Identifying and Developing Our Nation's Human Capital." Arlington, VA: National Science Foundation.

Newcombe, N. S., Uttal, D. H., & Sauter, M. (2013). "Spatial development." In P. D. Zelazo (Ed.), *Oxford Handbook of Developmental Psychology* (pp. 564–590). New York, NY: Oxford University Press.

Shea, D. L., Lubinski, D., & Benbow, C. P. (2001). "Importance of Assessing Spatial Ability in Intellectually Talented Young Adolescents: A 20-year Longitudinal Study." *Journal of Educational Psychology*, 93.

Shepard, R. N. (1978). "Externalization of Mental Images and the Act of Creation." In B. Randhawa & W. Coffman (Eds.), *Visual Learning, Thinking, and Communication* (pp. 133– 190). New York, NY: Academic Press.

Simonton, D. K. (2012). "Taking the U.S. Patent Office Criteria Seriously: A Quantitative Three-Criterion Creativity Definition and Its Implications." *Creativity Research Journal*, 24.

Snow, R. E. (1999). "Commentary: Expanding the Breadth and Depth of Admissions Testing," in S. Messick (Ed.), *Assessment in Higher Education* (pp. 133–140). Hillsdale, NJ: Erlbaum.

Thorndike, R. L. (1949). "Personnel Selection: Test and Measurement Techniques." New York, NY: John Wiley & Sons. U.S. Department of

Commerce. (2012). *The Competitiveness and Innovative Capacity of the United States.* Retrieved from http://www.commerce.gov/sites/default/files/documents/ 2012/january/competes_010511_0.pdf

Uttal, D. H., & Cohen, C. A. (2012). "Spatial Abilities and STEM Education: When, Why, and How." *Psychology of Learning and Motivation,* 57.

Uttal, D. H., Meadow, N. G., Tipton, E., Hand, L. L., Alden, A. R., Warren, C., & Newcombe, N. S. (2012). "The Malleability of Spatial Skills: A Meta-Analysis of Training Studies." *Psychological Bulletin,* 138.

Wai, J., Lubinski, D., & Benbow, C. P. (2009). "Spatial Ability for STEM Domains: Aligning Over Fifty Years of Cumulative Psychological Knowledge Solidifies Its Importance." *Journal of Educational Psychology,* 101.

Webb, R. M., Lubinski, D., & Benbow, C. P. (2007). "Spatial Ability: A Neglected Dimension in Talent Searches for Intellectually Precocious Youth." *Journal of Educational Psychology,* 99.

Joe Callahan, "No Homework in Ocala Elementary Schools," *Ocala StarBanner,* July 12, 2017

Whitney Ransome, "The Value of Single-Sex Education: All-Girls Schools Provide Lasting Benefits to Students," *Baltimore Sun,* January 23, 2012.

"Great Science for Girls" strategies can be found on https://www.fhi360.org/projects/great-science-girls, produced under a grant from the National Science Foundation.

Denisa, R. Superville, "Dallas Expands Choices with Single-Gender Schools," *Education Week,* October 5, 2016.

Carla Sparks and I spoke on this subject at the Gurian Winter Institute in Tampa in January of 2015.

Stephen Moore, "President Obama, Are You Listening?" *The Wall Street Journal,* May 2-3, 2015.

Corey Mitchell, "Boys-Only Programs Raise Legal Concerns," *Education Week,* March 4, 2015.

These articles refer to the ACLU and executive office attacks on single-gender schools. I have supported the ACLU over the years on free speech issues, but on gender issues both the ACLU and the Obama Administration fell on the wrong side of science and common sense. The ACLU began this trend by deciding to align with the few people I mentioned in the chapter who formed the "American Council for Coeducational Schooling (ACCS)" to attack the single-gender classroom movement in public schools. Using the "gender equality requires gender sameness" myth, these folks team up with the ACLU to accuse single-gender teachers and schools of illegal activity (gender discrimination) and severe danger to children's psyches via "gender stereotypes."

Some of the schools the Gurian Institute works with are co-educational schools that utilize single-gender classes to teach math/science and language arts, and we work with single-gender schools as well. These schools (see www.gurianinstitute.com/success) are having great success in closing achievement gaps and educating our nation's children, both female and male, but the

ACLU and the ACCS attack them and us with rhetoric that 1) shows no proof of danger to children in single-gender classes, and 2) pretends success of these classrooms doesn't exist. These ideologues even minimize the findings of their own scientific disciplines in the science of sex and gender. This is attack politics at its worst. Because the schools and districts don't have funding to battle the ACLU and these folks, the attacks close down these programs and schools—not because the attacker is right, but because the attacker is well-funded.

Two schools under siege by these people are Gurian Institute Model Schools (schools in which all personnel have been trained in nature-based theory and male/female brain difference) located in Hillsboro Country Public Schools. Their predecessor institutions were failing and nearly shut down. Now they are A schools with some of the best test scores and graduation rates in the state. They serve mainly disadvantaged populations and their brave teachers and staff have literally saved many young lives from crime and early death. Despite their clear success for (and lack of harm to) their hundreds of students, the ACLU manipulated Title IX and other laws to attack their single-gender option.

If you would like to witness the ACLU straw man arguments, go to the aclu.org website and obtain its "Teach Kids, Not Stereotypes" document. Reading it at first, you'll want to shut every person in America down who even thinks about a single-sex classroom! That is, until you realize that it is all ideological air. The "harm" only makes sense if you buy the DGP ideology that anything "boy" or "girl" is gender stereotyping, and thus inherently harmful because "boy" and "girl" are just patriarchal social constructs that damage children.

But if you don't start from the extreme DGP position, the ACLU position crumbles. Once you use cost-benefit analysis, you'll see how much disservice this kind of document does to children. Millions of dollars are spent in school districts such as Hillsboro to answer thousands of pages of ACLU and OPR (Office of Public Review) attack/inquiry. This is taxpayer money spent to defend schools—not against a valid or proven claim, but an ideology that focuses nearly always on what a certain group (the ACLU funders) think is good for girls (or not good).

Ragatz, Carolyn M. (2015). *Playing Vocabulary Games and Learning Academic Language with Gifted Elementary Students*. Dissertation. Publication Upcoming.

Ferriman, Kimberly, et.al., including David Lubinski and Camilla P. Benbow, "Work Preferences, Life Values, and Personal Views of Top Math/ Science Graduate Students and the Profoundly Gifted: Developmental Changes and Gender Differences During Emerging Adulthood and Parenthood," *Journal of Personality and Social Psychology*, Vol. 27. 2009.

Ming-Te, et.al., "Technology, Engineering, and Mathematics Not Lack of Ability but More Choice: Individual and Gender Differences in Choice of Careers in Science," *Psychological Science*. March 18, 2013.

Chapter 8

Frank Griffitts, et al. including Kathryn Boak McPherson, *Why Teens Fail*, Phoenix: Be the One, 2012. Frank is a great resource on cyberbullying and other aspects of online activity among children. He is President of the Aether Academy and Aether Media as well as a former police detective.

The suggestions in this chapter are taken from multiple sources integrated into our digital health programs. Those sources are listed here:

Denise Moreno, "Smartphones Reduce Your Brain Power, Even When They're Off and You're Not Using Them," *International Business Times*, June 27, 2017.

Denise Moreno, "Anxiety and Social Media: Brain's Addiction to Checking Accounts," *International Business Times*, August 2, 2017.

Diana Kruzman, "The Hot New Games Aren't on Your Phone, They're on the Table and Require (Gasp!) Other People," *USA Today*, August 1, 2017.

You can find Bill Gates interview with Australian television by googling "Bill Gates discusses his children's cell phone use."

Kaomi Goetz, "Not Your Average Gamer: Women Play to Socialize," *All Things Considered*, May 3, 2010.

Jenny Anderson, "A Study of Kids' Screen Time Explains the Vicious Cycle that Makes Parents Unable to Say No," *Quartz*. August 01, 2017.

Fred Maxwell, "Parents Cautioned About Phone App That Could Be Hazardous to Children," *Western Journalism*, July 14, 2017.

Rachel Alexander, "Digital Detox," *The Spokesman Review*, September 11, 2017.

Sandy Cohen, "Incivility Going Viral," *Associated Press*, July 13, 2017.

Alexia Elejalde-Ruiz, "Harsh on the Eyes," *Chicago Tribune*, January 12, 2016.

Charlie Wells, "Smartphones Go to School," *Wall Street Journal*, February 18, 2016.

Michelle Piper, "The Millennial Mindset," *Family Therapy Magazine*, March/April 2017. Much of this issue is devoted to understanding millennials who use technology for so much of their daily experience.

Rochelle Cade and Jasper Gates, "Gamers and Video Game Culture," *The Family Journal*, Vol 25., 2017.

Stuart Green, "I'm Banning Laptops from My Classroom," *Wall Street Journal*, July 11, 2016.

Ravizza, Susan M. et. al, "Logged in and Zoned out: How Laptop Internet Use Relates to Classroom Learning," *Psychological Science*, 2016.

Christopher Mims, "Limiting Screen Time Can Benefit Your Children," *Wall Street Journal*, October 24, 2016.

Jonei Aleccia, "How Much Digital Media is Ok for Kids," *Seattle Times*, October 25, 2016.

Kim Painter, "Limited Time Online Is OK for Toddlers, Doctors

Say," *USA Today*, October 1, 2016. This article refers to the new American Academy of Pediatrics study which suggests small children can relate to grandparents and others via Facetime and computer screens for very brief periods of time.

West, Greg L., et.al., "Video Games and Hippocampus-Dependent Learning," *Current Directions in Psychological Science*, Vol. 26, 2017. This study provides an interesting perspective on a backdoor way to help girls in spatial intelligence development—getting them into visuospatial-heavy video games like superhero/war games and NASCAR more deeply than most girls are interested in playing.

Eve Glazier and Elizabeth Ko, "Limit Screen Time, Caffeine to Sleep," *Andrews Mcmeel Syndication*, July 1, 2017.

Matt Richtel, "A Silicon Valley School that Doesn't Compute," *The New York Times*, October 22, 2011.

Jim Taylor, "Is the American Academy of Pediatrics Copping Out on Screens," *Psychology Today*, October 13, 2015.

Up-to-date "blue light" research is referenced in Alexia Elejalde-Ruiz's "Harsh on the Eyes," *Chicago Tribune*, January 12, 2016.

Catlin Tucker, "Creating a Safe Digital Space," *Educational Leadership*, October 2015.

Kevin Clark, "The NFL'S Laboratory for Millennials," *The Wall Street Journal*, September 15, 2015.

Joel Cooper and Kimberlee Weaver, *Gender and Computers: Understanding the Digital Divide*.

George, Madeleine J. and Odgers, Candice L., "Seven Fears and the Science of How Mobile Technologies May Be Influencing Adolescents in the Digital Age," *Perspectives on Psychological Science*, 2015, Vol. 10(6).

Sue Shellenbarger, "We Want Our Children to Code, Even If We Can't," *The Wall Street Journal*, February 10, 2016. This article contains an example of a family in which children are introduced to intense computer use through coding by age 6. If we could study children like these longitudinally, especially young males, I believe we will find in 20 years a high probability of social-emotional issues for children whose brains are linked to technologies so young.

Charlie Wells, "Smartphones Go to School," *The Wall Street Journal*, February 18, 2016.

Deborah Perkins-Gough, "Secrets of the Teenage Brain," *Educational Leadership*, October 2015.

Casey, B.J., et al. "Behavioral and Neural Correlates of Delay of Gratification 40 Years Later," *Proceedings of the National Academy of Sciences*, 2011, Vol. 108.

Galvan, A., et al. "Earlier Development of the Accumbens Relative to Orbitofrontal Cortex Might Underlie Risk-Taking Behavior in Adolescents," *The Journal of Neuroscience*, 2006, Vol. 26.

Amy Ellis Nutt, "Loneliness Can Be Lethal Health Risk, Scientists Say," *The Washington Post*, February 1, 2016.

You can learn more about obesity genetics and the new trend of genetic testing in workplaces in Rachel Emma Silverman, "Genetic Testing May Be Coming to Your Office," *The Wall Street Journal*, December 16, 2015.

See also:

Mead, Nathaniel, "Origins of Obesity: Chemical Exposures," *Environmental Health Perspectives*, 2004, Vol.112.

Berkey, Catherine, et al. "Activity, Dietary Intake, and Weight Changes in a Longitudinal Study of Preadolescent and Adolescent Boys and Girls," *Pediatrics*, 2000, Vol. 105.

Vandewater, Elizabeth, et al. "Linking Obesity and Activity Level with Children's Television and Video Game Use," *Journal of Adolescence*, 2004, Vol. 27.

Bob Granleese, "Why Are British Kids So Unhappy? Two Words: Screen Time," *The Guardian*, January 16, 2016.

Lindsay Holmes, "Sneaky Ways Technology Is Messing with Your Body and Mind," Huffington Post, December 5, 2014.

Joel M. Moskowitz and Larry Junck, "Do Cellphones Need Warning Labels?" *The Wall Street Journal*, May 23, 2016.

Nicholas Carr, "How Smartphones Hijack Our Minds," *The Wall Street Journal*, October 7-8, 2017.

Susan Pinker, "To Beat the Blues, Visits Must Be Real, Not Virtual," *The Wall Street Journal*, June 4-5, 2016. This is a pithy and very powerful article on the science of loneliness—and the necessity of real life to combat it. Virtual life can often amplify depression, not help it.

Bartholow, Bruce, et al. "Chronic Violent Video Game Exposure and Desensitization to Violence," *Journal of Experimental Social Psychology*, 2006, Vol. 42.

David Williamson Shaffer, *How Computer Games Help Children Learn*.

A somewhat different view than mine on technology and electronics appears in Danah Boyd's "Let Kids Run Wild Online," *Time*, March 24, 2014.

Jean M. Twenge, *An Aversion to Adulting*, Atria. New York, 2017.

Digital citizenship resource centers include:
- www.mediatechparenting.net
- www.edutopia.org
- www.safekids.com/family-contract-for-online-safety
- www.digitalcitizenship.net
- www.safesupportlearning.ed.gov.

Resources to help with cyberbullying pre- and post-intervention include: www.b4uclick.org and the Cyberbullying research center, www.cyberbullying.org.

Carmen Gonzalez Caldwell, "Know the Signs: Girls at Much Higher Risk for Cyberbullying Than Boys," *The Miami Herald*, July 19, 2017.

Daniel Amen, "Wi-Fi: More Addictive than Sex, Chocolate or Alcohol?" *Amen Clinics Newsletter*, December 6, 2016.

Bushman, Brad, et al. "Chewing on It Can Chew You Up: Effects of

Rumination on Displaced Aggression," *Journal of Personality and Social Psychology,* 2005, Vol. 88.

The January/February 2016 edition of the *Psychotherapy Networker* is dedicated almost exclusively to sex and sexuality. I highly recommend this issue for anyone interested in learning more about pornography, male/female differences in sexual interest, and the hook-up culture among our teens and young adults.

Joanna Ellington, *Slippery When Wet.*

Julie Schwartz Gottman and John Gottman, "Lessons from the Love Lab," *Psychotherapy Networker,* November/December 2015.

Cynthia M. Allen, "Faith, Education Dovetail After All," *Fort Worth Star-Telegram,* April 20, 2014.

To learn more about the girls' Christian rite of passage program please visit: www.timwrightministries.org.

William Watson, S.J., *Sacred Story.* To learn more about Fr. Watson's Forty Weeks Program visit www.sacredstory.net.

Melinda Gates wrote this very powerful article in the *Washington Post,* August 24, 2017.

Chapter 9

Marilyn Sewell (1991), *Cries of the Spirit,* Beacon Press. Boston.

Camille Paglia, "2013: The Year Men Became Obsolete?" *Time,* December 30, 2013.

Camille Paglia, "A Defense of Masculine Virtues," *http://online.wsj.com,* December 27, 2013.

Noretta Koertge, *A House Built on Sand,* Oxford University Press, 2000.

As noted in earlier notes, the 2013 national poll on modern parenthood was conducted by the Pew Research Center. The study asked mothers and fathers to identify their "ideal" working arrangement. Fifty percent of mothers said they would prefer to work part-time and 11 percent said they would prefer not to work at all. Fathers answered differently: 75 percent preferred full-time work. *And the higher the socio-economic status of women, the more likely they were to reject full-time employment.* Among women with annual family incomes of $50,000 or higher, only 25 percent identified full-time work as their ideal.

According to decades of research through the American Enterprise Institute, women's and men's pay for *equal work* is generally equal with some exceptions (for instance, the Women's World Cup Soccer team was paid less than male World Cup team members even though the women won the World Cup). These cases must clearly be redressed and various laws are being enforced to address them. When enforcement of those laws is not enough, tort and court systems under federal and state law provide the avenue for redress.

Meanwhile, my own work as a gender consultant in various Fortune

500 corporations, as well as the work of Barbara Annis who has provided consulting to dozens of these companies, show these issues beneath the surface on women's pay gaps.

- Women are less likely to self-promote or negotiate for raises than men (less naturally aggressive in the pay process); we must focus on mentoring them in self-promotion.
- Women often work fewer hours than men in the same job, choosing not to travel away from home as much as men.

Our gender consulting is set up to help women self-promote better and more aggressively so that they can be better paid. At the same time, if men put two more hours a day into their job via travel and commute, there will always be some pay gap that favors the longer-hour workday.

Meanwhile, while the 77 cents on the dollar figure is incendiary in the media, the truth is that, as we noted in the chapter, it is not a wage gap per se but, rather, an *aggregate income during work years* gap. Furthermore, it will never close since males tend to stay in the money-earning workforce throughout their lifetimes, gaining a higher aggregate income while the majority of their wives/partners, once children come, have chosen (if possible) to take many years off from full money-earning in order to care for children in the home. Thus, there is a pay gap of 77 cents on the dollar.

Given that the very men who earn more money during child-raising years give that money in partnership with their spouse to support women and children, simplifying the gender conversation to "77 cents on the dollar" does a grave disservice to women who have chosen their lives and men who help them make that life-choice possible by supporting them.

While protecting women who really are discriminated against in wage earning is sacred work and will continue via law and tort, the 77 cents on the dollar is a straw man argument we must rethink if we are to fully support our children and our families.

To explore straw men arguments in this area, you might find very helpful some short video clips by Christina Hoff Sommers at the American Enterprise Institute. These are on YouTube and you can use them in your meetings and community work. Some are:

- http://conversationswithbillkristol.org/video/christina-hoff-sommers/?start=15&end=376
- http://www.youtube.com/playlist?list=PLytTJqkSQqtr7BqC1Jf4nv3g2yDfu7Xmd

We must remember: the DGP assessment of males was created around 1960 before the brain sciences found full form. Now, we can and must move gender equity out of old paradigms, whether patriarchal or DGP, to fully protect women and girls (and boys and men) in ways that are equitable, complementary, and ultimately help our females as much as our males.

The WHO study and Global Disease Reports are very instructive and can be accessed via various sites and links. One to start with: http://www.who.int/gho/publications/world_health_statistics/2015/en/.

David Autor and Melanie Wasserman, *Wayward Sons: The Emerging*

Gender Gap in Labor Markets and Education, for The Third Way Think Tank. See www.thirdway.org.

Isaac Cohen, "An 'Ether of Sexism' Doesn't Explain Gender Disparities in Science and Tech," *Forbes Magazine,* July 30, 2014.

Christina Zander, "Even Scandinavia Has a CEO Gender Gap," *The Wall Street Journal,* May 22, 2014.

Sheryl Sandberg, *Lean In.*

Ferriman, Kimberly, et.al., including David Lubinski and Camilla P. Benbow, "Work Preferences, Life Values, and Personal Views of Top Math/Science Graduate Students and the Profoundly Gifted: Developmental Changes and Gender Differences During Emerging Adulthood and Parenthood," *Journal of Personality and Social Psychology,* Vol. 27. 2009.

Ming-Te, et.al., "Technology, Engineering, and Mathematics Not Lack of Ability but More Choice: Individual and Gender Differences in Choice of Careers in Science," *Psychological Science.* March 18, 2013.

Hillel Italie and Angela Charlton, "Kate Millett Authored 'Sexual Politics," *Arizona Republic,* September 8, 2017. I was speaking in Arizona when I read this article announcing the passing of Kate Millett, a second wave feminist who argued in *Sexual Politics* that the feminist cause must be about accelerating the demand of "freeing half the race from its immemorial subordination." This depiction of women as victims was incendiary but also helped create the issue we face now—men as villains, women as victims. Our paralysis in this gender war leads me to hope we will now move to a fourth or fifth wave of feminism in which actual science is used to show us all the ways we need to help girls and boys, and women and men.

Steven Pinker, "The Genetics of IQ," *The Wall Street Journal,* January 2, 2016.

www.playitsafe.org

I know that some of my points in this chapter may seem shocking to some readers, so I am including more analysis and references here. There is gold in each of these articles—gold for a new debate on gender equity.

Smith, Dominique, et.al., *Building Equity.* ASCD: Alexandria, Virginia, 2017.

Lindsey Bahr, "Actress Tackles Equal Pay and Female Action Stars," *Associated Press,* July 28, 2017.

Joann S. Lublin, "Ranks of Women CEOs Get Slimmer," *Wall Street Journal,* August 3, 2017.

Mattek, Alison, et.al., "A Mathematical Model Captures the Structure of Subjective Affect," *Psychological Science,* Vol 12(3). 2017.

Rachel Sandler, "Tech Start-Ups Founded by Women Hire More Women," *USA Today,* June 16, 2017.

Natalie Kitroeff, "Why Are So Many Women Leaving the Workforce?" *Los Angeles Times,* June 18, 2017.

Robert J. Samuelson, "Nation's Social Capital on Decline," *Washington Post,* June 13, 2017.

Steven T. Piantadosi and Jessica F. Cantlon, "True Numerical Cognition in the Wild," *Psychological Science*, Vol 28(4). 2017.

Jonathan Zimmerman. 2016. *Coddled on Campus*. Oxford University Press. Oxford.

KC Johnson and Stuart Taylor, Jr. 2017. *The Campus Rape Frenzy*. Encounter Books. New York.

Scott O. Lillenfeld, "Microaggressions: Strong Claims, Inadequate Evidence," *Perspectives on Psychological Science*. Vol. 12. 2017.

Stephen Baskerville (2017). *The New Politics of Sex*. Angelico Press. Kettering, OH.

Judith Grossman, "A Mother, a Feminist, Aghast," *Wall Street Journal*, April 16, 2013.

Stephen Henrick, "A Hostile Environment for Student Defendants: Title IX and Sexual Assault on College Campuses," *Northern Kentucky Law Review*, vol. 40, no. 1, 2013.

Wendy McElroy, *Rape Culture Hysteria*, 2016.

Shawna Thompson, "False Allegations Hurt Genuine Rape Claims," *Lincoln Journal Star*, Sept. 1, 2017.

Daphne Patai, *Heterophobia: Sexual Harassment and the Future of Feminism*, Lanham, Maryland: Rowman and Littlefield, 1998.

Jay Belsky, "The Politicized Science of Day Care," *Family Policy Review*, vol. 1, no. 2. Fall 2003.

"Persistent Myths in Feminist Scholarship," *Chronicle of Higher Education*, June 29, 2009 (http://www.aei.org/article/100695).

Every major news service, newspaper, and online outlet covered the Damore story at Google between about August 3 and August 15, 2017.

Kerr, B.A. and Multon, K.D. "The Development of Gender Identity, Gender Roles, and Gender Relations in Gifted Students," *Journal of Counseling and Development*, April 2015, Vol 3.

National Science Foundation (2003). "Gender Differences in the Careers of Academic Scientists and Engineers." Retrieved from *http://www.nsf.gov/statistics/nsf03322/pdf/nsf03322.pdf*.

Sarah Skidmore Sell, "Women Top CFO Pay Chart," *Associated Press*, December 19, 2015.

Ann Case and Angus Deaton, "Rising Morbidity and Mortality in Midlife Among White Non-Hispanic Americans in the 21st century," *Proceedings of the National Academy of Sciences*, Vol. 112, November 2015.

Rae Jacobson, "Helping Girls Deal with Unwanted Sexual Attention," *Child Mind Institute Newsletter*, 2017.

Mike Mariani, "The Neuroscience of Inequality: Does Poverty Show Up in Children's Brains," *The Guardian*, July 13, 2017.

Lyndsey Layton, "Study Influences Achievement-Gap Debate," *The Washington Post*, April 16, 2015.

Alison Gopnik, "The Income Gap in the Growth of Children's Brains," *The Wall Street Journal*, May 16, 2015.

Blair, C., et al. "Maternal and Child Contributions to Cortisol Response to Emotional Arousal in Young Children from Low-Income Rural

Communities," *Developmental Psychology,* Vol. 44.

Belsky, Daniel, et.al, "The Genetics of Success: How Single Nucleotide Polymorphisms Associated with Educational Attainment Relate to Life-Course Development," *Psychological Science,* 2016.

Laurie Meyers, "The Toll of Childhood Trauma," *Counseling Today,* July 2014, 29-36.

Alison Gopnik, "Genes' Unknown Role in a Vicious Circle of Poverty," *The Wall Street Journal,* September 27 – 28, 2014.

Robert Maranto and Michael Crouch, "Ignoring an Inequality Culprit: Single Parent Families," *The Wall Street Journal,* April 21, 2014.

Rachel Emma Silverman, "Working Parents Share the Load, Study Says," *The Wall Street Journal,* November 5, 2015.

Jena MacGregor, "Study Finds More American Workers Would Rather Work for a Male Boss," *The Washington Post,* November 14, 2013.

E-school News reported the gap in February 22, 2016 based on federal data. "Low-income students enroll in school having heard 30 million fewer words than their peers from more affluent homes, researchers have found. The gap is even wider for English-language learners."

Robert J. Samuelson, "Jobless Young Pose Global Risks," *The Wall Street Journal,* June 9, 2015.

Ruth Simon, "Gender Gap Widens for Entrepreneurs," *Wall Street Journal,* May 14, 2015.

Gerald Skoning, "The Mythical 'Pay Equity' Crisis," *The Wall Street Journal,* October 14, 2014.

Sherry Jones and Janet Chung, "Pregnant Workers Measure Overdue," *The Spokesman-Review,* February 13, 2016.

Amartya Sen, "Women's Progress," *The Wall Street Journal,* January 2-3, 2016.

Joanna L. Krotz, "Being Equal Doesn't Mean Being the Same," joannakrotz.com, January 21, 2016.

Epilogue

St. Catherine is quoted from *Love Poems by God,* translated by Daniel Ladinsky.

E.O. Wilson, *The Meaning of Human Existence.*

E.O. Wilson, *Consilience.*

Rita Dove is quoted from *Best American Poetry (2000).* New York: Simon & Schuster.

Virginia Woolf's *The Waves* has some of the most beautiful passages of language I have ever read. The italicized sections depicting the day's transitions from sunrise to sunset over the ocean are stunning.

Bibliography

Amen, Daniel. (2017) *Memory Rescue.* Tyndale. Coral Stream, IL

_____. (2013) *Unleash the Power of the Female Brain.* Bantam. New York

_____. (2010) *Change Your Brain, Change Your Life.* Bantam. New York.

_____. (2006) *Healing A.D.D.* Bantam. New York.

_____. (2005) *Sex on the Brain.* Bantam. New York.

Arnot, Robert. (2001) *The Biology of Success.* Little Brown & Company. Boston, MA.

Baron-Cohen, Simon. (2003) *The Essential Difference.* Basic Books. New York.

Bear, Mark; Connors, Barry; Paradiso, Michael. (1996). *Neuroscience.* Williams and Wilkins. Baltimore, MD.

Benbow, Camilla and Lubinski, David. (1997) *Intellectual Talent.* Johns Hopkins University Press. Baltimore, MD.

Blum, Deborah. (1998) *Sex on the Brain.* Penguin Books. New York.

Borba, Michelle. (2016) *Unselfie.* Touchstone. New York.

Brizendine, Louann. (2007) *The Female Brain.* Three Rivers Press. New York.

_____. (2011). *The Male Brain.* Harmony. New York.

Bly, Robert. (1996) *The Sibling Society.* Addison-Wesley Publishing. Boston, MA.

Carbone, June and Cahn, Naomi. (2014) *Marriage Markets.* Oxford University Press. Oxford.

Campbell, Joseph (reprint, 2008) *The Hero with a Thousand Faces.* New World Library. New York.

Carr-Morse, Robin. (1998) *Ghosts from the Nursery.* Atlantic Monthly Press. New York.

Carter, Rita. (1998) *Mapping the Mind*. U. of CA Press. Los Angeles, CA.

Coloroso, Barbara (2002, 2015). *The Bully, The Bullied, and the Not-So-Innocent Bystander*. William Morrow. New York.

Cooper, Joel and Weaver, Kimberlee. (2003) *Gender and Computers*. Lawrence Erlbaum. Mahwah, NJ.

Damour, Lisa. (2017) *Untangled*. Ballentine. New York.

Deak, JoAnn. (2003) *Girls Will Be Girls*. Hyperion. New York.

Ellington, Joanna. (2015) *Slippery When Wet*. JDK Publications. Spokane, WA.

Faludi, Susan. (2000) *Stiffed*. Harper Perennial. New York.

Farrell, Warren. (2000) *The Myth of Male Power*. Berkeley. New York.

Flinders, Carol. (2002) *The Values of Belonging*. Harper. San Francisco, CA.

Friedan, Betty. (1963) *The Feminine Mystique*. Norton. New York.

_____. (1981/1998). *The Second Stage*. Harvard University. Cambridge, MA.

Fogarty, Robin. (1997) *Brain Compatible Classrooms*. Skylight Professional Development. Arlington Heights, IL.

Gilligan, Carol. (1998). *In A Different Voice*. Harvard University Press. Boston, MA.

Goleman, Daniel. (1995). *Emotional Intelligence*. Bantam. New York.

Griffitts, Frank, et.al., including Kathryn Boak McPherson. (2012) *Why Teens Fail*. Be the One. Phoenix, AZ.

Gurian, J.P. & J. (1983) *The Dependency Tendency*. Rowman and Littlefield. Lanham, MD.

Gurian, Michael., et.al. (2011) *Boys and Girls Learn Differently! A Guide for Teachers and Parents*. Jossey-Bass. San Francisco, CA.

Gurian, Michael, with Kathy Stevens. (2005) *The Minds of Boys*. Jossey-Bass. San Francisco, CA.

Gurian, Michael. (2007) *Nurture the Nature*. Jossey-Bass. San Francisco, CA.

_____. (2006) *The Wonder of Boys*. Tarcher-Putnam. New York, Tenth Anniversary Edition

_____. (2002) *The Wonder of Girls*. Pocket Books. New York.

Harris, Judith R. (1998) *The Nurture Assumption*. Free Press. New York.

Jensen, Eric. (1995, 2000 Rev.) *Brain-Based Learning*. The Brain Store. San Diego, CA.

Jessel, David and Moir, Anne. (1989) *Brain Sex*. Dell. New York.

Jung, Carl, edited by Claire Douglas. (1997) *Visions*. Princeton University Press. Princeton, NJ.

Kandel Eric; Schwartz, James; Jessell, Thomas. (1995) *Essentials of Neural Science and Behavior*. Appleton & Lange. Norwalk, CT.

Karges-Bone, Linda. (1998) *More Than Pink & Blue*. Teaching and Learning Company. Carthage, IL.

Koertge, Noretta. (2000) *A House Built on Sand*. Oxford University Press. Oxford.

Kundtz, David. (2004) *Nothing's Wrong*. Conari Press. Boston, MA.

Ladner, Joyce. (2003). *Launching Our Black Children for Success*. Jossey-Bass/John Wiley. San Francisco, CA.

Legato, Marianne J. (2014) *Eve's Rib: The New Science of Gender-Specific Medicine*. Open Road Media. New York.

Levine, Mel. (2002) *A Mind at a Time*. Simon & Schuster. New York.

McElroy, Wendy. (2016). *Rape Culture Hysteria: Fixing the Damage Done to Men and Women*. CreateSpace. Seattle, WA.

Moir, Anne and Bill. (1999). *Why Men Don't Iron*. Citadel. New York.

Moir, Anne and Jessel, David. (1990) *Brain Sex*. Laurel. New York.

Paglia, Camille. (1991) *Sexual Personae*. Vintage. New York.

Payne, Ruby. (2000) A Framework for Understanding Poverty. AhaProcess, Inc. Highlands, Texas.

Pease, Barbara and Allan. (1999) *Why Men Don't Listen, And Women Can't Read Maps*. Broadway Books. New York.

Pinker, Steven. (2003) *The Blank Slate*. Penguin. New York

Ratey, John and Eric Hagerman. (2008) *Spark*. Little Brown. New York.

Ravitch, Diane. (2003) *The Language Police: How Pressure Groups Restrict What Children Learn*. Alfred A. Knopf. New York.

Rhoads, Steven E. (2004) *Taking Sex Differences Seriously*. Encounter Books. San Francisco, CA.

Salomone, Rosemary C. (2003) *Same, Different, Equal*. Yale University Press. New Haven, CT.

Sandberg, Sheryl. (2013). *Lean In*. Knopf. New York.

Sax, Leonard (2005). *Why Gender Matters*. Doubleday. New York

_____. (2013). *Girls on the Edge*. Basic Books. New York.

Schlosser, Eric (2012). *Fast Food Nation*. Mariner. New York.

Shaffer, David Williamson. (2006) *How Computer Games Help Children Learn*. Palgrave Macmillan. New York.

Sichel, Deborah and Jeanne Watson Driscoll. (2000) *Women's Moods*. Harper. New York.

Siegel, Daniel J. (1999) *The Developing Mind*. Guilford Press. New York.

Simmons, Rachel (2011). *Odd Girl Out*. Mariner Books. New York.

Sommers, Christina Hoff. (2013) *Freedom Feminism*. AEI Press. Washington, D.C.

Sousa, David. A. (2001) *How the Brain Learns*. Corwin Press. Thousand Oaks, CA.

Sprenger, Marilee. (2002) *Becoming A "Wiz" at Brain-Based Teaching: How to Make Every Year Your Best Year*. Corwin Press. Thousand Oaks, CA.

Sykes, Bryan. (2003) *Adam's Curse*. W.W. Norton & Company. New York.

Szalavitz, Maia. (2016) *Unbroken Brain*. St. Martin's Press. New York

Tannen, Deborah. (1991) *You Just Don't Understand*. William Morrow. New York.

Taubes, Gary. (2015) *The Case Against Sugar*. Knopf. New York.

Taylor, Shelley E. (2002). *The Tending Instinct*. Times Books. New York.

Tournier, Paul. (1964) *The Whole Person in a Broken World*. Harper & Row. New York.

Walsh, William. (2014) *Nutrient Power.* Skyhorse Publishing. New York.

Wilson, E.O. (2015) *The Meaning of Human Existence.* Liveright. New York.

_____ (1999) *Consilience* Vintage. New York.

Wiseman, Rosalind. (2016, reprint) *Queen Bees and Wannabes.* Harmony. New York.

Wolfe, Patricia. (2001) *Brain Matters.* Assoc. for Supervision and Curriculum Development.

Woody, Jane DiVita. (2002) *How Can We Talk About That?* Jossey-Bass. San Francisco, CA.

About the Author

Dr. Michael Gurian is a marriage and family counselor in his twenty-sixth year of private practice and a New York Times bestselling author of twenty-eight books in seven disciplines, with more than one million copies in print (www.michaelgurian.com). The Gurian Institute, which he co-founded in 1996, conducts research internationally, launches pilot programs, and has trained more than 60,000 professionals in the last twenty years (www.gurianinstitute.com).

Michael has been called "the people's philosopher" for his ability to bring together people's ordinary lives and scientific ideas. Gurian provides between twenty and thirty keynotes and trainings per year and consulting to community organizations, schools, governmental agencies, corporations, medical personnel, and faith communities.

Michael previously taught at Gonzaga University, Eastern Washington University, and Ankara University. His academic speaking engagements include Harvard University, Johns Hopkins University, Stanford University, Morehouse College, the University of Colorado, the University of Missouri–Kansas City, and UCLA. His multicultural philosophy reflects the diverse cultures (European, Asian, Middle Eastern, and American) in which he has lived, worked, and studied.

Michael's work has been featured in numerous professional journals and the major media, including *The New York Times, The Washington Post, USA Today, Newsweek, Time, Psychology Today, AARP Magazine, People, Reader's Digest, The Wall Street Journal, Forbes Magazine, Educational Leadership, The American School Board Journal, Counseling Today, Parenting, Good Housekeeping, Family Therapy Magazine, Redbook,* and many others. Gurian has also made multiple appearances on *Today, Good Morning America, CNN, PBS, National Public Radio,* and many others.

Michael lives in Spokane, Washington with his wife, Gail, a family therapist in private practice. The couple has two grown daughters, Gabrielle and Davita.

About the Gurian Institute

THE GURIAN INSTITUTE, founded in 1996, provides professional development, training services, and pilot programs in gender diversity and gender dynamics. All the institute's work is science-based, research-driven, and practice-oriented.

Institute staff, trainers, and coaches work with parents, mental health professionals, teachers, counselors, school districts, corporations, the legal system, medical professionals, and others who serve boys and girls, and women and men. The Gurian Institute has more than 150 trainers throughout the world.

The Gurian Institute provides online courses as well, along with DVDs, books, workbooks, newsletters, and a user-friendly website at www.gurianinstitute.com. In 2018, the institute began a subscription service. To learn more, visit www.michaelgurian.com and www.gurianinstitute.com.

The Gurian Institute also provides consulting for schools and agencies, as well as licensing services for increasing school and agency outreach. We believe this work constitutes a growing social movement and supports agencies, schools, and parents with a commitment to helping achieve the goals of social justice and social change.

The Gurian Institute Corporate Division provides training and consulting in gender diversity for businesses, corporations, and governmental agencies. This work has inspired the book *Leadership and the Sexes*, which looks at both women and men in our workforce from a gender science perspective. For more about this work, see www.gender-leadership.com.

Membership in the Gurian Community

We hope you will join our community. To learn more and to register, please go to www.michaelgurian.com and click the Membership button.

The Gurian Foundation

THE GURIAN FOUNDATION was co-founded by Michael Gurian and Gail-Reid Gurian. It is a 501(c)(3) corporation that can take donations and help with grant funding. Please go to www.gurianfoundation.org to learn more.

If you feel so moved, please donate toward summits, initiatives, and community work in your area through the Gurian Foundation. Donations and some grant funds are eligible for tax deduction.

To reach the foundation directly, please contact Gail Reid-Gurian or Michael Gurian at michaelgurian@comcast.net.

Index

A

B

C

D

E

F

G

Limbic system 74
Literacy 30, 31
Lubinski, David 205, 246-248, 254, 257

M

Male emotional intelligence 124, 125
Male/female brain difference 25, 143, 147, 150, 154, 229, 236, 248
Male privilege 57, 193, 203, 210, 221
Masculinity 195, 210, 221
Math/Science 30, 31, 143, 147, 149-151, 154, 156, 157, 159, 161, 162, 216, 247
Maturation 72, 79, 80, 99, 120, 128-134, 136, 162, 175, 177, 178, 180, 188
McPherson, Katey viii, 167, 219, 249, 258
Media literacy 169
Medication 50, 51, 64, 102, 182, 230, 231, 233, 238
Mental illness 74-76
Meta-analysis xii, 221
Meta-study 25, 88, 99, 119
Microaggressions 182, 192, 193, 196, 216, 217, 222
Mirror neurons 82, 126
Montessori 155
Movies 89, 134, 170, 175, 181, 191

N

Natural girl 3, 25, 93, 168, 178, 181
Nature-based theory 5, 23, 118, 216, 248
Neurobiology x, 226
Neuropsychology x
Neuroscience 107, 142, 180
Neurotoxins ix, 72, 95, 97-103, 105, 108, 109, 111, 175, 182, 238, 239
Non-interventionist 87
Nucleus accumbens 177
Nurture the nature x, 51

O

Obama, President 199, 247
Obesity ix, 59, 62, 75, 97, 101, 168, 177
Obesity genes 176
Obesity genetics 63, 103, 231, 251

OPRMI 121, 242
Oxytocin 12, 26, 27, 76-78, 80, 94, 125, 126, 178

P

Paglia, Camille 195, 252, 259
Patriarchy x, 195, 196, 200, 213, 221
Pell Institute 221
Phthalates 102
Pinker, Steven 3, 205, 222, 254, 259
Plastics 98, 99, 101, 102, 104, 105
Prefrontal Cortex 231
Preschool 43, 79, 128, 152, 157
Pruning 177, 178

R

Ped dye 105, 242
Resilience 7, 19, 35, 60, 115-117, 119, 120, 122-125, 127-130, 133-137, 193, 196, 197, 210, 221, 244
Resilient 121
Rite of passage 188, 252
Role models 95, 108
Rumination 60, 74-76, 80-84, 86-88, 125, 178, 184, 185, 234

S

Safe emotional container 133
Sandberg, Sheryl 195, 254, 260
Sax, Leonard 80, 101, 103, 105, 222, 235, 236, 239, 241, 260
Screen-time 175, 176
Self-esteem 36, 70-72, 76, 77, 122, 126, 127, 131, 151, 152, 154, 185, 205, 208, 209
Sexism viii, 96, 108, 142, 144, 146, 208-210, 216
Single-sex classrooms 154
Single-sex schools 154
Smart phones 8, 24, 169, 189
Sommers, Christina Hoff 245, 253, 260
Spatial-mechanical 145, 157, 204
Sports 44, 133, 176, 208, 209, 235
Stages 161, 170, 173, 175, 217, 225

CPSIA information can be obtained
at www.ICGtesting.com
Printed in the USA
LVHW101645171122
733396LV00003B/307

9 780983 995975